Charles E. Faupel

# Shooting
# Dope

*Career Patterns*

*of*

*Hard-Core*

*Heroin Users*

*University of Florida Press*

*Gainesville*

*Library of Congress Cataloging-in-Publication Data*

Faupel, Charles E.
Shooting dope: career patterns of hard-core heroin users /
Charles E. Faupel.
    p.   cm. — (American social problems)
    Includes bibliographical references and index.
    ISBN 0-8130-1070-5
    1. Heroin habit—United States.   2. Narcotic addicts—
United States.   3. Narcotics and crime—United States.
I. Title.   II. Series.
HV5825.F38   1991
364.2′4—dc20                                        91-92

This research was sponsored in part by DHEW Grant No.
1 R01 DA01827 from the Division of Research, National
Institute on Drug Abuse. Views expressed are those of the
author and do not necessarily reflect the position of the National Institute on Drug Abuse.

The University of Florida Press is a member of the Univer-
sity Presses of Florida, the scholarly publishing agency of
the State University System of Florida. Books are selected
for publication by faculty editorial committees at each of
Florida's nine public universities: Florida A & M University
(Tallahassee), Florida Atlantic University (Boca Raton),
Florida International University (Miami), Florida State
University (Tallahassee), University of Central Florida (Or-
lando), University of Florida (Gainesville), University of
North Florida (Jacksonville), University of South Florida
(Tampa), and University of West Florida (Pensacola).

Orders for books published by all member presses should
be addressed to University Presses of Florida, 15 North-
west 15th Street, Gainesville, FL 32611.

**Shooting Dope**

*American Social Problems*

To Martha

# Contents

**James A. Inciardi**

# Foreword

███████████ Decades of drug research by social scientists have exposed a finite number of recurring research and policy issues that continue to beg for empirical evidence. The nature of the relationship between drug use and criminal behavior is but the most persistent of these knotty issues, and it has occupied much of my own professional career. Are addicts forced into crime because of their compulsive need for expensive drugs? Or, are they rather drawn into a criminal life-style for many of the same reasons they experiment with drugs, namely, that it is held out as an attractive life-style by those whose opinions they regard highly? These are questions that continue to occupy the debate over the so-called drugs-crime nexus. Beyond this, the quality of addict criminality has been the focus of scholars across disciplines. The question of whether addicts are skilled professionals or undisciplined opportunists continues to fuel debate in the literature. The ethical character of addict behavior is an issue that has captured the imagination of the popular media as well as the scholarly community. The popular cultural portrayal of the addict as a moral degenerate has been challenged in much of the ethnographic research on the subject.

Charles Faupel has used these three recurring issues as a forum for elaborating the complex nature of addict careers. The career paradigm elaborated here is rooted firmly in the experiences of the participants in the heroin subculture itself. Faupel has managed to avoid an over-simplified view of addict careers that might result from merely overlaying the career metaphor on addict life-styles. Rather, sensitive to the experiences and perspectives of the participants in the subculture, revealed through hundreds of hours of life history interviews, he has identified two dominant features of addict life-styles that tend to shape the direction of their careers. These contingencies—drug availability and life structure—form the basis for a career typology that is not merely an extension of conventional careers, even though it shares many dynamics with these more respectable careers. Addict careers are so profoundly affected by the uncertainty of dependable supplies of quality heroin and potential disruptions to daily routines that any sort of linear progressive career path would be quite unrecognizable to most addicts.

Understood in the context of these career contingencies, the recurring research issues mentioned above take on a new focus. The question is not so much "Do drugs cause crime?" but rather "Under what conditions do addicts feel compelled to commit crime to satisfy their habits?" It is not so much a matter of whether addicts are criminal specialists or opportunistic hustlers but rather when in their careers they manifest these various characterizations. Faupel's delicate understanding of the ethical conduct of heroin users suggests that throughout most of their careers addicts are faithful to the ethical code in the subculture, but that there are times in their careers when they must abandon these proscriptions. Faupel's treatment of these issues represents a major challenge to much of the literature making claims about *the* relationship between drug use and crime or *the* nature of addict criminality. Social life is more complex than these reductionist findings imply, and this study makes an important contribution to this literature by reminding us of these complexities.

Another contribution of this book is the sober look that it takes at important policy issues, particularly the debate over legalization. Faupel's position is fairly clear: legalization represents a positive step forward toward a rational drug policy in this country, even though it is not a panacea. Advocates of both sides of this issue will find ammunition in this position, but they will be confronted with the shortcomings of their own positions as well. Regardless of one's position on this important issue, however, Faupel's analysis is intriguing because it emerges directly from the career paradigm that he develops throughout the book. I know of no other treatment of the legalization issue that so comprehensively examines it from the perspective of its impact on heroin-using careers.

The concluding chapter addressing the implications of a career para-digm for treatment policy raises some important questions about cur-rent treatment priorities. Throughout the book, Faupel demonstrates that addiction is fundamentally a *social* process. Any treatment effort that fails to address the social nature of addiction is doomed to failure, in his view. Our history of narcotics treatment in this country has been dominated by physiological and psychological paradigms. They have not had a strong track record. Drawing upon the therapeutic community as a point of reference, Faupel outlines in this chapter some of the critical elements of a socially based treatment policy and its implementation.

In this book Faupel takes a refreshing look at the phenomenon of heroin addiction and the policy issues attached to it. Not only is it read-able; its examination of heroin addiction as a career renders the life-style of the heroin addict comprehensible and familiar to those with limited or no exposure to this feature of social life. At the same time, he has succeeded in addressing some of the most perplexing issues in the field today. The issues raised and the discussion they entail here should promote discussion in the field for some time.

*University of Delaware, Newark*

# Preface

My introduction to this research was in no way spectacular. I was a graduate student in sociology at the University of Delaware, and, though specializing in social deviance, I knew absolutely nothing about the phenomenon of drug use other than a casual knowledge of Merton's "retreatist." Moreover, growing up in the rural Midwest, the only knowledge that I had about heroin addiction came from the occasional themes on television serials and periodic doses of fire-and-brimstone sermons on what would happen if I were to start messing around with the stuff. So I was caught a bit off guard when Jim Inciardi invited me to join his research staff to elicit life history data from hard-core heroin users. I would discover later that this very naïveté could prove to be an asset.

Needless to say, in spite of the methodological training I received in various graduate and undergraduate courses, I was not fully prepared for 18 months of intensive interviewing with these hard-core addicts. Early in the project, before entering the field, I found it advisable to familiarize myself on a firsthand basis with the reality of heroin use. At the invitation of Ed "Doc" Preble, I visited New York City's Spanish Harlem for a week, an experience that profoundly affected my subsequent fieldwork. It was the first time I had been to New York City, much less to Spanish Harlem. The heightened insecurity that I was experiencing was not lessened when my taxi driver informed me that most drivers would not venture into that part of the city. After what seemed like an excruciating number of hours, we finally reached 105th Street where Doc's storefront field office was located at the time. Again, I was not prepared for what I met. As I peered into the dimly lit room (illuminated only with a single, bare light bulb), behind a rather broken-down table (which I later found out was the executive desk) sat a gaunt-looking man in his late fifties whom I took to be Doc. "Howdy," I said as I mustered up all of the impression management skills I could, "my name's Chuck." "Hey, Chuck," he replied, "where you from, Chuck?" surmising from my midwestern accent that I was not from New York City. "Bad Axe, Michigan," I responded, to his great amusement. I would never be "Chuck" to Doc again, and on a subsequent visit after his death I noted that I was entered in his Rolodex as "Bad Axe."

I learned a great deal during the week I spent at the storefront office, including something about the life-style of heroin addicts, the techniques of shooting up, the argot, and the criminal specialties of street addicts. More important, I encountered a philosophy of ethnographic research that shaped my entire fieldwork experience. From the moment I met Doc, I had the sense that I knew this man as one might know a long-term friend, an experience that I later learned was shared by nearly everyone who knew him. It is this quality that I also learned was most critical to interpersonal rapport. Doc eschewed highly sophisticated expressions of methodology and technique in the ethnographic research role. Such research, he said, is first and foremost a social relationship and the interview principally a conversation. The rules that guide this conversation are not fundamentally different from those that guide casual relationships in which any sensitive individual finds himself or herself. The simplicity of this philosophy certainly does not preclude the necessity of arduously developing research skills, a caveat to which Doc's long and illustrious career as an urban ethnographer attests. It does, however, remind us that good ethnography is more than technique and that no level of sophistication in technique can replace a fundamental honesty and sincerity in the way we relate to the participants in our research. As Doc said on one occasion, when asked how one goes about establishing an ethnographic field station, "To ask how you set up and operate an ethnographic field station is like asking how you write a poem, paint a picture or throw a ball. The answer can be very simple or very complex. Until now I've taken the simple course by answering 'There's nothing to it, be yourself, use your common sense. Just don't be a jerk.' And if the person is one, then I say 'Forget it'" (Preble,

1982). All beginning field researchers should be as fortunate as I to have this sound advice hammered home as forcefully as it was for me throughout that week with Doc in New York.

There are numerous others whose contribution to this project must be acknowledged. Jim Inciardi had the foresight to recognize the need for systematically gathered life history data to reveal more about the complexity of the elusive relationship between expensive drug use and criminal behavior. Jim has built on his academic career by crunching numbers and otherwise keeping computer specialists busy, but I've always suspected he has felt more at home hanging out with junkies and their dealers on the street, pumping them for whatever information he could get over a cigarette or a beer. There is probably no single personal quality that gets in the way of good ethnography more than taking oneself too seriously as a scholar or academician. It not only interferes with developing the necessary rapport with respondents but also prevents researchers from seeing the world through the eyes of those they are studying. Jim's success as a street ethnographer is testimony to his ability to divest himself of academic titles, vocabulary, concepts, and theories, the preoccupation with which he has referred to on more than one occasion as "intellectual masturbation." Jim's orientation to the academic enterprise was a liberating experience that taught me that I didn't have to be bound by conventional methodological or theoretical wisdom as I explored the subcultural experiences of heroin-addicted criminals.

Keeping me from becoming too careless, however, was the co-principal investigator and project director, Anne Pottieger. Anne is one of the most meticulous methodologists I know, and I don't think there was a step in this entire process of which she was not cognizant. It was Anne who continually held my feet to the ground by such questions as "Why are you doing this?" "What would happen if you did it this way instead?" "Have you ever thought about how you are going to analyze this stuff?" "How are you assessing the reliability and validity of your data?" Anne has this way of answering queries and giving direction by strategically posing such questions and patiently waiting for me to work them through, even though it probably would have been easier for both of us had she simply offered her opinion.

Two other individuals played an instrumental role in the substantive development of this book. During the early months of the data-analysis process, Carl Klockars invited me to discuss the project at a paper session on qualitative methodologies at the American Society of Criminology meetings in Washington, D.C. I received several helpful criticisms from those attending that session. Carl took a very active interest in the project from that point, which culminated in a coauthored article. As I began to formalize ideas for the book, I came to rely heavily on Charles Watson at Troy State University. I met Charles during my rookie year at Auburn, when he was there on a temporary assignment. I quickly came to appreciate his academic rigor and have worked with him on several projects since then. Charles demonstrated an interest in the ideas I was developing early in our relationship, offering criticisms and helping to shape the conceptual ideas contained here even before I began formally writing the book. In addition, he reviewed each of the initial drafts of these chapters with a fine-tooth comb (and a bright red pen).

There are, of course, numerous others whose contribution was vital to a project of this scope. I am especially grateful to Leonard Beeghley at the University of Florida for his thoughtful criticisms and especially for his encouragement and support. He had a difficult job, but he made this experience an enriching and rewarding one for me. Bruce Johnson at Narcotic Drug Research Incorporated and Lonn Lanza-Kaduce at the University of Florida served as early reviewers of the manuscript and offered many thoughtful suggestions and criticisms, many of which have been directly incorporated into this final version. Nancy Quillen at the University of Delaware was helpful in the early stages of data analysis, typing difficult transcripts from tape-recorded interviews. Geraldine Lyle at Auburn University typed and retyped various versions of papers and drafts of chapters with unequaled turnaround time. I would also like to thank my colleagues at Auburn for their many suggestions, my wife, Martha, and children, Jennifer, Alison, and Christina, for their patience while daddy went down to his basement office to work instead of playing their favorite bedtime games.

Finally, I owe a deep debt of gratitude to 30 men and women in the Wilmington, Delaware, area who were gracious enough to share the details of their biographies with me. I hope above all that I have been faithful to their accounts in this analysis.

# Participants
# in the Study

Below is a brief description of the participants in this study. Because confidentiality was guaranteed to each of these individuals, the names are pseudonyms.

**Mario** is a white male in his early 30s. He first used heroin at age 17. His primary criminal activities are burglary and drug dealing.

**Pagie** is a black male in his early 30s. He first used heroin at age 21. His primary criminal activity is burglary.

**Eddie** is a white male in his late 20s. He first tried heroin at age 18. His primary criminal activity is check forgery.

**Mona** is a white female in her late 20s. She first used heroin at age 19. Her main criminal activity is to serve as an accessory to her husband, Ike, who is involved primarily in burglary.

**Richard** is a black male in his early 30s. He first used heroin at age 17. His primary criminal activities are pimping and shoplifting.

**Harry** is a white male in his late 20s. He first used heroin at age 18. His principal crimes are burglary, drug dealing, and con games.

**Helen** is a white female in her mid 30s. She first became involved with heroin at age 20. Her primary means of criminal income is prostitution, although she has engaged in a variety of crimes such as pickpocketing, check forgery, con games, and drug dealing.

**Shannon** is a black female in her early 20s. She first tried heroin at age 17. Her primary crimes are prostitution, pimping, and drug dealing.

**Bobbie** is a white female in her early 20s. She first used heroin at age 16. She is involved primarily in drug dealing, pimping, and pickpocketing.

**Gloria** is a black female in her mid 20s. She first used heroin at age 20. Her major crime is shoplifting.

**Carol** is a black female in her early 20s. She first used heroin at age 15. Her primary crime is shoplifting.

**Bertha** is a white female in her mid 20s. She first tried heroin when she was 18 years old. Her primary criminal activity is drug dealing.

**Stephanie** is a black female in her mid 20s. She first tried heroin at age 17. She is the only participant in this study who did not ever use heroin on a regular basis. She used primarily methamphetamines ("speed") and minor tranquilizers such as Valium. Her primary crime is check forgery.

**Penny** is a black female in her mid 20s. She first used heroin at age 24. Her major crimes are prostitution, drug dealing, shoplifting, and con games.

**Belle** is a black female. She is a veteran addict in her early 40s. She first tried heroin when she was 23 years old. She is almost exclusively involved in prostitution.

**Sandy** is a black female in her mid 20s. She first used heroin at age 17. She is involved in shoplifting, drug dealing, pimping, and con games.

**Rose** is a black female in her early 20s. She first tried heroin at age 14. She is involved primarily in prostitution and secondarily in shoplifting.

**Little Italy** is a black male in his late 20s. He first used heroin at age 16. His principal crime is drug dealing.

**Slick** is a white male in his mid 20s. He first tried heroin at age 16. His major crime is shoplifting.

**Old Ray** is a black male. He is a veteran addict in his mid 40s. He first used heroin at age 22. His primary criminal activities are drug dealing, burglary, shoplifting, and check forgery.

**Ron** is a black male veteran addict in his mid 40s. He first used heroin at age 20. His primary crime is drug dealing.

**George** is a black male addict in his early 30s. He first used heroin at age 21. He is involved primarily in robbery.

**Boss** is a black male in his late 20s. He first used heroin at age 15. He has been involved in a wide variety of crimes, including pickpocketing, robbery, and pimping.

**John** is a black male in his mid 20s. He first used heroin at age 24. His principal crimes are drug dealing and pimping.

**Ted** is a black male in his late 20s. He first used heroin when he was 15 years old. He is involved primarily in pimping and drug dealing.

**Fred** is a black male in his early 30s. He first used heroin at age 22. He is almost exclusively involved in drug dealing.

**Booter** is a black male in his mid 30s. He first used heroin at age 23. He is involved primarily in pimping and check forgery.

**Spence the Fence** is a black male in his early 20s. He first used heroin at age 19. His primary crimes are fencing, drug dealing, and burglary.

**Horace** is a black male addict in his early 40s. He did not become initiated into heroin use until age 33. His criminal activities are primarily drug dealing and fencing.

**Joe** is a black male in his mid 20s. He first used heroin at age 15. He is involved primarily in shoplifting.

# 1

# Introduction

━━━━━━━━━━━━━━━ This book is about heroin addicts. The lives of these individuals are in most ways no different from those of their friends and neighbors who do not use heroin. Many heroin addicts work at legitimate jobs. They have families. They enjoy many of the same types of recreational activities as those of us who do not use heroin. Yet the world of heroin use is quite segregated from the day-to-day lives of most Americans. Consequently, numerous stereotypes of heroin addiction have been cultivated, many of which bear little resemblance to the experience of most addicts. In this book, I seek to portray heroin use and addiction from the perspective of those who participate in the heroin-using subculture.

Heroin is part of a rather large family of drugs known as opiates or, more commonly, narcotics. Natural opiates are those drugs that derive from the poppy plant, and they include opium, morphine, and codeine. Synthetic opiates are pharmacologically similar to natural opiates but are artificially manufactured in a laboratory. The most common of these are Demerol, Darvon, and Methadone. Heroin is a partially synthetic drug, the product of treating morphine with acetic anhydride. Heroin was originally introduced into medicine as a cough suppressant by the Bayer Company in 1898. It was banned from medical use in 1924, although virtually all of the other opiates have legal medical uses in the United States today.

Physiologically, narcotics act to depress the activity of the central

1

nervous system, as do other depressants such as alcohol, barbiturates, and tranquilizers. Users commonly report drowsiness following the ingestion of narcotics, sometimes taking a rather extreme form when, in the street vernacular, the user goes *on the nod* (a sleep-like trance). Unlike many of the other depressants, most narcotics are extremely effective as analgesics, which is their primary medical function.

The most commonly recognized physiological effect of narcotics is addiction. Users develop a tolerance for heroin rather quickly, requiring increased dosages of the drug to get the same effect. When tolerance levels increase substantially, for most users it is no longer a matter of getting high but rather of avoiding withdrawal symptoms. Other drugs, particularly depressants such as alcohol, barbiturates, and tranquilizers, have a similar effect. This addictive property is especially problematic with heroin, however, because of the high cost of the drug. Indeed, the economic demands of heroin addiction are far more consequential than those associated with addiction to legal drugs.

Unlike most other depressants that can be purchased legally over the counter or with a doctor's prescription, heroin can be obtained only through illegal means, a reality with profound consequences for the habitual user. The drug's illegal status in American society results in addicts being disenfranchised from the cultural mainstream. Heroin addicts are pariahs in their communities. Users of alcohol and other depressants that have similar physiological effects share little of the social stigmatization borne by heroin addicts. Even users of other narcotics such as Demerol or Dilaudid, drugs that can be obtained through doctors' prescriptions, are not marginalized in this way. Indeed, these narcotics are frequently the drugs of choice among health professionals (McAuliffe et al., 1984; Maddux et al., 1986; Winick, 1961).

Consequently, the dynamics of heroin use and addiction cannot be understood simply in terms of pharmacological properties. The heroin user is a participant in a social world, largely segregated from conventional society. Heroin is a part of that world, as are crime, legitimate employment, housekeeping and domestic duties, and other activities that may or may not be shared by the larger culture. This subculture of heroin use imposes its own normative system, confers status and prestige, and engages its participants in an extensive socialization process that involves both technical knowledge and normative values. Thus, this book views narcotics addiction—from experimentation to the pains of withdrawal to "burning out"—as fundamentally a social experience.

Although narcotic drugs have been used for millennia (Scott, 1969) and their use in the United States and the Western world has been well documented (Brecher, 1972; Inciardi, 1986; Musto, 1973), commentary on the social dynamics of narcotics use has largely been limited to the twentieth century. Since the passage of the Harrison Act in 1914, a voluminous literature has emerged on various aspects of narcotics use and addiction. Most of the early writers understood addiction in quasi-medical terms—as a disease of sorts that renders its victim powerless to resist. Social reformers quickly seized upon the medical metaphor in their portrayals of the hopeless plight of drug addicts. Leading the crusade against narcotics was Richard Pearson Hobson, a celebrated Spanish-American War hero who described heroin as a "vampire" seeking to create a population of "living dead." "Many of the daylight robberies, daring hold-ups [and] cruel murders," he maintained, "are now known to be committed chiefly by drug addicts who constitute the primary cause of the crime wave . . ." (Epstein, 1977:28). Hobson had no doubt as to why heroin made criminals of addicts:

> The entire brain is immediately affected when narcotics are taken into the system. The upper cerebral regions, whose more delicate tissues, apparently the most recently developed and containing the shrine of the spirit, all those attributes of the man which raise him above the level of the beast, are at first tremendously stimulated and then—quite soon—destroyed . . .
>
> At the same time the tissues of the lower brain, where resides all the selfish instincts and impulses, receive the same powerful stimulation. With the restraining forces of the higher nature gone, the addict feels no compunction whatever in committing any act that will contribute to a perverted supposition of his own comfort or welfare. (Epstein, 1977:27)

This moral crusading by Hobson and others such as Harry Anslinger and Mrs. William Vanderbilt was not totally lost on the scientific community. Despite a handful of early naturalistic studies that attempted a more subjective understanding of drug-using life-styles (e.g., Becker, 1953; Hughes, 1961; Lindesmith, 1968), most of the early studies as well as much of the recent research have invoked a medically based "disease" paradigm for explaining narcotics use and related behavior. The search for the "addictive personality" (Chein et al., 1964; Platt, 1975) is but one application of the disease metaphor. Those studies that cloak their explanations in more value-neutral terms also reveal their ideological positions when they seek to explain drug use in terms of "retreatism" (Merton, 1938) or "double failure" (Cloward and Ohlin, 1960). Indeed, the very fetish for "cause" manifest in the use of medical referents such as "etiology" and "epidemiology" presupposes that there is some malady or pathology whose cause and prevalence must be explained.

Recent decades, however, have witnessed what Matza has called an "appreciative" understanding of deviant behavior: "Appreciating a phenomenon is a fateful decision, for it eventually entails a commitment—to the phenomenon and to those exemplifying it—to render it with fidelity and without violating its integrity. . . . This does not mean the analyst always concurs with the subject's definition of the situation; rather that his aim is to comprehend and to illuminate the subject's view and to interpret the world *as it appears to him*" (1969:24–25; italics in original). Among the first to assume such a posture toward narcotics use and addiction was the urban ethnographer Edward Preble. In his pioneering work "Taking care of business—the heroin user's life on the street," coauthored with John Casey in 1969, the addict is portrayed not as a withdrawn "retreatist" or "double failure" but rather as one who is engaged in purposive behavior, actively constructing a social identity in a challenging social environment. "The heroin user is, in a way, like the compulsively hard-working business executive whose ostensible goal is the acquisition of money, but whose real satisfaction is in meeting the inordinate challenge he creates for himself" (Preble and Casey, 1969:21).

Preble and Casey were not alone in their quest for a subjective understanding of the world of heroin addiction. At about the same time that they were working in the Upper East Side of New York City, Harvey Feldman was actively studying the drug scene in the Lower East Side, reporting his findings in his "Ideological supports to becoming and remaining a heroin addict" in 1968. Similar research was being conducted on the West Coast, particularly that of Sutter (1966, 1969, 1972), and by Hughes (1977) in Chicago. These studies and others, individually and collectively, have refocused our attention from drug addiction as a pathology to be explained to drug addiction as a social experience to be understood.

## The Orientation of This Book
━━━━━━━━━━━━━━━━━━━━━━ The research presented here joins an ever-
expanding ethnographic literature seeking to portray the social experience of drug use, including Patricia Adler's (1985) ethnography of
high-level "wheeling and dealing"; Biernacki's (1979) study of "junkie
work"; Goldstein's (1979) *Prostitution and Drugs;* the empathetic *Life
with Heroin: Voices from the Inner City,* recorded by Hanson et al.
(1985); and Rosenbaum's (1981) important documentation of the
vicissitudes in the lives of women on heroin. These and other studies
like them view drug addicts not so much as passive objects of external
forces but rather as active subjects who confront and respond to these
external constraints and opportunities.

Throughout this book, addicts will describe their experiences in
their own vernacular. This specialized vocabulary which has evolved in
the heroin-using subculture carries rich meaning which in many cases
cannot possibly be captured with conventional language, and reveals
important insights into the career dynamics of these users.

In the following pages I also attempt to represent heroin addicts as
responsive subjects. In so doing, I have adopted a biographer's perspective, permitting respondents to describe their careers as heroin users.
The concept of career is usually invoked in reference to the work histories of incumbents of legitimate occupations, although it is by no means
new to the study of deviance generally (e.g., Becker, 1963) nor to the
study of drug use specifically (e.g., Coombs, 1981; Crawford et al.,
1983; Rosenbaum, 1981; Rubington, 1967; Waldorf, 1973). The career concept is particularly helpful in understanding heroin addiction
for two reasons.

First, while there are certainly features of heroin-using careers that
are unique, there are many ways in which these drug-using careers
closely resemble conventional careers. Both conventional and heroin-
using careers, for example, traverse identifiable phases often marked by
major turning points. Both types of careers are subject to certain constraints and opportunities that are important in shaping the direction
that careers will take. In chapter two, I elaborate the nature of these
constraints and opportunities—which I call *career contingencies*—and
explore the various ways in which addicts respond to these contingencies throughout their lives. Because conventional careers are also characterized by many of the same broad dynamics associated with heroin-

using careers, the career concept provides a conceptual framework for understanding heroin-using life-styles in terms familiar to non–heroin users. That is, understanding heroin addiction as a career renders the phenomenon more familiar and hence less unique and exotic.

Second, the career paradigm more faithfully captures the complexity of heroin use and addiction than does the more mechanistic, pathological model. Understanding addiction as a career precludes simplistic cause-effect explanations. Similarly, intervention strategies that fail to recognize the complex nature of addict careers will surely be frustrated. Understanding addiction as a career has profound implications for a number of recurring research and policy issues that are discussed throughout this book. I have previously examined three of these issues from a career perspective: the drugs-crime connection (Faupel and Klockars, 1987); the extent to which addicts are criminal specialists (Faupel, 1987a); and the nature of addict ethics (Faupel, 1987b). These issues are highlighted below and form a substantive focus for the career dynamics discussed later in the book. I draw from these earlier studies as I explore how these thematic features of addict life-styles are affected by changing career contingencies.

*The Drugs-Crime Connection*

The causal relationship between the use of expensive drugs and crime has occasioned a long-standing debate among drug researchers, generating a voluminous literature over the past half century. A survey of this literature by Gandossey et al. (1980) lists over 450 citations to books, articles, and reports that specifically address the heroin-crime relationship. Early researchers assumed that heroin, because of its addictive nature and high cost, causes criminal behavior. As tolerance for and physical dependence upon heroin increase and as the cost of progressively larger doses of heroin escalate proportionately, addicts are driven to criminal means to support their habit. Tappan reflected this understanding nearly 30 years ago when he wrote, "The addict of lower socio-economic class is a criminal primarily because illicit narcotics are costly and because he can secure his daily requirements only by committing crimes that will pay for them" (1960:65–66).

Studies conducted since the 1950s, however, indicate that most addicts have criminal records prior to the onset of addiction (for overviews of this literature, see Austin and Lettieri, 1976; Gandossey et al.,

1980; and Greenberg and Adler, 1974). These findings seriously call into question the causal nexus between drug use and criminal behavior, giving rise to a second hypothesis about the relationship between heroin use and crime. This hypothesis maintains that the "principle explanation for the association between drug abuse and crime . . . is likely to be found in the subcultural attachment" (Goldman, 1981:162) composed of the criminal associations, identifications, and activities of those persons who eventually become addicted. This explanation is couched in the context of the contemporary sociolegal milieu in which heroin use takes place. Since heroin was criminalized in 1914, the social world of narcotics use has become increasingly intertwined with a broader criminal subculture (Musto, 1973). Consequently, would-be heroin users inevitably associate with other criminals in the highly criminal *copping* (drug-purchasing) areas of inner cities and are often recruited from delinquent and criminal networks. Through these associations the individual is introduced to heroin, and both criminal activity and heroin use are facilitated and maintained.

Still more recent studies, however, find that regardless of whether addicts have criminal records prior to addiction, their criminal activity increases substantially during periods of increased drug consumption. Rather than determining the age at onset of crime and drug use, these studies attempt to address the far more difficult issue of untangling the drugs-crime relationship as it is manifest over the careers of addicts. Ball et al. (1981, 1982, 1983) interviewed Baltimore addicts regarding levels of criminal involvement during periods of addiction and during periods of abstinence while they were "at risk" (not in prison or a residential treatment program). The researchers then calculated the total number of "crime days" (any 24-hour period in which one or more crimes were committed) per year at risk for periods of abstinence and for periods of addiction. Hence, rather than merely assessing the sequence of initiation into drug use versus crime, Ball et al. attempted to ascertain the relationship between drug use and crime throughout the careers of the addicts in their study. Examining the frequency of criminal behavior and drug use over time in this manner led to some startling results: "A . . . major finding of the study was that addiction status had a marked influence on criminality among these males. Thus, it was found that the number of offenses increased sixfold when these subjects were addicted. . . . These research findings pertaining to the impact of addiction on criminality were surprising and unexpected. Thus, we did not expect this marked increase, given the known involvement of this population in crime. Conversely, one might say that we were unprepared for the decrease that occurred when addiction ceased" (Ball et al., 1981:61).

A similar strategy was employed by Anglin and Speckart among clients of methadone-maintenance programs in California (Anglin and Speckart, 1986, 1988; Anglin and Yih-Ing Hser, 1987; Speckart and Anglin, 1986). These researchers established critical dates and time periods in addict careers: first narcotics use (FN), first daily use of narcotics for 30 days (FDU), the last time narcotics were used for 30 consecutive days (LDU), starting date of methadone maintenance (M), and date of methadone discharge (MD). Levels of criminal activity were then examined with respect to these critical dates. The findings are quite clear. While there is certainly evidence for preaddiction criminality, there is a substantial increase in criminal activity after addiction (FDU) and a substantial decrease following the addiction period (LDU). Anglin and Speckart concur with the conclusion by Ball et al. that there is a monotonic and causal relationship between narcotics use and criminal behavior.

While the Baltimore and California research was under way, Bruce Johnson and his associates were devising a novel strategy in New York City (see Johnson et al., 1985). This methodology was unique because, unlike the earlier studies, Johnson et al. interviewed cohorts of addicts daily for a period of five days followed by weekly interviews over the next four weeks, for a total of nine interviews over a 33-day period. During each session, respondents were asked to relate specifically what crimes they had committed and what drugs they had used that day or during the preceding week.

The findings of Johnson et al. are not as dramatic as those reported by Ball et al. or by the Anglin and Speckart team. While daily heroin users had more criminally active days than did less-frequent users, the frequency of crime per criminally active day was not appreciably different between user groups. Moreover, there was little difference across user groups in the amount of overall income derived from crime. While the authors conclude that daily heroin users do commit more crime than less-frequent users, their findings are much less definitive with regard to the drugs-crime nexus than are those of the Baltimore and California studies. This is likely due in part to another important finding by the Johnson et al. study: heroin users rely on a myriad of quasi-criminal strategies for enhancing drug availability. The addicts in the study reported that much of their drug income derived from such activities as *touting* and *steering* (directing potential customers to fellow dealers), *renting* their *works* (making syringes and other drug paraphernalia available for a fee), *hitting* (injecting) less-experienced users, and *testing* drugs for local dealers. Some of these individuals would act as *runners*, transporting large quantities of drugs from one place to another, or *holders*, maintaining possession of a dealer's drugs and dispensing it to customers after receiving hand signals from the dealer as to the amount sold. These are valuable services to dealers since in the event of an arrest they do not have the drugs on their person. Still other respondents reported running *shooting galleries*, usually abandoned buildings where addicts could come in off the street to *shoot up* (inject heroin). All of these activities are remunerated—sometimes in cash, sometimes in the form of free drugs. Hence, the Johnson et al. study reveals that addicts enhance the availability of drugs in many ways, including but not limited to predatory criminal activities.

The superior character of these methodologies notwithstanding, caution must be taken in interpreting the data. While these authors have clearly established that there is a relationship between addiction and crime throughout the careers of addicts, their data fail to establish causality definitively. While the conclusion that increased addiction causes criminal behavior is certainly a reasonable one, it is just as reasonable to conclude that increased criminality facilitates addiction. I contend that the ongoing debate over the causal relationship between drug use and crime fails to appreciate the dynamic character of addict careers. These activities are subject to all those contingencies that shape the broader careers of which they are a part. I shall attempt to demonstrate that, in fact, both the "drugs cause crime" and "crime causes drugs" explanations may accurately explain the drugs-crime connection at different periods in an addict's career.

### Criminal Specialization

Understanding addiction as a career also has implications for how we conceptualize the nature of addict criminality. Early literature addressing this issue depicts the addict as suffering from a pathological personality (Chein, 1956), as a "retreatist" who has withdrawn from meaningful social participation (Merton, 1938), and even as a "double failure" who has failed not only in the legitimate marketplace but as a criminal as well (Cloward and Ohlin, 1960). These depictions contribute to an understanding of addict criminality as highly impulsive and opportunistic, motivated by driving physiological and psychological needs for drugs.

Recent research, however, questions this presumption (Agar, 1973; Biernacki, 1979; Faupel, 1986, 1987a; Gould et al., 1974; Hanson et al., 1985; Preble and Casey, 1969; Sackman et al., 1978). These observers view criminal addicts as skilled entrepreneurs who must develop a profitable *hustle* (criminal activity) if they are to survive on the street. In the legitimate occupational marketplace, the current high level of career specialization has only come about through an increasingly refined division of labor. Letkeman suggests that the criminal enterprise is similarly affected when he writes that "an increasingly complex technology encourages criminals to specialize" (1973:159).

The extent to which addict criminals specialize, however, has been debated, even among those who reject the earlier pathological, impulsive model. Preble and Casey, on the one hand, assert that there is considerable specialization: "As with non-addicted criminals, addict criminals tend to specialize in certain activities, depending on their personalities, skills and experience" (1969:17). Similarly, James et al. report that "women tend to choose one cluster of criminal activities in which they excel through experience or innate skill" (1976:453). Other recent observations, however, contradict these claims (Goldstein, 1981; Johnson et al., 1985; Rosenbaum, 1981). Goldstein, for example, concludes that "the majority of subjects engaged in theft by 'grabbing what they could'" (1981:70). Similarly, observing the behavior of female addicts, Rosenbaum asserts that "basically, because her life is chaotic, all work takes the form of odd jobs rather than occupations; she may burgle today, forge tomorrow, and prostitute next week" (1981:74–75).

This discrepancy in observations reflects a continuing disagreement among observers of the criminal-addict subculture regarding the nature and extent of criminal sophistication among heroin addicts. A more moderate position is suggested by Gould et al.: "The average middle of the road dope fiend is much more successful than these losers. He usually has one or two hustles which he is fairly good at, but he knows enough about other hustles to be able to boost [shoplift] at Christmas time, work the parking lots in June when the universities are having graduation, and deal a little dope on the side to make ends meet" (1974:52). This observation, which characterizes the *main hustle* (Biernacki, 1979; Faupel, 1986, 1987a; Fields and Walters, 1985), suggests that although addicts may not be highly sophisticated criminals, they do tend to gravitate toward a restricted number of select crimes at which they become relatively skilled. Also implied in the main hustle, however, is that there are circumstances under which addicts may depart from their criminal propensities and flirt with other forms of criminal behavior as the need or opportunity arises. Furthermore, I illustrate in later chapters that the variable contingencies of heroin-using careers may not allow addicts to be highly selective during lean periods, while during more prosperous times criminal activity may be restricted to a single preferred hustle.

*Addict Ethics*

Perhaps the most commonly stereotyped attribute of heroin addiction is an inevitable deterioration of moral values and ethical standards. This belief, which Lindesmith (1940) calls the "dope fiend mythology," holds that as the addict becomes hopelessly enslaved to the addictive powers of heroin, all ethical constraints dissolve and a process of moral degeneracy inevitably ensues. A vice squad officer interviewed by Leroy Gould and his colleagues stated quite poignantly: "These junkies become so degenerate it is sad. They live in such filth. You should see some of the apartments I've been in. What's more, junkies have no consideration for their families and their friends. . . . I think the drug does something basic to a person. I don't know what it is. I'm not an expert on that sort of thing, but it seems as if drug users just don't have any morals left after awhile" (Gould et al., 1974:71).

Implied in this statement is the belief that the addict is willing to victimize anyone indiscriminately, without regard to friendship or even family ties. One San Francisco journalist has flatly asserted: "He's after that money; he needs it to buy heroin. And he'll take it from you if you are his nearest and dearest friend, even if he has to kill you to do it" (quoted in Silver and Aldrich, 1979:42).

Recent research questions this depiction of the inevitable morally destructive effects of heroin use. Numerous studies (e.g., Ashley, 1972; Hanson et al., 1985; Hughes, 1977; Preble and Casey, 1969; Rosenbaum, 1981; Waldorf, 1973; Zinberg, 1984) suggest that most heroin addicts maintain a sense of ethical responsibility in their social worlds. Contrary to popular belief, this research consistently reports that heroin addicts are not indiscriminate in their choice of victims. Rosenbaum finds that not only do addicts espouse a distinct code of ethics but that the inclination and ability to adhere to this code vary with one's standing in the world of heroin use: "A code of ethics is, in fact, a part of the stratification system in the addict world. Theft, for example, is graduated. The more impersonal the target of stealing, the better; the closer to home the worse the addict feels about it. While it is seen as all right, even courageous and bold, to steal from a large store or a person unknown to the addict, stealing from friends, family and, to a lesser extent, other addicts is not sanctioned" (1981:54).

In spite of this growing body of research, we do know that most addicts have engaged in behaviors that violate the standards and norms of their subculture. Despite ethical protestations to the contrary, most addicts have, at one time or another, victimized those nearest and dearest to them. Heroin addicts are by no means unique in their capacity to violate their own ethical standards. Situational exceptions to idealized cultural standards can be observed throughout all sectors of the population, and it should not be surprising that there are times, places, and circumstances in which normative standards of the heroin subculture are also violated. As Meier argues, the more important empirical challenge is to determine the circumstances under which these standards are breached: "The concept of norm . . . does not require a correspondence between what persons say and what they do; discrepancies are to be expected. . . . Because norms identify behavior that 'ought' or 'ought not' to occur, behavior may (and often does) depart from norms. . . . The more relevant consideration includes the conditions under which this potential for deviance is realized and the conditions under which norms guide specific conduct" (1981:14).

I contend that all heroin users are indeed capable of violating their sense of ethical responsibility at one point or another in their careers. There are certain periods, however, in which normative indiscretions are more likely to occur than in others, and the ability of addicts to maintain ethical standards is shaped by the constraints and opportunities encountered throughout the course of their careers (Faupel, 1987b).

These are issues with which criminologists and drug researchers have wrestled for decades. My purpose in writing this book is to elaborate a framework for interpreting the complexities addressed by these and other important research questions. Moreover, the answers to these questions—and the conceptual perspective of *career* in which both the questions and the answers are structured—provide a perspective from which to evaluate existing strategies and policies. Law enforcement agencies, for example, understand drug use as essentially a criminal problem calling for more effective interdiction, thereby eliminating or at least reducing supplies of illegal drugs. Treatment agencies, by contrast, typically approach drug use and the various behavioral dynamics associated with it as a medical issue that calls for a reduction in demand through treatment and, it is hoped, a "cure."

The career framework elaborated here reflects the fundamentally social nature of drug use and related behaviors. That which predisposes these careerists to use or not to use drugs, to engage in criminal activity or to desist, is more than simply the plentifulness of drugs, the threat of arrest, or physiological craving for a particular substance, although these are all conditions that may indeed play a role in motivating behavior. As with conventional careerists, there is a host of factors that predispose addicts to do this or that. By examining addict behavior as a response to external career contingencies, this analysis provides a framework for evaluating drug policy that reflects the perspectives and experiences of the career participant. These considerations are formally addressed in chapters eight and nine.

### The Fieldwork Methodology

This research is a part of a larger, ongoing study of the relationship between use of expensive drugs and criminal behavior that began in 1977. In an effort to move beyond the standard methodology employed in the literature, which simply established the sequence of onset of drug use versus criminality, the decision was made to build in a qualitative component composed of life history interviews with hard-core heroin-using criminals in the Wilmington, Delaware, area. This methodology places limits on generalizations that can be made from the data. Controlled users, or *chippers,* will not have experienced many of the dynamics reported here. Similarly, physicians, nurses, and middle-class "prescription users" are not usually subject to many of the constraints experienced by lower-class street users. Hence, it is important to emphasize that the findings I report here are intended to describe hard-core urban heroin addicts. The first part of this section describes the life history technique as it was employed in this study. This discussion is followed by a brief description of the data-analysis process.

### The Life History Technique

Despite its limitations, the life history technique has made a substantial contribution to our understanding of social life, as evidenced by Thomas and Znaniecki's pioneering work *The Polish Peasant in Europe and America* (1927) along with Sutherland's *The Professional Thief* (1937) and Shaw's *The Jack Roller* 1930). More recently, work on professional fences by Klockars (1974) and Steffensmeier (1986) has substantially enhanced our knowledge of the criminal enterprise by providing rich accounts of this important component of the underground economy.

The life history contributes substantially to our understanding of the social world in several ways. First, it serves as a valuable reality check with which to evaluate existing ideas, theories, and statistical data. Second, because of the wealth of data contained in the life history—data that are not predetermined by existing theoretical constructs—previously untapped areas for theoretical development may be suggested. Third, of all possible methodologies, the life history is most insightful of the subjective nature of social reality. The "commonsense" view of social reality emanating from the experience of the actor is critical for a comprehensive understanding of the social world of drug use. Finally, the life history method is particularly appropriate to the study of social process. While quantitative analysts frequently draw conclusions regarding the dynamics of social process, their methodologies do not allow them to analyze the processes they assert. Denzin brings this valuable contribution into clear focus as he responds to Lundberg's charge that the life history lacks any scientific base: "There certainly is no better way to establish covariance and time order between a set of variables than with a method that explicitly focuses on events over time" (1970:239).

The life history technique employed here departs somewhat from the traditional methodology in two ways. First, several life histories were obtained rather than a single, in-depth case study. A total of 30 addicts from the Wilmington area were interviewed. All of the respondents had extensive contact with the criminal justice system, and, at the time of interview, 24 were under correctional supervision (either incarcerated, on work release, or on probation or parole). Women are slightly overrepresented, constituting 12 of the 30 respondents. Ethnically, the sample consists of 22 blacks and 8 whites. Hispanics are not represented because there is not a sizable Hispanic drug-using population in the Wilmington area.

Second, while the interviews spanned the entire biographies of each of the respondents, the primary focus was on that period in their lives in which they used drugs and/or committed crimes on more than an experimental basis. In this respect, it might be more appropriate to refer to these interviews as *career histories*. While the interviews were consciously conducted in an open-ended format, certain broad focal areas for questioning were designated prior to going into the field to allow some degree of comparability across the sample. These broad areas include (1) early pre-drug-using and criminal experiences that may have served as predisposing factors contributing to the respondent's drug using and criminal career, (2) initial experimentation with drug use and criminal behavior, (3) the evolution of drug use and criminal patterns over time, (4) patterns of activity during peak periods of drug use and criminal behavior, including descriptions of typical days during those periods, (5) respondent's perceptions of the cultural milieu in which drug using and/or criminal behavior takes place, including normative proscriptions, status distinctions in the subculture, and requisite skills and knowledge for successful functioning in the subculture, (6) encounters with the criminal justice system, and (7) treatment experiences.

In order to insure a higher response rate, respondents were paid $5 per hour for their interview time. Respondents were informed of this remuneration at the time the project was introduced to them. It was clearly specified that they were being paid for their time just as anyone would be paid for their time. They were not being paid for information, as might have been their experience, for example, with the police seeking information on other addicts. This initial explanation was necessary to avoid the potential problem of respondents telling me what they anticipated I wanted to hear. Respondents were also promised confidentiality during this initial explanatory session and were told that they could withdraw from the interview at any point.

The interviews ranged from 10 to 25 hours in length, with each session lasting from 2 to 4 hours. With a single exception, all of the interviews were tape-recorded. Respondents were told, however, that they could request that the tape recorder be turned off at any time they felt the information was too sensitive to record. There were a few occasions when such a "blackout" was requested, although in most cases it was simply a matter of a respondent wanting to gossip about a particular person and not wanting it taped. Respondents were not hesitant to speak openly of their drug using and criminal careers, and more often than not they found it to be a rewarding experience.

Prior to going into the field I established contact with an ex–treatment counselor who had a long-standing rapport with Wilmington's drug-using population. His "good guy" reputation was firmly established some years earlier when he successfully instigated much-needed reforms in one of the local treatment centers. Later, I made contact with another treatment professional, which facilitated my entry into the prison subculture. Fortunately, the director of the prison treatment program was regarded as highly trustworthy by the inmates in the prison. He was perceived as an ally in the quest for better living conditions in the prison, a reputation enhanced by the uneasy relationship between prison officials and the treatment program itself, which was still relatively new at that time.

The tactical strategy of using treatment personnel, while potentially a liability, proved invaluable for two reasons. First, as I have already suggested, I was quite fortunate in that the personnel available to me were positively regarded by area drug users. The tasks of soliciting cooperation and subsequently establishing rapport were thus facilitated by my association with these individuals. Second, I avoided many of the problems typically associated with using indigenous informants as points of entry. The professionals I contacted, for example, did not have a vested interest in introducing me to a select group of their friends who could benefit from the financial reward offered for their participation. Indeed, their position placed them in contact with multiple networks of drug users. Moreover, these professional contacts were already familiar with the nature of social research and were readily trainable with regard to the specific nature and goals of this research project. Consequently, they not only functioned as a point of entry into the drug subculture but also served to screen out those potential respondents who did not have extensive drug-using and criminal histories.

My entry into the field was relatively smooth, facilitated greatly by the ex–treatment counselor who introduced me to some key contacts. My naïveté was quite obvious, of course, as I was continually having to ask respondents to define what became new words in my vocabulary—

words like *jones, cut, bundle, boy,* and *girl.* Moreover, I'm sure my surprise and disbelief at the life-style dynamics did not go unnoticed by the participants in the project, particularly during the early days of the fieldwork. I made no attempt to hide my naïveté, however, as I soon learned that it could be quite advantageous. Upon learning that I truly was *square* (I had smoked marijuana on two occasions—hardly enough to qualify as an experienced drug user), respondents quite readily assumed the role of teacher and exerted themselves to "tell it to me like it really was."

As the fieldwork progressed I became less naïve, to be sure; I did, however, consciously cultivate a naïveté in my relationship with the research participants in a number of ways. I would typically introduce the project by stating that research on heroin addiction is decades old, but there have been few studies that have sought out the heroin user's perception of addiction, crime, treatment, and other relevant aspects of drug use; that what I wanted to do was to go away with a more thorough understanding of the heroin-using world as the participants experienced it, and only they (the participants) could adequately provide me with that understanding. Similarly, when querying participants regarding their criminal modus operandi and the requisite skills involved, I explicitly placed them in the role of a teacher who was to assume that I knew nothing about crime. What would I have to know? What skills would I have to learn? How would I go about committing such a crime without getting caught? Later in the fieldwork process as I began to formulate some theoretical ideas, I would routinely ask respondents to reflect on these ideas and provide me feedback. In one instance, I asked a participant to read and respond to a draft of a paper I was working on. Strategies such as this that appeal to the expertise of the participant inevitably entail the assumption of a social role in the interview process. The respondent is no longer a research subject but is an expert, a teacher.

This strategy was often less than comfortable for me as a researcher because it meant abandoning my role as expert, a role that academicians are only too ready to assume. It also meant relinquishing some control over the interview process itself as the participants in this project played a much more dominant role in defining the direction of the interview. But I am convinced that the value of this strategy greatly outweighed whatever disadvantages it may have incurred. It was fascinating to observe these respondents as they took on the expert role. They became more assertive, more animated, and generally more visibly interested in the interview. In the first moments of the interviews, respondents were often vague and even careless in their responses, but as they took on the role of expert, their responses were invariably more painstaking as they attempted to represent themselves and their world as accurately and completely as possible.

The research methodology used here does raise some validity and reliability issues. One such issue is the use of incarcerated offenders as respondents. This group does not necessarily represent the broader population of heroin users. These are, after all, addicts who were caught. Moreover, because they are a captive population with excess time on their hands, it is certainly conceivable that these incarcerated addicts may have embellished their biographies, especially given that they were paid on an hourly basis. The reader is thus cautioned to recognize this special character of the sample. Nevertheless, the dynamics expressed in these pages do not contradict other similar studies, particularly those of an ethnographic nature. Moreover, while the participants in this research differ on various specific points, there is remarkable consistency across all 30 (street and incarcerated) respondents with regard to the broader career dynamics described here. Finally, I would argue that there is little incentive to deceive. It was made clear to each respondent that this was independent research, not affiliated with any agency of the criminal justice system. Most of the respondents readily accepted this portrayal and did not question the project's integrity. Hence, unlike criminal justice and treatment personnel who often hold a big carrot or stick, these respondents recognized that I was not in a position to affect their destiny in any way. There was no "correct" response that would place them in a more favorable position. All that I wanted was their most honest and candid recollection of the events of their careers. Indeed, I am confident that the roles of "expert" and "student" the participants and I played respectively actually served to enhance data validity. The role of student allowed me to ask "dumb" questions and to query apparent contradictions in a less-threatening way, thus clarifying and qualifying the information I received. Participants in the study, thrust into the role of experts, were visibly conscientious about representing themselves to me in the most accurate way that they could.

Memory is almost surely a more knotty validity issue than is deceit. Respondents were asked to recall events from years earlier in their lives.

While I was not interested in such specific details as, say, how many times a respondent may have committed a shoplifting offense in 1963, it was necessary to learn how much an individual respondent was criminally involved at one time relative to another, to learn something of the sequence of increases in crime and drug use, and so on. In an effort to minimize such errors of memory, I would frequently ask for the same information in a different way. Respondents would often supply further information later in the interview that allowed for further clarification of earlier responses. In addition, it was relatively common for a respondent to give contradictory information, which provided an opportunity for further clarification by my exposing the contradiction. I also learned that like the rest of us, heroin users tend to organize their biographies around important incidents in their lives. I thus created a "time line" of key events in their biographies. Such events included first times for committing a crime, using drugs, getting caught for a crime, and for going to prison, as well as other significant occurrences such as the death of a family member, getting married, etc. The time line not only provided a concise overview of crucial biographical episodes but also served as a valuable tool for clarifying the temporal sequence of these events. I might typically ask, "Now you said your heroin use increased somewhere around the end of the 1960s. Do you remember if it was before or after you committed your first robbery? Was it before or after you went to prison the first time?" While questions such as these did not always allow me to affix a specific date on a particular incident, the time line did permit me to locate that event within the context of the respondent's biography.

Finally, because Wilmington is a smaller locale than major drug centers such as New York or Miami, there may be some differences in career dynamics for the addicts in this sample. Law enforcement officers readily recognize many of the addicts on Wilmington streets. Similarly, many—perhaps most—of the addicts in Wilmington know each other, including at least four of the addicts in this sample.[1] In short, there may be a more cohesive subculture in smaller urban areas such as Wilmington that may affect the careers of these addicts in ways that are not possible in larger drug centers. Moreover, Wilmington addicts must travel to major cities to obtain large quantities of wholesale *dope*, a limitation not confronted by addicts in larger urban centers. Hence, while the dynamics reported here reflect the experiences of hard-core urban addicts as opposed to middle-class or occupationally related addicts, there may be some features of these careers that are not shared by career addicts in larger metropolitan areas.

*Analysis of the Data*

It is perhaps a bit artificial to speak of "data analysis" as a separate process, since to a large extent the data were constantly being analyzed and interpreted throughout the research process. This approach is the essence of what Glaser and Strauss call "grounded theory," which involves a union of data and theory generation: "Generating a theory from data means that most hypotheses and concepts not only come from the data, but are systematically worked out in relation to the data during the course of the research" (1967:6). Hence, in addition to tape-recording the interviews, which provided the basis for a more formal and thorough subsequent analysis, notes were taken during the interviews. Following each two- to four-hour session, these notes were translated into longhand and organized and typed when possible. This process of note taking, organizing, and rewriting provided an initial data analysis that proved valuable in suggesting some preliminary theoretical ideas that, in turn, informed subsequent lines of questioning.

All but one of the interviews were tape-recorded. Upon completion of the interviewing process, the nearly 500 hours of tape recordings were subject to a more detailed analysis than was possible with the field notes. A content analysis was performed, using essentially the same categories that guided the interviews themselves. Several types of information were coded on the content analysis: (1) locator information, including case number, sex of respondent, and location of the material on the tape or transcript; (2) substantive content, including summary statements and quoted material; and (3) theoretical and methodological notes.

The following pages represent the most complete analysis of these data to date. Chapter two elaborates the conceptual framework from which the data are interpreted. It does this by situating heroin addiction within the broader spectrum of activities that constitute careers as understood by sociologists, discussing the temporal quality of careers, and by elaborating those special dynamics and contingencies that shape the direction of heroin-using careers. The career concept has been applied to deviant life-styles with great frequency, but with few exceptions (e.g., Luckenbill and Best, 1981) there has been little refinement or clarification of the concept in the deviance literature. Hence, I devote the following chapter primarily to conceptual and theoretical concerns.

Chapters three through six consist of detailed discussions of each of four broad but clearly discernible phases of heroin-using careers that emerge in relation to these contingencies. Moreover, these chapters address the dynamics implicit in each of these phases for the various research and policy questions discussed earlier. Finally, chapters seven through nine systematically summarize the research and policy implications of the career paradigm elaborated throughout the book. Among other issues, these chapters examine implications for law enforcement, treatment, drug legalization, and the viability of official data on drug use and crime.

# 2

# Drug Use as Career

══════════════════════════ The concept of career first appeared
in the sociology of occupations to refer to "the sequence of movement
from one position to another in an occupational system by any individual who works in that system" (Becker, 1963:24). As used in the sociology of occupations, the concept is typically linked to an organizational
system, as in Becker's (1952) study of the career of the Chicago public
school teacher and Hall's (1948) classic study of the stages of medical
careers.[1] The concept was introduced into the deviance literature in
Goffman's (1959, 1961) discussions of the moral careers of mental patients and was later extended by Becker (1963) to deviant careers generally. Subsequent to these pioneering works, career has been used as an
interpretive framework to study numerous manifestations of deviance,
including prostitution and other forms of sexual behavior (Best, 1982;
Bryan, 1965; Buckner, 1970; Skipper and McCaghy, 1970; Weinberg,
1966); fencing (Klockars, 1974; Steffensmeier, 1986); professional
crime (Inciardi, 1975; Letkeman, 1973; Sutherland, 1937); skid row
alcoholism (Wiseman, 1970); gambling (Hayano, 1982; Lesieur, 1977);
and narcotics addiction (Coombs, 1981; Faupel, 1987a; Fiddle, 1976;
Rubington, 1967).

This chapter examines drug addiction as a career by (1) defining career as a sociological concept, (2) identifying types of careers with a
special focus on the typological nature of drug use, and (3) examining

the temporal quality of careers. The chapter concludes with a discussion of the contingencies that shape heroin-using careers.

## Career as a Sociological Concept

Van Maanen's description of career provides a starting point for a sociological definition of heroin-using careers: "The career then is simply a series of separate but related experiences and adventures through which a person passes during a lifetime. It is shorthand notation for a particular set of activities with a natural, unfolding history—involvement over time in a given role or across a series of roles. A career can be either brilliant or disappointing, a success or a failure. In the work world, therefore, prostitutes, plumbers, doctors, factory workers, managers, housewives, bartenders, waitresses, lawyers, criminals, and cops all have careers" (1977:1).

It has not been customary in common parlance to regard activities that are not related to professions or occupations as careers. Stereotypically, homemakers care for their families, but they do not "work." Stamp collecting and other hobbies are forms of relaxation, a hiatus from a stressful career perhaps, but they are not usually understood as careers themselves. Heroin addicts are defined as "retreatists" or as suffering from an "addictive personality." Their behavior is frequently described in terms of pathology or compensation but is seldom defined in terms of meaningful activities and roles organized around the pursuit of rational goals as is, say, the hectic schedule of a doctor or Wall Street broker. A subjective understanding demands that we describe these otherwise disparate activities in terms that reveal their commonality. More than a quarter century ago, Everett C. Hughes insightfully observed that "we need to rid ourselves of any concepts which keep us from seeing that the essential problems of men at work are the same whether they do their work in some famous laboratory or in the messiest vat room of a pickle factory. Until we can find a point of view and concepts which will enable us to make comparisons between the junk peddler and the professor without intent to debunk the one and patronize the other, we cannot do our best work in this field" (1958:48).

Despite the stereotypes, all of the activities mentioned above can be described in terms of career. More significant than the specific nature of a given set of activities is the way in which they relate to one's biography. Are these behaviors systematically organized in relation to social roles or are they disparate, unrelated events in the life of the actor? Do they serve as meaningful acts that serve to organize one's biography or are they incidental to one's definition of self? Again Van Maanen provides a useful benchmark: "What is most significant about a person's career is, however, the degree to which it serves as the principle around which the individual organizes his or her life. And this depends not only upon the status, direction, tempo, and length of the career, but upon the meaning the individual ascribes to the career as well" (1977:1).

Van Maanen identifies three essential qualities common to all careers. First, careers have a temporal character. A single action does not constitute a career; rather, a career is a series of activities played out over time in a given role or a series of roles. Second, and perhaps most important, this sequence of related activities serves as a significant reference point around which an individual organizes his or her life. Hence, it is not appropriate to label the daily purchasing and reading of a newspaper a career (unless, of course, one is employed as a librarian for a major newspaper whose job it is to do just that). For most people, however, daily newspaper reading is quite incidental to those activities that they do regard as significant. People read the paper before they go to work, on a break from work, or after they get home from work, but not as part of their work. As important as it may become in one's daily routine, newspaper reading is not an important principle around which most people organize their lives—it is not a career in the sense that being a doctor, lawyer, business executive, homemaker, or even a prostitute or criminal is a career. All of these signify a constellation of activities that make up a coherent framework from which an individual acts in a reasonably organized and predictable manner. Finally, it is in relation to this framework that individuals interpret the meaning of events in their lives. That is, a career is more than a series of observable activities; it is also a subjective experience and identity deriving from the meanings attached to these activities, a feature which has received considerable commentary (Blankenship, 1973; Goffman, 1961; McCall and Simmons, 1966; Stebbins, 1970, 1971). For our purposes, then, *career* is defined as *a series of meaningfully related statuses, roles, and activities around which an individual organizes some aspect of his or her life.*

## Types of Careers

——————————— It is immediately apparent that if lawyers, doctors, homemakers, stamp collectors, prostitutes, criminals, and drug users may all be defined as careerists, there are also obvious and important differences in the nature of these careers. The careers of homemakers encompass an entirely different complex of statuses and roles than do those of lawyers. Doctors do not face the same problems and opportunities confronted by drug users. Hence, while adoption of a common vocabulary and conceptual framework to describe these activities has been a watershed in the study of deviant behavior, it is also important to recognize that there are ways in which these various activities differ. While careers may vary in any number of ways, there are two broad dimensions discussed in the literature that capture most of these important differences. The first is a normative dimension, distinguishing between *deviant* and *respectable* careers. The second dimension distinguishes between *occupational* and *nonoccupational* careers.

### Deviant versus Respectable Careers

Since Goffman (1959) and later Becker (1963) extended the application of career to deviant conduct, the concept has come into wide use in the sociology of deviance. This literature reveals a number of qualities of deviant biographies that make them analogous to conventional careers. It reveals something of the way in which deviant careers are launched as well as exited. It describes a hierarchy of statuses and associated role expectations. These studies also reveal the nature of the norms and maxims that guide the conduct of prostitutes, fences, and other deviant careerists, and of the socialization processes whereby these norms and maxims are learned. Also highlighted are those features of the careers of shoplifters, strippers, burglars, and drug addicts that are shared by the careers of physicians, lawyers, and even ministers. In short, this literature provides a common vocabulary and conceptual framework for both deviant and respectable careers.

It has also been recognized, however, that there are important points of divergence between deviant and respectable careers. These breaches in the career analogy have been succinctly summarized by Luckenbill and Best (1981). The overriding characteristic of deviant careers that distinguishes them from their respectable counterparts is the threat of punitive sanctions. Deviant careerists must often carry out their activities in secret, or at least segregate them from conventional friends and associates. Furthermore, these punitive sanctions introduce an additional cost, or potential cost, to these lines of activities which does not have to be calculated by conventional careerists. Moreover, unlike most respectable careers, deviant careers are not usually enacted in a highly structured formal environment (though see Hughes, 1937, for a brief discussion of less-structured respectable careers). As a consequence, Luckenbill and Best maintain that the sequence of statuses and roles characterizing the deviant career is less predictable than that for most respectable careers in highly structured organizational contexts.[2] The deviant career does not, for example, usually begin with any formal educational process; nor are there usually any formal rites of passage as one traverses the sequence of statuses. Hence, it is often difficult to measure the development or direction of deviant careers. That is, because there are no formally recognized standards against which to assess the direction of deviant careers, it is difficult to determine whether incumbents are progressing or retrogressing, moving upward or downward in their careers. Unlike the aspiring executive who is moved through various positions accompanied by appropriate increases in salary, the pattern of progression is usually not so clear with deviant careers. Indeed, the stigmatization process that often accompanies deviant careers frequently results in what most observers regard as downward mobility. Drug addicts who become known to the police, for example, may be courted by law enforcement agencies and pressured to become informants. When this happens, it is difficult to maintain quality *connections* (dependable sources of drugs), and, lacking a sufficient quantity of drugs, the publicly labeled addict is forced to live a meager existence. At the same time, however, having "done time" in prison usually contributes to the prestige that one enjoys on the streets. But the critical feature of deviant careers is their lack of clear demarcation relative to most respectable careers.

### Occupational versus Nonoccupational Careers

Luckenbill and Best also distinguish between occupational and nonoccupational careers. This dimension has received less attention in the literature but nevertheless reveals important differences in career dynamics and therefore merits further elaboration. Occupational careers are organized around those statuses and roles associated with the activities that one engages in for purposes of making a living—commonly called *work*. Nonoccupational careers, on the other hand, consist of the sequence of statuses, roles, and activities organized around pursuits not related to making a living.

When sociologists speak of occupations, they usually refer to fairly narrowly defined, regularly occurring patterns of activity for purposes of sustaining a livelihood. Form defines occupations as "relatively continuous patterns of activities that provide workers a livelihood and define their general social status" (1968:245). Similarly, Slocum defines occupation as "the kind of work an adult does on a regular basis. Usually it is an activity performed for wages, salary, commissions or other forms of money income" (1966:4).

There is considerable disagreement, however, about the relationship between occupation and career. Some definitions practically identify career with occupation by focusing on occupational achievements as the essence of career (Form, 1968). More commonly, occupational sociologists understand career as a series of related occupations through which workers move on their career paths. Implied in these definitions is the possibility of upward mobility through a sequence of positions and occupations characterized by ever-increasing prestige. But as Krause has noted, "Career is a minority, elite institution in Western society, if by this term we mean a graduated sequence of ever-increasing responsibilities within an occupation, a profession, or an organization, with recognized and known signposts along the way" (1971:41). Working- and lower-class occupations do not constitute nearly so stable a progression and are, according to Wilensky (1961), "disorderly" in contrast to the "orderly" careers of professional occupations.

There are also definitions that dissociate career from the concept of occupation altogether, rejecting the existence of an occupation as a precondition for career. Hughes explicitly embraces an extraoccupational understanding of career:

> Careers in our society are thought of very much in terms of jobs. . . . But the career is by no means exhausted in a series of business and professional achievements. There are other points at which one's life touches the social order, other lines of social accomplishment—influence, responsibility and recognition.

A woman may have a career in holding together a family or in raising it to a new position. Some people of quite modest occupational achievements have careers in patriotic, religious, and civic organizations. They may, indeed, budget their efforts toward some cherished office of this kind rather than toward advancement in their occupations. It is possible to have a career in an avocation as well as in a vocation. (1958:64)

It is this broader understanding of career that I have elaborated earlier in relation to Van Maanen's work. It is also this broader definition that is implicitly held by most sociologists of deviance who employ the career concept and to which I adhere. This point of view is reflected in Figure 1.

The typology presented in the figure is a heuristic device intended to illustrate the polytypic nature of career as a sociological concept. Two important features of Figure 1 should be highlighted. First, the occupational status of a career varies independently of its normative status. That is, both respectable and deviant careers may be occupational in nature; conversely, both may take place outside of an occupational framework. These two dimensions of careers and examples of the kinds of

### Figure 1: Types of Careers

Occupational

| | |
|---|---|
| TYPE I | TYPE III |
| *Respectable-Occupational* | *Deviant-Occupational* |
| Professions | Professional crime |
| Blue-collar | Theft |
| | Prostitution |

Respectable _____|_____ Deviant

| | |
|---|---|
| TYPE II | TYPE IV |
| *Respectable-Nonoccupational* | *Deviant-Nonoccupational* |
| Homemakers | Homosexuality |
| Volunteer careers | Mental Illness |
| Avocations, hobbies | Alcoholism |
| | Nudism |

Nonoccupational

careers that represent each type are shown here.[3] Second, the normative and occupational dimensions are represented here as continua; a given career is more or less deviant or more or less occupational in character. Consequently, there may be career experiences that defy classification in a single type. Moreover, some careers may contain features of more than one of these types. Despite such complexities, this typology does sensitize us to the multidimensional nature of career. Furthermore, it provides a useful framework for locating deviant careers—and, more particularly, drug-using careers—within the broad spectrum of activities that are understood as careers.

## Career Attributes of Drug Use

————————— Any discussion of the use of expensive illegal drugs must address two related but distinct sets of activities, which Goldman (1981) labels "consumer activities" and "income generating activities." Consumer activities refer essentially to behaviors associated with locating, purchasing, and using drugs. Income-generating activities involved raising the necessary funds, typically through criminal means, to purchase expensive drugs. These two sets of behaviors are, of course, highly interrelated and, in some cases, almost indistinguishable. Frequently, drug users who have wholesale connections will purchase a quantity of drugs and sell at retail only enough to cover their original purchase, a procedure known as *juggling*. In this way, drug dealing is for many users simply a means of financing their own habits.

### Drug Use and Career Types

Goldman's distinction is essential to the career typology outlined here. Users of expensive illegal drugs pursue multidimensional careers—that of drug consumer and (typically) that of criminal.[4] As criminals, these individuals are engaged in profit-making activities not only to maintain current levels of drug consumption but also to support a life-style with which they are comfortable. They are, in short, making a living, just like individuals in respectable occupations. As Pagie, a respondent in my study, explained: "It was business to me then. My addiction was business. What I had to sell was business. I was very businesslike in manner too. Because it wasn't a game I was playing."

Pagie's remarks illustrate that heroin users regard their income-generating criminal activity as work, an observation that has been frequently made (Agar, 1973; Biernacki, 1979; Faupel, 1986; Hanson et al., 1985; Sackman et al., 1978). As criminals, these individuals are involved in a myriad of occupational roles and activities, even within a given hustle. For example, burglars *case* (stake out) residences or businesses during the day, usually perform the act of burglary and theft at night, and fence the proceeds of their crime as soon as possible. This last act thus concludes a series of income-generating activities. Similarly, drug dealers must cultivate wholesale connections, usually in major cities in the region. After purchasing quantities of the drug, they must then test the drug for purity and *step on it* (dilute it) if it is sufficiently concentrated. The drug is then bagged and sold to retail customers. All of these are income-producing activities that reflect the dynamics of deviant-occupational careers (Type III in Figure 1).

There is, however, another aspect of drug-using careers that is interdependent with, but nevertheless conceptually distinct from, this income-generating criminal dimension. These consumer activities comprise those behaviors and statuses organized around the acquisition and consumption of drugs. As drug users, criminal addicts engage in a variety of nonoccupational consumer activities. They learn to *cop* (purchase), *cook* (prepare), and *spike* (inject) the drug. Similar to other nonoccupational careerists, addicts as consumers also develop social identities. Some are *dope fiends* (heavily involved but respected addicts), others *down-and-out junkies,* a term usually carrying the derogatory connotation of an addict who has lost respectability. Some have a reputation for being able to shoot up *righteous dope* (highly concentrated heroin), while others are known as *cotton shots* (down-and-out junkies who glean the residue from the cotton that other addicts have used to filter out impurities in the heroin). These features associated with drug use as a consumer activity predominantly reflect the dynamics of deviant-nonoccupational careers (Type IV in Figure 1).

These consumer features of addict careers are not isolated from the Type III income-generating criminal activities that most addicts are simultaneously pursuing. This dual quality of addict careers is a theme that runs through the biographies of all the addicts I interviewed. As I highlight throughout the remaining chapters of this book, the careers of addicts as criminals play a critical part in shaping the careers of addicts as users. Similarly, an individual's drug-using patterns provide both opportunities and obstacles to the successful performance of his or her criminal role. In other words, these roles are not merely parallel careers that happen to be pursued simultaneously. Rather, they are interdependent features that are inextricably linked in the dual-dimensional career of the criminal addict.

### The Temporal Quality of Careers

Careers have a temporal character, which implies that they pass through stages or phases, each of which poses certain obstacles and opportunities that, in turn, further define the nature and direction of the career. Although the term *career* was not commonly applied to drug-using activities until the late 1960s (Rubington, 1967), the social basis of addiction was recognized as early as 1947 by Lindesmith (1968). Subsequent research has further demonstrated the social process of addiction. Becker (1967) explored the social process of getting high. In the literature of the last two decades, the temporal dynamics of drug use and addiction are discussed with some frequency. Fiddle's ethnography describes the "sociopharmacological model of 'graduation': from nose to muscles to veins, from matchbox cover to the *works* or *equipment*, the slow filtering through the body to the *rush* or *buzz* and swift diffusion of ecstasy" (1976:558; italics in original). Social scientists who study occupational careers have identified any number of phases that, while not perfectly analogous to heroin-using careers, do illustrate dynamics characteristic of deviant careers as well.

**Career Choice and Entry.** The early period that marks the beginning of a career has been variously labeled but generally consists of the related processes of career choice and career entry. While some, such as Ginzberg et al. (1951), have argued that this is a rational, purposive process, most sociologists emphasize the situational character of choosing and entering a career. Katz and Martin view career initiation as follows:

> The process of entry into an occupation may be looked upon as the cumulative product of a series of specific acts, which may or may not be directly focused upon a deliberate career choice. . . . We suggest conceiving career choices as courses of action which are composites of adaptations—by individuals, to be sure—to meet the exigencies of particular, immediate situations. . . . The decisions

which underlie embarkation on a nursing career *for at least some persons* revolve around limited, situational contingencies—in which the matter of nursing-as-career enters only tangentially or not at all. Such "situationally delimited" decisions, we are suggesting, do not involve definite career decisions in terms of a subjective career commitment, but nonetheless these decisions constitute the active steps toward entry upon a career. (1962:149–50; italics in original)

Drug-using careers, I contend, are initiated in the same manner. Almost without exception, studies report that beginning users are *turned on* (introduced to the drug) by close friends and acquaintances, who themselves are often just experimenting with the drug (Chein et al., 1964; Crawford et al., 1983; Feldman, 1968; Rubington, 1967). Harry, a respondent in my study, described his first experience with amphetamines: "This girl was on a diet in school. She came into school and said, 'Man, they [amphetamines] make you really feel good. Look how much weight I lost. They just make you high.' I said, 'Well, let me try one.' I tried them, and I was, shit, 'motor man.'"

Experimentation with heroin is often a less-positive experience. Much like one's first encounter with alcohol, early experiences with heroin are often unpleasant, accompanied by nausea and other adverse physical reactions. It is, however, an experience that marks the beginning of a career in heroin use and is consequently a memorable event for many users, as borne out by the following interview excerpt:

[**Belle**] He was telling me how good it was—'cause I was doggin' him for it. I said, "Give me a try." And I didn't like it and I threw up and everything . . . I said, "I'm not gonna do that shit no more." Next day the same thing.

[**Interviewer**] Why did you go on using after the first time, since it was so unpleasant?

[**Belle**] I guess it was just like drinkin' . . . you get so shit-faced you wake up the next day and say, "Man, I ain't gonna do that shit no more. Goddamn, it was decent, but I feel like shit." Couple days later you forget about that—you're sitting there with a martini in your hand. . . . It's like that.

While the circumstances under which addicts first use heroin are varied, initiation into heroin-using careers is usually unintentional. For many, the setting is a party or similar social occasion in which the drug is being shared. Women frequently get turned on by their boyfriends. One respondent in this study had been lending money to a drug-using friend for months, and when he wasn't getting paid back, he insisted that the borrower give him some dope as collateral. Some days later he and another friend experimented with it. As these experiences suggest, beginning heroin users are not consciously initiating heroin-using careers. Despite the voluntary nature of early experimentation described by nearly all of the addicts that I interviewed, entry into heroin-using careers is not purposive but is quite situational and, in some cases, even serendipitous.

**Career Mobility.** Somewhere between entering and exiting a career are encountered the opportunities, obstacles, decisions, and activities that make up one's career. This phase, which can be broadly termed the period of *career mobility,* refers to all of the vicissitudes encountered in the course of one's career. This broad application is at variance with much of the occupations literature, which views career mobility as a "commitment to moving upward through a series of related occupations and statuses according to a schedule" (Form, 1968:252). The deviance literature, in contrast, depicts deviant careers in a much less orderly fashion. As Luckenbill and Best point out, mobility need not always imply a vertical progression:

> Riding escalators between floors may be an effective metaphor for respectable organizational careers, but it fails to capture the character of deviant careers. A more appropriate image is a walk in the woods. Here, some people take the pathways marked by their predecessors, while others strike out on their own. Some walk slowly, exploring before moving further, but others run, caught up in the action. Some have a destination in mind and proceed purposively; others view the trip as an experience and enjoy it for its own sake. Even those intent on reaching a destination may stray from the path; they may try to shortcut or they may lose sight of familiar landmarks, get lost, and find it necessary to backtrack. Without a rigid organizational structure, deviant careers can develop in many different ways. (1981:201)

Deviant careers are by nature composed of multiple career shifts and temporary exiting and reentering. Lesieur (1977), for example, finds that compulsive gamblers experience repeated cycles of abstinence and relapse in their careers. Similarly, Irwin (1970) found that risk of arrest frequently forces habitual property offenders to engage temporarily in some other type of work. Failing to do so before getting caught often results in arrest and confinement, which serve to substantially interrupt one's career. Reentry for many of these felons means a return to their former criminal life-styles, or, in some cases, they will take up new hustles.

Like other deviant careers, drug-using careers closely reflect what Wilensky (1961) calls disorderly careers. Nearly three decades ago, Ray (1961) described a cycle of abstinence and relapse among the heroin addicts he interviewed. These patterns have also been observed by others (e.g., Akers et al., 1968; Coombs, 1981; Waldorf, 1971). Similarly, with regard to criminal occupations that sustain drug-using careers, a pattern of frequent occupational shifts has often been observed (Biernacki, 1979; Fiddle, 1976; James et al., 1976). Indeed, Rosenbaum has described the career of the female addict as "chaotic": "The activities that are part of the addict's life make establishing a structured routine nearly impossible. With the first event of the day—waking up sick— chaos begins. A woman who is desperate does not have the patience to think out her moves, to execute an ordered plan; therefore, her hustling patterns are both sporadic and chaotic. She may prostitute one day, boost the next, forge after that—each without much plan or attention to detail. Her skills are never highly developed in any one occupation, so she doesn't have one to fall back on" (1981:50–51).

As I elaborate more fully below, there are a host of factors in the subculture of heroin use that affect the addict's ability to sustain a reasonably stable life-style, and Rosenbaum's observations clearly apply to portions of the careers of both the men and women I interviewed. While there are stable periods in heroin-using careers, from an overall perspective heroin addiction can be characterized as anything but orderly.

**Exiting the Career.** The process of exiting a career in the world of conventional occupations is most commonly thought of as retirement, which is normally understood as an earned right, the legitimate and logical culmination of one's career. This ideal is probably less commonly realized than might be expected. There is a growing literature that suggests that most occupational careerists do not cease labor market activity upon exiting their original careers (Gray and Morse, 1980; Lieberman and Lieberman, 1983; Parnes and Nestel, 1981; Skoglund, 1979; Stagner, 1979). Moreover, I maintain that the concept of retirement itself presupposes an orderly, usually professional career. In contrast, disorderly careers involve frequent career disruptions and forced changes (Wilensky, 1961) such that in many cases retirement amounts to little more than another disruption or career shift. Retirement from disorderly careers certainly does not represent the culmination of a lifetime of career activity as it does in more orderly, professional careers.

I suggested earlier that deviant careers more closely reflect disorderly careers than orderly careers, and this is also borne out by the retirement process. Criminal careerists do not have retirement and pension funds from which to draw an income. In most cases, exiting a criminal career is a gradual and uncertain process. Irwin (1970) found that the felon's return to conventional society was an uneasy transition. Aspirations are high but opportunities are limited, and the ex-convict finds "doing good" enormously difficult. Harris's (1973) study of the Dilly Boys, male prostitutes in London's West End, reveals a similar pattern, an exit process that is anything but smooth. Some male prostitutes become drug addicts; others take up petty crime; still others gravitate to the gay bars that previously served as their business hangout. Most do eventually return to conventional society, but the process is anything but orderly.

Heroin addicts, like other deviant careerists, do not retire as from an orderly career. The criminal dimension of most street heroin-using careers is typically occupational in nature, and I have suggested elsewhere (Faupel, 1986, 1987a) that hard-core heroin addicts regard their criminality in occupational terms. The occupational character of addict criminality translates into the street argot as "hustling," and insofar as criminal hustlers develop an occupational commitment, they assume a "main hustle" that implies a degree of specialization (Faupel, 1986). Addicts do not, however, maintain the same main hustle throughout their careers and, in point of fact, typically pursue a series of criminal occupations prior to their exiting the criminal world. Moreover, these criminal careers are commonly pursued simultaneously with conventional ones, since many addicts hold legitimate jobs and moonlight in the evening and on weekends for extra cash. These are jobs that addicts may assume on a full-time basis when, for whatever reason, they leave the hustling life-style. It is clear that retirement from criminal activity is not, for most addicts, the rationally planned culmination of a lifetime career.

The nonoccupational dimension of heroin-using careers comprises the consumer (drug-using) activities of heroin addicts. This aspect of heroin-using careers is characterized by a great deal of fluctuation as addicts go through periods of withdrawing and cutting back in heroin consumption only to relapse days, weeks, or months later (Ray, 1961). Winick (1962) has suggested that addicts eventually "mature out" of narcotic addiction, implying a certain rite of passage analogous to the retirement experience of respectable, occupational careerists. Waldorf (1983) finds that while some addicts do indeed exit their careers through a process of maturation, there are also other patterns of retirement. Some become converts to religious or other social causes. Still others become alcoholics or join the ranks of the mentally ill. Waldorf also found that some quit using heroin but do not leave the life-style completely; they still hang out in the copping areas, dabble in crime, and so on. In short, while most addicts do eventually quit using heroin more or less permanently at some point in their lives, they do not necessarily "mature out" in the manner described by Winick. Addicts frequently encounter such obstacles and seemingly insurmountable difficulties in maintaining their life-styles that they feel they have very little choice but to quit. Booter described just this situation: "And I ran into some problems. . . . I couldn't work no more, see, the job is getting in my way. My paycheck is Friday, but I gotta have a shot today . . . so you start throwing away stuff. You don't dress nice no more. . . . I started giving all my time to shooting dope. I don't want no more job no more. I ain't interested in clothes. I used to buy records all the time. [Now] I ain't interested in no records. I ain't interested in nothing now but getting this bag. And that was one more reason to quit."

In contrast to the idea of "maturing out," retirement by "burning out" is seldom rationally anticipated, and for this reason it more closely resembles the retirement experiences of those in disorderly careers.

I have attempted in this section to highlight the evolving and interactional quality of heroin-using careers. The deviant and nonoccupational features of these careers certainly pose realities that distinguish them from conventional occupational careers. These disparities notwithstanding, there are underlying processes equally familiar to heroin addicts and to conventional careerists. Both types of careers involve temporal phases, commonly described as career choice and entry, mobility, and retirement. Heroin addicts, to be sure, use a different vocabulary to describe these phases. Rather than choosing and entering a career, they are experimenting or *turning on*. Career mobility is more aptly described as *getting hooked* (becoming addicted), *jones-ing* (withdrawing), developing a *main hustle, getting busted* (caught by the law), *taking care of business* (supporting one's habit), or any other of a myriad of experiences that define the direction of a given addict's career. Retirement from heroin addiction is commonly described as *burning out* or, in some cases, *shaking the monkey*. All of these descriptions, however, refer to career dynamics that, in the broadest sense, are familiar to plumbers, architects, and even physicians and lawyers.

Moreover, just as job markets, "golden opportunity" job offers, and domestic considerations all affect both career choice and mobility for conventional careerists, the careers of heroin addicts are also shaped by contingencies that are often beyond the control of the addict. Fluctuating prices of heroin, the risk of arrest, loss of a copping connection, and other eventualities all affect the direction that these careers will take. The following section examines those contingencies that are instrumental in shaping heroin-using careers.

## Contingencies of Heroin-using Careers

Becker (1963) has defined career contingencies as structural and subjective factors that determine movement from one social position to another. The careers of heroin addicts are profoundly affected by such factors. The addicts I interviewed related many situations in their lives that bore directly on their drug-using and criminal patterns. Some were major events that marked turning points in their careers. A major *score* (proceeds from a criminal act) may establish the reputation of an addict as a big-time hustler, thereby launching a new criminal career. Getting busted, on the other hand, may serve to extend the addict's reputation into the criminal justice system, forcing the abandonment of a particular criminal career, at least temporarily. It is not only the major events in the lives of addicts that shape their careers, however. The addicts in this study reported that such relatively insignificant occurrences as learning how to prepare and inject heroin themselves profoundly affected their consumption patterns.

While the situations and circumstances that shape heroin-using lifestyles are many and varied, they affect addict careers in similar ways. Among the addicts who participated in this study, two broad contingencies emerged that are particularly significant in understanding the direction of addict careers. These contingencies, which I call drug availability and life structure, account for a variety of discrete and otherwise unrelated circumstances that have similar effects on addict careers.

### Drug Availability

I use the term *drug availability* in the broadest sense to refer to all of the eventualities that make possible the introduction of a quantity of drugs into one's system. Thus, the term encompasses more than mere access to dealers who have quantities of the drug to sell, although this is certainly an important aspect of availability. In one interview, Eddie, a white addict in his late twenties, reflected, "You might have money in your pocket and you go up there and you wait until five o'clock that afternoon [for a dealer]; or you might go up there and he's sitting there at ten o'clock and you don't have any money. By the time you get money, he's gone." These difficulties in connecting with a dealer with quality dope are, of course, part of the challenge of the addict life-style.

But there is more to drug availability than simply finding a dealer who is willing to sell a quantity of drugs. Heroin is expensive. The *street price* (retail cost) of a bag of heroin (about 90 milligrams) in Wilmington at the time I was interviewing was $20. Even a modest habit for a Wilmington addict using street dope is extremely costly at this price. Hence, a critical factor in drug availability is affordability. There are, in essence, two strategies for making heroin more affordable, both of which were extensively implemented by the addicts I interviewed: increasing income and reducing costs.

**Enhancing Availability through Increased Income.** Regular heroin users almost universally report a heavy reliance on criminal or quasi-criminal activity to obtain sufficient funds to sustain their drug use. While it is true that "chippers," those who use heroin sporadically, may be able to support their consumption from legitimate income (e.g., see Zinberg, 1984), most regular users do not find themselves in such fortunate straits. Using heroin on a daily basis or even every other day requires substantially more funds than most addicts with limited conventional occupational skills are capable of generating legitimately. It is not unusual for heroin users to experience a relatively sudden escalation in their heroin consumption upon developing criminal skills. Moreover, some crimes are more lucrative than others, and it is not uncommon for addicts to learn a new crime that is perceived to be more profitable than their current hustle. One common hustle that is significant in terms of enhancing availability is drug dealing. This is not only a highly lucrative enterprise, but it can easily be assimilated into other ongoing criminal routines. Insofar as they are successful at these routines, addicts who take up criminal activity almost always report a substantial increase in their drug consumption.

This career-shift dynamic is not unique to heroin addicts, of course. Occupational shifts occur in the conventional world as well. In some cases, these shifts are forced upon conventional careerists because of economic hard times, perhaps resulting in downward social mobility. Occasionally, however, those in conventional careers are presented with possibilities of different kinds of work that offer them a substantially higher standard of living. When such opportunities occur, conventional careerists experience not only increased income but expanded consumer life-styles as well. While narcotic drugs are not usually part of this life-style, the point is that consumer behavior is a function of means, and means are directly related to one's position in the occupational and economic hierarchy.

**Enhancing Availability through Lowered Cost.** Lowering the purchase price of the drugs they consume is a primary means by which experienced heroin addicts enhance availability. This is done by purchasing heroin in quantity, usually by the *bundle* (25 bags), which, at the time I was conducting this fieldwork, sold for about $75 in Philadelphia and New York. This brings the cost to about $3 per bag, a hefty reduction from Wilmington street prices of $20 per bag, and is tantamount to increasing one's income by $17 for every bag purchased—a 600% increase in availability. It is commonplace for experienced addicts to buy their dope in bundles, sell four or five of the bags to less-experienced users at street prices, and use that money to *re-up* with (buy) another bundle at wholesale prices. The enterprising addict has, in effect, covered the cost of 20 bags of wholesale heroin by retailing a meager five bags, a process known as *juggling*. An addict named Shannon recalled in her interview with me how her habit suddenly escalated to a *quarter* (about 15 bags) per day after she started juggling: "I started dealing. I was around it; and it seems like I wanted to get higher and higher. Where before I was buying it myself. When you get it like that [wholesale, in quantity], you do it like that. I'm not realizing how much dope I'm gonna shoot when I just pour it in the cooker like that."

Addicts also find other creative ways of reducing the monetary cost of their heroin consumption. Many of the women I interviewed reported that at one or more times in their careers they were living with drug dealers who supplied them with all the heroin they wanted. Goldstein (1981) found that New York addicts obtained their drugs through bartering and other forms of in-kind payments. Many of them exchanged services for drugs with local drug dealers. One such service, also reported by several of the addicts I interviewed, is to become a *tester* for a wholesale or even street-level retail dealer. Because the purity of drugs transacted in the illicit marketplace is so variable, a drug dealer will frequently rely on users who have not developed a great tolerance for heroin to test the quality of the dealer's drugs by injecting a small quantity into their veins. If the tester easily gets high on this small amount, the dealer knows that he or she can step on, or dilute, the drug, thereby increasing the quantity he or she has to sell. This is an important service, and the tester is frequently remunerated not only by the free test drug but by additional quantities as well. Penny reported: "He [dealer friend] made me his tester, and I finally realized he not only made me his tester, he made me a dope fiend because I didn't have to pay for it. . . . He gave me so much I didn't have to ask."

**Enhancing Availability by Learning How to Use Heroin.** Making drugs more affordable, either through increased income or decreased cost, is not the only condition enhancing availability. Addicts may acquire a sizable *stash* (supply) of heroin, but if there is no available means of introducing it into the bloodstream, they have not, in effect, enhanced availability at all. They must learn to *cook* (process) the drug, to *tie up* (expose a vein), and to *spike* (inject). Acquiring these skills increases the availability of heroin in at least two ways. First, helping others to get high, or *get off*, is almost always done on a fee-for-service basis. Older, experienced, but temporarily down-and-out junkies will frequently offer their services for a share of the dope. Needless to say, having to share one's supply of heroin in this way reduces the quantity available for one's own consumption. Second, learning to self-inject allows addicts to shoot up whenever and wherever they choose, unhampered by the need to have someone else present to get off. It is not surprising, then, that once addicts learn these valuable skills, heroin consumption escalates dramatically. "Just by me getting my own works and taking off by myself . . . my shot [habit] progressed," recalled Old Ray, a veteran addict. "[Learning to inject yourself] is like opening up a dam. Easy access—opportunity."

In summary, drug availability refers to all of those conditions that facilitate the possibility of introducing a quantity of a narcotic substance into one's system. Increased income and decreased cost are certainly major components of the equation, but availability has a broader referent than financial affordability. Addicts are also confronted with numerous obstacles and opportunities of a noneconomic nature that profoundly affect availability. All conditions related to drug availability are enhanced through involvement in the heroin-using subculture. Some fifty years ago, Sutherland postulated that criminal behavior is learned through association with other criminals who serve as agents of socialization, a process he referred to as "differential association" (Sutherland and Cressey, 1974). Through this process of differential association, would-be criminals learn not only the values, norms, and motivations for committing crime but also the skills, knowledge, and techniques necessary for successfully maintaining criminal life-styles. These differential associations are no less important to heroin addicts who seek to enhance availability by learning new and more lucrative hustles, cultivating contacts with wholesale dealers, or simply learning techniques for getting off.

Those situations that enhance (or limit) availability inevitably affect one's drug-using career. In particular, conditions of availability are instrumental in dictating the level of drug consumption one can expect to experience at any given point in time. The fundamental operating principle here is obvious to the point of a truism: we cannot consume what we do not have. Certainly, our capacity to want is virtually limitless; hence, these wants and needs must be defined and regulated. Durkheim recognized this axiom nearly a century ago when he wrote, "The more one has, the more one wants, since satisfactions received only stimulate instead of filling needs. . . . To achieve any other result, the passions first must be limited. Only then can they be harmonized with the faculties and satisfied. But since the individual has no way of limiting them, this must be done by some force exterior to him" (1951:248). Durkheim further points out that people's needs are defined by their social position: "According to accepted ideas, for example, a certain way of living is considered the upper limit to which a workman may aspire in his efforts to improve his existence, and there is another limit below which he is not willingly permitted to fall unless he has seriously bemeaned himself. . . . Likewise, the man of wealth is reproved if he lives the life of a poor man, but also if he seeks the refinements of luxury overmuch. . . . A genuine regimen exists, therefore . . . which fixes with relative precision the maximum degree of ease of living to which each social class may legitimately aspire" (1951:249).

The point is simply that wants and needs, and the means available to satisfy them, are constrained by one's position in the broader social structure. Consumer cravings are defined by the opportunity structures available to satisfy them—not vice versa. Addiction to heroin and other illicit drugs is not fundamentally different from other aspects of consumer behavior. Ironically, however, drug use is one of the few consumer activities that is believed to have a causal effect on income-generating opportunities, a phenomenon commonly expressed as "drug use causes crime." It is popularly believed that heroin is such a powerfully addicting substance that users quickly lose their ability to limit consumption. The inherently addicting qualities of heroin are blamed for somehow "causing" crime.

As I point out in subsequent chapters, however, many addicts use heroin on an occasional basis for weeks, months, and even years before increasing their consumption of the drug. Only when opportunities for obtaining increased quantities of the drug present themselves do these people escalate their drug use. This principle of consumer behavior was recognized by Winick (1974) when he argued that drug dependence could only be understood in terms of increased access to the drug, removal of normative proscriptions against its use, and role strain and/or role deprivation that may predispose an individual toward such use. Winick's understanding of role strain/deprivation is particularly insightful and incorporates much of what I understand to be life structure.

*Life Structure*

Like those individuals pursuing conventional careers, heroin addicts engage in a host of activities that are linked to the various positions and identities they hold. These roles serve to structure an addict's daily routine and provide the basis for what I mean by *life structure,* which refers to the constellation of roles that patterns behavior in a regular and predictable manner. Recent ethnographic accounts of heroin-using careers in several American cities reveal that, like their nonusing counterparts, most addicts maintain reasonably predictable daily routines (Beschner and Brower, 1985; Walters, 1985). Throughout their lives, the respondents I interviewed fulfilled, to one degree or another, conventional as well as criminal and other subcultural roles. Indeed, most of these addicts reported that throughout much of their drug-using careers they spent substantially more time engaged in conventional role activities than in criminal or deviant ones.

Unlike most conventional careers, however, routine criminal activity is also an important source of life structure for most of the addicts I interviewed. Burglars spend time staking out business establishments and residential areas. Shoplifters typically establish regular sequences of stores from which they *boost* (steal) during late morning, noon, and early afternoon hours, saving the later afternoon for fencing what they have stolen. Prostitutes usually keep a regular evening and nighttime schedule, which normally runs from about 7 P.M. to 3 A.M. Mornings are usually spent sleeping, and afternoons are taken up by domestic duties.

It is within this structure of conventional and criminal roles that copping, juggling, and shooting dope take place. Following is a typical day as recalled by an addict known as Little Italy for a period quite early in his drug-using career. During this time, he was working as a salesman at a men's clothing store, dealing drugs, and pimping on a small-time basis.

*Typical Day for Little Italy*
*While Working at the Clothing Store*

*(Capitalized items indicate drug/crime-related activities)*
    7:30 A.M.   Get out of bed
               SHOOT UP ("wake-up shot"—3 bags)

|          | Get ready for work |
|----------|--------------------|
|          | SELL DRUGS |
| 8:30 A.M. | Leave for work |
| 9:00 A.M. | Begin work |
| 1:00 P.M. | Off for lunch |
|          | SHOOT UP (3 bags) |
|          | SELL DRUGS (most sales during this time) |
| 2:00 P.M. | Back to work |
| 5:00 P.M. | Off work |
|          | Eat dinner |
| 6:00 P.M. | SHOOT UP (after-dinner shot—3 bags) |
|          | Relax around the house |
| 7:30 P.M. | Hit the streets |
|          | SELL DRUGS |
|          | Party, gamble, etc. |
|          | SPEND TIME WITH HIS PROSTITUTES |
| 11:00 P.M. | Back home |
|          | SHOOT UP (3 bags) |
| 11:30 P.M. | Go to bed |

This daily schedule is, of course, an approximation—Little Italy was recalling a period several years earlier in his career. His reconstruction does represent, however, a reasonably structured daily routine, organized primarily around conventional employment and secondarily around his leisure-time and criminal-hustling activities. Within this daily routine, Little Italy structured his drug-using and drug-dealing activities.

Life structure might be understood to represent the degree of stability in one's life-style. The regularity of events defines necessary action people must take, allows them to gauge their progress, and helps them curb an otherwise insatiable appetite. Without such regularity, there is a lack of normative clarity by which to define appropriate actions and, indeed, to limit appetites. Durkheim (1951) termed the societal manifestation of this condition as *anomie*, referring to the lack of moral regulation that takes place during times of social upheaval. Such disruptions may also occur within the more immediate social milieu of an individual's life. When this occurs, regardless of the cause, people typically experience a loss of control over their environment and even their behavior. Cigarette smokers and coffee drinkers frequently have this experience when they find themselves on vacation or at conventions or on other occasions when their regular daily routine is somehow temporarily disrupted. The routine breaks in the morning and afternoon that are the normal times for smoking and drinking coffee are replaced by a comparatively unstructured day. At such times, consumption of nicotine and caffeine frequently picks up dramatically, often unconsciously.

These experiences are also common to heroin addicts. While it is true that they have reasonably stable routines throughout much of their careers, there are any number of circumstances that may alter their life structure. Many of these occurrences are not appreciably different from the crises faced by conventional careerists. Heroin addicts also experience the pain of divorce, the frustration of being fired from a job, or the embarrassment of having to drop out of school. Little Italy reported that one of the most significant events in his life was when his fiancée Vonda broke up with him: "February is when I started everything [drugs]. Vonda had kept giving me a lot of rejection. I couldn't take it no longer. I just said, 'Well, fuck it.' . . . I say, 'Well, what do I have to lose?' . . . I said, 'I don't have her so I don't need nothin' else.'"

In addition to the vicissitudes common to most of us, the peculiar life-style of heroin addicts leaves them vulnerable to a host of additional risks and problems that threaten a stable life structure. Occasionally, for any number of reasons, an addict may lose a wholesale copping connection. The connection may have been arrested, or perhaps the connection suspects that the *heat* (pressure of the law) is on the addict who might therefore become an informant. Loss of a wholesale connection often means that an addict will have to rely on lower quality, higher priced *street dope* (retail) until another connection is reestablished. These difficulties inevitably disrupt the normal pattern of daily activity. Similarly, if an addict hustler's modus operandi is deciphered by local law enforcement agencies, he or she will have to alter the routine, if not get into a different hustle altogether.

These disruptions in life structure can have a profound effect on the nature and extent of one's heroin consumption. The participants in this study indicated that they experienced such disruptions when their drug habit got out of control. With no familiar roles to pattern their daily activities, these addicts had no mechanism to regulate their consumption. Old Ray offered his philosophy as to why drug consumption is so affected by life structure: "Usually the person that gets involved in drugs is not totally involved in anything else. I was on the street at the time [I started using more]. I just got laid off. . . . I had encountered a situation of economic castration. . . . This made me susceptible to the street. . . . A man would become involved in anything—negative or positive—as long as he's involved. You must have some activity. Drugs is a commitment." Another participant, George, discovered the importance of such involvements and commitments rather involuntarily when his girlfriend died: "That's when I didn't care too much about myself. The woman that dated me died. . . . I got no sense of direction. I just don't care if I got no job. I'm gonna take now. I'm stealing, so ain't no problem in getting high now. [I'm] using a whole lot more."

Earlier in this section, a typical daily schedule for Little Italy was presented, demonstrating how drug copping, selling, and using fit into his routine. But his life structure was seriously disrupted when he lost his job at the clothing store. As his daily routine was drastically altered, Little Italy was left with extended periods of free time, which profoundly affected his use of drugs.

*Typical Day for Little Italy*
*after Losing His Job at the Clothing Store*

*(Capitalized items indicate drug/crime-related activities)*
  9:00 A.M.  Get up (no breakfast)
  Morning  Stay at home playing cards
            Wait for customers (drugs)
            SHOOT UP (5 bags)
12:00 P.M.  Eat lunch
 Afternoon  SHOOT UP (5 bags)
            Hit the streets
            SPEND TIME WITH HIS PROSTITUTES
  6:00 P.M.  SHOOT UP (5 bags)
  Evening  Hit the streets
            SPEND TIME WITH HIS PROSTITUTES
            SHOOT UP (5 bags)
11:00 P.M.  Go to bed

It is not difficult to understand how Little Italy's drug consumption nearly doubled (from about 12 bags per day to 20 bags per day) after he lost his job at the clothing store. He suddenly had more unstructured time, making it much more difficult to regulate his consumption behavior. Just as cigarette smokers and coffee drinkers rely on regularly scheduled coffee breaks to gauge their consumption of nicotine and caffeine, a highly structured daily routine is essential in regulating drug-consumption behaviors of heroin users as well.

## A Typology of Heroin-using Careers

Drug availability and life structure are critical dimensions of the dynamics of addiction careers. I have already demonstrated how each of these dimensions individually influences levels of drug use. However, the life histories of the addicts I interviewed also reveal that these two dimensions are closely interrelated and jointly affect the nature and direction of addict careers. That is, concomitant variation in these two dimensions is often beyond the addict's control, and differences in the way addicts respond to and manage these variations combine to produce discernible stages in their careers. Just as conventional careers are understood in terms of rather predictable phases that serve to define one's stature or position—entry, early socialization, upward mobility, retirement, etc.—so are heroin-using careers defined in terms of movement from one phase to another. The interaction of drug availability and life structure may be understood to describe addict-career phases that are familiar to members and observers of the heroin-using subculture.

Figure 2 identifies four such career phases, each of which is marked by a different interaction of drug availability and life structure. It is important to note that while each phase denotes an addict "type," none of these individual types implies a single career pattern. That is, throughout their drug-using careers, addicts typically move through periods in which they may at one time be described as one type and later as an-

### Figure 2: A Typology of Heroin-Using Career Phases

| Availability | Life Structure | |
| --- | --- | --- |
| | High | Low |
| High | The stable addict | The freewheeling addict |
| Low | The occasional user | The street junkie |

other type, as the circumstances that define drug availability and life structure may change. It must also be remembered that social reality does not lend itself to such discrete taxonomic categories in pure form. That is, both drug availability and life structure are continua. It is not always readily apparent whether drug availability or life structure is "high" or "low" for a particular addict at any given point in time. Indeed, what is "high" for one addict may be "low" for another. Hence, levels of drug availability and life structure are only meaningful relative to the overall career of each addict. More significant than the absolute levels of availability and structure is whether these dimensions are increasing, decreasing, or remaining constant over a period of time. Figure 2 is thus a static representation of a dynamic model, as significant changes in levels of drug availability and/or life structure cause the addict to move from one career phase to another.

As portrayed in Figure 2, availability and structure are interactive dimensions. Indeed, it is often the case that changes in one of these contingencies affect the other. Losing wholesale connections, for example, not only reduces availability but may also disrupt life structure because addicts must alter their routines to accommodate lower levels of availability. Similarly, a sudden windfall or the obtaining of high-quality inexpensive dope gives an addict the luxury of abandoning a rigorous hustling routine for a period of time.

In the chapters that follow, each of these career phases, representing unique combinations of drug availability and life structure, will be elaborated. The dynamics of transition to and from each phase—the occasional user, the stable addict, the freewheeling addict, and the street junkie—will be highlighted. In addition, those long-standing controversies among observers of the drug scene discussed in chapter one will be addressed as these issues relate to the career phase of heroin addicts.

# 3

# Getting into Drugs:
# Occasional Users

▬▬▬▬▬▬▬▬▬▬▬ The occasional-use phase, defined by a low level of drug availability but a high degree of life structure, designates two critical periods in the careers of heroin addicts. Those addicts at the end of their careers, seeking to withdraw permanently, often attempt to reduce drug availability by enrolling in drug-free treatment programs and severing ties with the drug subculture. At the same time, these individuals seek to rebuild a life structure around conventional rather than criminal routines. This "retirement" phase of heroin addiction is briefly examined later in the chapter. More commonly, however, occasional users are those just getting acquainted with the drug scene. Hence, this chapter is primarily about the early period of occasional use when participants are just beginning their addiction careers.

### Initiation as Occasional Use
▬▬▬▬▬▬▬▬▬▬▬ Most heroin users begin their careers quite young. The addicts in this study averaged 18 years of age when they began using heroin; with one exception, they were under the age of 25 when they first tried the drug, the youngest initiate being 14 years old. Many novices, particularly the younger ones, are still in school and hence are situated in a structured environment. Those who are beyond school age or who have dropped out by the time they are introduced to narcotics often maintain a reasonably structured routine by working

full- or part-time or fulfilling domestic and child-care duties. The respondents in this study reported a variety of activities that structured their daily routines at the time they were first turned on to heroin. Mario was working as an apprentice for a local optician. Pagie was working full-time at a local factory. Eddie was a full-time student at the local university. Bertha was a barmaid in a tavern and caring for an infant son. Mona was living at home with a stable family and working full-time doing clerical work.

Indeed, the lives of most of these persons were anything but dramatic at the time they were first introduced to heroin. Using attendance in school and employment as indicators of life structure, 19 of the 30 respondents were either in school or employed full-time when they first began using heroin. Only five respondents were definitely out of work and not in school when they first tried the drug; the status of the remaining six respondents is not clear.[1] There are, of course, other roles that serve to structure daily activities. Many of the women in this sample had time-consuming domestic responsibilities when they first tried heroin. Referring to the early period of their heroin use, some of these individuals described themselves as "closet addicts." They tried to arrange their drug-using activities inconspicuously around the structure of existing responsibilities and tasks.

Such structures provide a degree of insulation from becoming heavily addicted. In his pilot study of occasional users, Powell observes the importance of daily conventional routines in controlling heroin use: "To the extent our subjects were involved in something which interested them, they were relatively free of heroin use. To the extent that they were . . . 'between things' they felt vulnerable to continuing heroin use" (1973:592). Moreover, these routine conventional activities fail to provide the initiate with a high level of drug availability.

It is true that most young users have had some criminal experience. There has been a remarkable consensus in the literature of the last half of the twentieth century that crime precedes heroin use as measured by median or average age at onset (e.g., see Greenberg and Adler, 1974). Almost without exception, the addicts in this study also reported that their first criminal act preceded their first experience with heroin (and with most other drugs except alcohol and marijuana). We cannot assume, however, that one's first criminal act marks the launching of a systematic criminal career. These initial criminal acts are usually isolated events that bear little relationship to a full-fledged criminal career.

Eventually, of course, heroin addicts begin to experiment with various types of crime on a more regular basis, experiences that are more accurately considered the beginning of their criminal careers. But their early flirtation with crime does not usually net the profits to sustain a high level of expensive drug use.

The beginning user, then, is almost always an occasional user as a result of the comparatively high level of life structure provided primarily by conventional roles combined with limited drug availability. These contingencies are important in defining the nature of early heroin-using careers. Some of the more important features of this period are discussed in the sections that follow.

*Turning On: Seduction or Experimentation?*

One of the more widespread beliefs about heroin addiction is that the initiate is a helpless victim who has been seduced by an unscrupulous entrepreneur seeking to spread his or her evil wares by turning young children on to deadly drugs (Ashley, 1972; Eldridge, 1967; Lindesmith, 1940; Rubington, 1967). "Every addict," maintain Anslinger and Tompkins, "knowing himself to be a moral and social outcast, delights in bringing others into the outcast fold" (1953:272). This belief rests on several popular views of the nature of narcotics use and addiction. First, there is the view that heroin addicts are inevitably moral degenerates whose ethics suffer certain deterioration with increased addiction (Lindesmith, 1940). Second, it is often presumed that drug dealers face fierce competition and must expand their markets in order to stay in business. Young children are especially lucrative targets, not only because they are naive and vulnerable, but because they represent a potential long-term clientele. Finally, there is also the perception that the victim, seduced by and at the mercy of the *junk peddler* (drug dealer), will unwittingly become immediately enslaved by a *taste* (sample of free heroin) to this deadliest of all drugs.

These popular, seemingly obvious views have proven to be misconceptions, unsupported by recent ethnographic evidence. While it is true that many—perhaps most—people who experiment with heroin go on to use the drug on a regular basis, a sizable body of research suggests that there are many individuals who do not (Blackwell, 1983; Powell, 1973; Zinberg, 1984; Zinberg and Jacobson, 1976). These findings question the "enslavement" theory of addiction, which suggests that there is something inherent in the pharmacology of heroin that causes addiction. Neither is there support in recent research for the image of the veteran addict/dealer promiscuously turning on the young and vulnerable. Most young users were first turned on by close friends who were themselves just beginning to experiment with drugs (Ashley, 1972; Blum, 1972; Blumer et al., 1976; Crawford et al., 1983; Eldridge, 1967; Hughes, 1977; Sutter, 1969; Voss and Clayton, 1984). Indeed, Sutter insists that turning someone on "is an expression of trust, friendship and acceptance. Most lower strata youth were introduced to drugs by a close friend or relative. After they learned to use drugs for pleasure, being turned on and turning others on became an established social practice, similar to the convention of buying a friend a drink or offering a drink to a guest when he comes to your house" (1969:807).

These sentiments were strongly echoed by the addicts in this study. Virtually all of them strongly insisted they would never turn on a young neophyte. Bertha was the most adamant in her commitment never to introduce youngsters to heroin: "I wouldn't deal to just anybody and I don't fool with young kids 'cause I think the son of a bitch that deals to young kids, they ought to hang that bastard up for life. I'm not talking about doing time—I'm talking about killing that sucker. Every kid deserves a chance [not to use drugs]."

Closer questioning, however, revealed that there were circumstances under which these addicts did in fact introduce others to heroin. Most commonly, these individuals remembered sharing drugs with nonusing friends during the early, experimental stage of their careers. Ron recalled how he introduced his close friend Belle to heroin: "Early in my career . . . Belle had approached me and said, 'C'mon man, it's my birthday. Share some with me.'" This early phase is often a time when young users are just experimenting themselves. Occasional users have not yet spent enough time in the subculture to be fully cognizant of, much less to have internalized, the normative proscriptions against turning others on. Moreover, they have not yet attended the "school of hard knocks." They have not yet *done time* (been jailed or imprisoned) and may have never even been arrested for possession or any other offense. Chances are that these occasional users have not even experienced the pains of their first *jones* (withdrawal). Hence, turning friends on to heroin is tantamount to sharing with them the excitement of one's first sexual experience. The scenario of the "merchant of death" seeking to victimize innocent neophytes is simply an inaccurate stereotype of the heroin subculture. The more realistic image is a much more innocent one, analogous to adolescents sneaking behind the barn to share a smoke from a cigarette purloined from a father's coat pocket. Ron recalled his experience with turning a friend on: "We couldn't find any marijuana. Then it dawns on me that I had this thing [bag of heroin] in my pocket. So I think, 'Should I tell him about it?' And I say, 'Might as well, we got nothing else.' And when I think about that situation, that happened fairly easy. There was no concern about what was happening to him nor what was happening to me. So when I look at that I can say, no, I don't see myself having as much a problem at that stage as I did later."

If it is the beginning user who is most likely to introduce novices to heroin, then it is also surely true that most addicts were themselves introduced to heroin by friends who were probably experimenting with the drug—that is, by other occasional users. The addicts I interviewed do not remember having been "seduced" into trying heroin for the first time. They did not mention unscrupulous dealers "hooking" them with free samples. More commonly, their initiation into heroin use—and drug use generally—was through the generosity of occasional-user friends. Harry reported that he had been using a number of drugs, including barbiturates, marijuana, and amphetamines, before he began using heroin at age 18. Similar to his initial experience with these drugs, his first encounter with heroin was with a friend of his who had been using only a short time.

> [Interviewer] How did you cop the heroin the first time? Did you go out and get it for yourself or did someone give it to you?
>
> [Harry] A buddy of mine . . . started using it in that interim. He had already made a connection for it. So he came around to me and said, "Do you want to shoot some dope?" I said, "Shit, yeah!"

Moreover, even those individuals who were initially turned on by older, experienced addicts were hardly seduced as innocent victims. Rather, they were active participants seeking out those users they knew had supplies of drugs. They describe their initial attempts to secure a taste of heroin in terms of sheer determination. "I was doggin' him for it," Slick recalled, describing his repeated efforts to get a more experienced friend to turn him on. Some of the women in this study also reported harassing their boyfriends to turn them on.

The common theme that runs through all of these accounts is the voluntary nature of initiation. There have been several motives offered for turning on to drugs. Brown et al. (1971) report that curiosity and influence of friends are dominant reasons for initial experimentation with heroin. This finding concurs with the accounts of the addicts in this study. "I was looking for something different," recalled Booter. "I was in a rut. . . . Then too, that's when my friend came home from the service."

*Experimentation with Crime*

By the time they have had their first encounter with heroin, most addicts have also had some criminal experience (Greenberg and Adler, 1974). The participants in this study also report prior criminal involvement. These respondents were a median age of 14 years old when they committed their first crime, in contrast to a median age of 18 when they first used heroin. The dynamics of criminal behavior during this early, experimental period are therefore worthy of investigation. Specifically, three separate but related issues continue to generate disagreement among scholars: the drugs-crime relationship, the extent of criminal specialization, and the ethical and normative features of addict criminality. I suggested in chapter one that these issues are controversial because researchers fail to see that addict life-styles are variously affected by two major career contingencies: drug availability and life structure. As these conditions of subcultural involvement change, we should also expect that the dynamics of addict criminality will vary throughout the careers of these individuals. The following discussion addresses these issues as they are expressed in this early occasional-use period of criminal-addict careers.

**The Drugs-Crime Connection.** The finding that criminal involvement precedes the onset of heroin experimentation, by months and even years, raises serious questions about the role of drug use in criminal behavior and vice versa. As I pointed out in chapter one, research on this subject offers two competing hypotheses. One proposes that the high cost of heroin, combined with its addictive nature, requires criminal involvement to pay for it. The other hypothesis suggests that the associations and subcultural attachments formed through early criminal exploits pave the way for experimentation with heroin and other drugs.

Both alternatives, which I have earlier characterized as "drugs cause crime" versus "crime causes drugs" (Faupel and Klockars, 1987), over-simplify the complex nature of the drug-crime connection. When examining this relationship over the careers of addicts, I shall demonstrate that both characterizations may apply but at different times during a given addict's career. Presently, however, I want to address this relationship as it applies to beginning occasional users.

First, it is necessary to understand clearly what the onset of criminality actually means. Early studies addressing this issue typically asked addicts how old they were when they committed their first crime. By virtue of their research design, these works defined the onset of criminality as one's first criminal experience. I have already suggested, however, that one's first crime seldom signifies the beginning of a criminal career.[2] These initial experiences are often quite accidental, separated in time and often of a different nature from later criminal careers, as the life histories in this study attest. Harry's first crime, for example, was stealing a bicycle at age 13. He stole the bike to demonstrate his bravado in order to be accepted into a neighborhood street gang. It was not until several years later that he became involved in burglary and drug dealing on a regular basis. Joe reported that his first crime was shoplifting at age 8. He was with a group of friends who decided to play hooky. Joe stole a toy bubble-gum machine. He did eventually go on to shoplift on a more regular basis, but this was some nine years later, when he was 17 years old. Similarly, Horace remembers stealing a quantity of soft drinks from a vendor's truck as his first crime at age 11. Horace did not become systematically involved in crime until he was in his early 30s, however, at which time he was forging checks, dealing drugs, and pimping as major means of income. Slick's first crime was stealing candy from a candy store. "I didn't even think of it as stealing," he recalled. "I just took it. I didn't see nothing wrong with it." These are the types of behaviors that most juveniles have committed at one time or another, and they do not represent a commitment to a criminal life-style. Singular behaviors are hardly an adequate indicator of a career. As discussed in chapter two, a career implies a series of related activities or roles around which people organize some aspect of their lives.

Stealing candy or bubble-gum machines may have been the first crimes that these individuals committed, but these activities were not systematically undertaken in a manner consistent with a criminal career.

Eventually, these young, would-be criminals begin to experiment voluntarily with various types of criminal activities. This experimentation frequently originates as a form of group delinquency, through involvement with friends who are collectively looking for some excitement. There are also serendipitous opportunities that provide new vistas for criminal experimentation. Harry described how he learned of the lucrative nature of drug dealing from his friend Bart: "And he said you can buy it for $x$ amount of dollars, and right away the dollar signs started clicking. I said, 'Well, shit, if I can buy a pound [of marijuana] for $150 (back then it was pretty cheap), then I can break that into ounces and sell them for $25 apiece—shit man!' You know? So it just started registering that I could do that."

The significant feature of this realization is that it was not driven by a need to support a drug habit. Harry had experimented with marijuana by this time, but it was not until two months later that he would try heroin for the first time. Moreover, Harry's first encounter with narcotics was related to his recently acquired criminal propensities only in a most indirect fashion. He had been arrested on a dealing charge, and many of his friends were avoiding him because they knew he was *hot* (under police surveillance) and might be pressured to put the heat on them. He was also experiencing hassles at home because of his arrest. His father responded punitively by taking the keys to the car that Harry himself had bought. Harry's initiation into the world of narcotics use was with morphine, an act that symbolized a retaliation of sorts against his father: "My friends walked out on me because I got popped. So my parents tried to take my car from me. You know, the keys are like a super phallic symbol. They represent power. My old man was trying to take my balls away from me. . . . I was incensed. I said, 'That bastard! I'll get back at them.' So I went and shot dope." Harry then went on to try heroin for the first time one month later when a friend of his—who was himself just experimenting—turned him on.

Despite the interesting particulars of how Harry was introduced to heroin use and crime, there is an underlying pattern that he shares with the other participants in this study. The road that led to his initial criminal experimentation was quite separate and distinct from that which led to his experimentation with narcotics. His introduction to drug dealing involved entirely different circumstances and social relationships from those surrounding his initial encounter with morphine and later heroin. Harry was, in short, experimenting with drug dealing and he was experimenting with heroin. While his drug bust was the trigger that predisposed him to shoot the morphine when he did, his early experimentation with drugs and with crime were essentially separate activities that, to be sure, would intersect later in his career.

By way of summary, I am suggesting that there is little evidence for a causal relationship between heroin consumption and crime during this early occasional-use period of addict careers. These novice careerists are experimenting both with a variety of drugs including heroin and with various types of criminal ventures. Each activity is pursued for the intrinsic reward that it offers. While the subcultural relationships associated with each may overlap, this is not necessarily the case. As often as not, those friends who first turn the occasional user on to heroin or other drugs are from entirely different social networks from those that expose one to the possibilities of various criminal ventures. Only later in a person's career do these activities become closely intertwined in ways that I shall examine in later chapters.

**Criminal Specialization.** In addition to the causal nexus between heroin use and crime, a related debate in the literature concerns the nature of addict criminality, specifically, whether heroin addicts are indiscriminate, random, and even impulsive in carrying out their criminal activities, or whether they are skilled criminal entrepreneurs. I pointed out in chapter one that both of these portrayals fail to represent the nature of addict criminality in a realistic way. A more accurate depiction is expressed in a street term, the *main hustle*. Implied in the notion of a main hustle is that heroin addicts tend toward committing a small number of crimes at which they become comparatively adept. Also implied in this street term, however, is that there may be times when addicts depart from their usual criminal routines.

Occasional users at the beginning of their heroin-using careers have not yet settled into a main hustle. These are often young persons who are still in school and living with their families or perhaps working full- or part-time at legitimate employment. Criminal conduct during this phase is usually sporadic, although some noncriminal activities are more conducive to criminal expression than others. Penny-ante gambling, pool hustling, and other leisure-time activities among school-age boys,

for example, provide valuable socialization experiences for more systematic criminal careers. An addict named Boss described to me how
his career as a pimp (one of his many hustles) originated in the normative culture of teenage sexual relationships where he grew up: "It
was nothing to have our girlfriends selling their bodies for us. That was
mandatory. If you didn't have your girlfriend selling her body for you,
you were sorry. You weren't even worth hanging out with."

The occasional-use phase is also a time of purposive criminal experimentation, a period in which novices often follow the lead of more experienced users. I described earlier how Harry became interested in
drug dealing when his friend Bart explained to him how much money
could be made. Bart's influence was not restricted to drug dealing; he
was instrumental in introducing Harry to other profitable hustling possibilities as well. Harry described his friend's influence on his early
criminal career: "I had to be free and independent [of my folks]. I had
to make my own mind, my own life, and since it didn't work out in
sports and most of the other things I tried, the criminal activity was
there. . . . So I went about doing it. And Bart was a good role model.
. . . I always need a good role model to keep sustaining my growth pattern and Bart was a good role model. He had been a fucking criminal
since he was eight years old. He knew the ropes. So I was attracted to
him like a magnet."

Harry's early criminal career is virtually a smorgasbord of hustling
experiences. As I indicated earlier, he began his criminal exploits by
stealing a bicycle in order to gain entry into one of the neighborhood
gangs. Following this, he engaged in petty theft from family members
and experimented with shoplifting before ultimately settling into burglary and, secondarily, drug dealing. Harry's experience mirrors the biographies of others in this study. These addicts remember the initial period of their drug-using and criminal careers as a time of experimental
criminal behavior. They had not yet spent enough time in the subculture to ascertain their criminal propensities and to learn the necessary skills for developing a main hustle.

The experimental nature of this early period of criminality should
not be confused with the opportunistic, impulsive, and desperate criminal behavior often attributed to addicts. These depictions of addict
criminality are premised on a causal relationship between drug use and
crime. The image portrayed is of the down-and-out junkie experiencing

the anguish of withdrawal, desperately looking for any opportunity to scrape together enough money to secure his or her next *fix* (dose of heroin). Occasional users do not find themselves in these desperate straits. Many of them have not yet even experienced the pain of withdrawal. Indeed, most of these individuals have engaged in a good deal of criminal experimentation before trying heroin for the first time.

The random and experimental nature of criminality during the occasional-user phase is more accurately viewed as the manifestation of a lack of sufficient socialization into the addict/criminal subculture. Early in their careers, heroin users have not yet properly assessed their criminal penchants and abilities since they have not learned the various hustling possibilities. Such persons are similar to college freshmen or sophomores sampling a variety of classes from different disciplines before ultimately deciding on a major. Indeed, it is common for college students to declare two or three majors before ultimately settling into that course of study best suited to their interests and abilities. The occasional user is, in many respects, a "freshman" addict criminal. Criminal routines have not yet been established; nor have most occasional users worked out a stable criminal identity. Hence, while they have not developed criminal specializations, or main hustles, neither is their criminality of an impulsive nature motivated by desperation. They are, to borrow yet another metaphor, still "playing the field."

**Criminal Ethics.** Corresponding to the image of the heroin addict as an impulsive, desperate criminal who will respond indiscriminately to any criminal opportunity in order to score is the widely held perception that heroin addicts quickly lose all sense of moral propriety. I pointed out in chapter one that this "dope-fiend mythology" has been vigorously rejected by numerous observers of the drug scene over the years. They argue that criminal addicts are guided by a rather well developed normative system.

The existence of such norms does not mean that addicts are always successful in adhering to them. Like other people, addicts occasionally violate norms. Indeed, it is my contention that all heroin users are capable of violating their sense of ethical responsibility at one point or another in their careers. Normative indiscretions are more likely to occur in the occasional-user phase than in any other.[3] As I pointed out earlier, it is during this phase that users are most likely to turn young friends on to heroin—not with the malicious purpose of getting them hooked, but as one would share a drink or a cigarette with a friend. I found that even dealers at this early stage in their careers sold quite readily to uninitiated youngsters. Ron, who was heavily involved in drug dealing, reflected on his choice of customers:

[**Ron**] Youngsters, children. That was out. Period. . . . See, I have kids who are teenagers. I'd hate to see that that was happening to them.

[**Interviewer**] Did you always feel that way about selling to young-sters and nonusers?

[**Ron**] I guess not in the early years, when I was dibbling and dab-bling, no.

The occasional user is also likely to violate other subcultural codes. During this early period of drug and criminal experimentation, dipping into the family's petty-cash box or into a parent's wallet for drug money is common. Nor is it rare for young users to steal goods that can be swapped for cash from local neighborhood markets, a practice that is usually later curtailed. Such behaviors are also common among nonus-ing teenagers who need extra money to purchase alcohol, to go to movies, or to obtain the latest fads and fashions that they cannot afford on their allowance or part-time income. Indeed, occasional users share some of these same motivations for crime. Novice users have not yet developed high tolerances for heroin that might serve to undermine their ethical integrity. While they may use the proceeds of their crime to pay for heroin or other illegal drugs, they are in no way "driven" to commit these acts as the "dope-fiend mythology" would suggest. Hence, these normative violations should not be construed as instances of moral degeneracy.

Normative deviation among beginning occasional users is instead a result of their inexperience. These young novices have not yet had the benefit of learning from the school of hard knocks. Most of them have not yet had the experience of an involuntary "jones" resulting from a lack of drugs or the money to buy them. They have not yet been ha-rassed by police who play a good-guy, bad-guy routine with them in order to *flip* (manipulate) them into informing on their friends and acquaintances. Chances are that these entry-level addicts have had only the opportunity to experience the excitement of making a successful score and subsequently getting off. Consequently, the normative proscription against turning other novices on to drugs has very little relevance to them. Far from engaging in a malicious or self-serving act for the purpose of getting someone hooked, these entry-level occasional users are instead turning their friends on to a newfound life-style that, from their perspective, promises a high level of excitement and reward.

The school of hard knocks is but one component of a broader socialization process that is part of the day-to-day life of the heroin-using subculture. The education acquired in this subculture is not essentially different from that obtained in conventional contexts in that here too the young careerist develops skills, rehearses the rhetoric, and internalizes the values, norms, and rationalizations that order social relationships. The entry-level occasional user, however, has not yet spent sufficient time in the subculture to have fully internalized these normative expectations. The ethical constraints espoused by most experienced addicts develop only with increased involvement in the subculture. As Belle, a veteran prostitute and drug user, explained, the normative breaches of the occasional user are not so much violations of an internalized ethic as they are manifestations of inadequate socialization at this early stage of one's career: "When you're real young and you're tricking [prostituting], you don't have the same kind of ethics as when you get older. . . . All you think about in the beginning is just getting the money. But after a while, as you go through the years and you suffer a little knocks and bangs, you begin to see that this is not the right way."

Finally, in addition to their insufficient socialization, beginning occasional users are also constrained by the realities of low drug availability and high life structure (see Figure 2, chapter two). The occasional user's life structure does not afford a high level of drug availability. Roles associated with school, family obligations, and legitimate employment, while providing a basis for a comparatively stable life-style, do not provide the means for even a modest level of heroin consumption. Moreover, especially in the case of very young initiates, even sporadic, experimental use of heroin requires economic resources beyond these users' legitimate capabilities. In the absence of internalized normative proscriptions, it should not be surprising that entry-level addicts will readily resort to subculturally proscribed means for obtaining experimental drugs.

### Exiting as Occasional Use

━━━━━━━━━━━━━━━ I indicated earlier that the occasional-user phase may also designate the career period in which the addict is attempting to exit from a career of crime and addiction. Those who seek to exit their careers through formal drug-free rehabilitation programs submit themselves to conditions of low (ideally no) drug availability combined with a high level of life structure provided by a very rigid daily routine (Faupel, 1985). Indeed, these residential programs, frequently referred to as therapeutic communities, go far beyond simply limiting physical access to drugs. All references to the drug-using lifestyle are discouraged, including association with street acquaintances, wearing of street clothes, and use of street names. Eddie recalled the rules of East Coast House: "No girlfriends. If you were married, your wife; but no girlfriends. Straight-legged pants. No psychedelic T-shirts. Your hair was kept short. . . . The reason behind it was to strip down the image. . . . Everyone looked alike." Residential programs are, in short, "total institutions" (Goffman, 1961) that attempt to isolate addicts as completely as possible from any association with the drug-using world. At the same time these centers attempt to provide a highly structured environment as a way of allowing addicts to gain self-control and rebuild their lives.

Recent evidence suggests that many addicts are successful in exiting their heroin careers voluntarily and without the aid of treatment. Waldorf found that addicts who are successful in voluntary withdrawal employ a number of "action strategies" to facilitate this process: "In general, the pattern of action for our untreated ex-addicts involved two distinct strategies: 1) movements away from the drug and the drug scene, and 2) efforts to develop a new lifestyle which could supplant the one they were abandoning" (1983:267). Specific strategies involved moving to new areas, even across the country; finding conventional employment; becoming involved in existing institutions such as church, college, or other voluntary associations; and building or rebuilding family relationships. The significant feature of these strategies is that they facilitate the termination of drug-using careers by imposing conditions of low drug availability and a high level of daily routine organized around conventional activities and responsibilities.

The occasional-user phase in the careers of criminal addicts is defined by a high level of structure in daily routine combined with a low level of access to heroin and other expensive drugs. The occasional user may be an initiate who is just getting into the drug scene or an experienced addict wishing to exit a drug-using career. But aside from these career entry and exit points, addicts may experience the occasional-use phase at any point in their careers. Indeed, a number of studies (Blackwell, 1983; Powell, 1973; Zinberg, 1984; Zinberg and Jacobson, 1976) report that many users maintain occasional or "controlled" use throughout their careers. The dynamics of occasional use may be brought on involuntarily—for example, during periods of imprisonment when access to drugs is minimal and one is forced to conform to a highly structured daily regimen. Moreover, it is common for addicts to simulate conditions of occasional use on a temporary basis as a mechanism for lowering their tolerance to heroin so they could get their lives back in order. Nearly all of the addicts I interviewed reported that they would occasionally enroll in methadone programs, not to find a "cure," but to reduce their tolerance to heroin, and thereby rebuild family relationships, search out legitimate employment, etc. Old Ray is representative of many of the addicts in this study in his efforts to reduce his tolerance level periodically: "Usually in the course of some commitment I had made prior—to stop dealing, to back off, to get my jones down, to stop messing around—I might wear it all the way down to break off my connections. I'd go through that phase too, usually to make a better relationship with my woman or [because of] some small minor arrest that I could easily get out of if I cleaned up and got in a drug program."

Many of these individuals hope to successfully maintain a *chippy* (a small habit, typically restricted to weekend use). Among those interviewed in this study, such strategies were usually temporary, and after a period of time, those users would resort to previous levels more characteristic of stable addicts. Most of these individuals remained in the heroin-using subculture where the drug was readily available. Insofar as these users had maintained a reputable identity, their friends were eager to share their dope with them and dealers were willing to extend them credit. It is difficult to remain an occasional user under such conditions. In this way, heroin addicts are similar to alcoholics. While there are many people who use alcohol on an occasional basis for many years, it is difficult for alcoholics to maintain this modest level of consumption. Generous friends buy rounds of drinks and bartenders are willing to extend credit. Controlled drinking is difficult when an individual has an alcoholic identity. For the same reason, confirmed addicts who attempt to sustain a modest level of drug consumption usually find that they must either withdraw from a heroin-using life-style altogether or revert to a pattern of heavier use.

While there is nothing inherently chronological about this or any other career phase, the defining characteristics of the occasional-user phase (low availability, high life structure) typify the conditions surrounding those who are just getting started in careers of crime and addiction. Beginning users often find themselves in situations of comparatively structured daily routines, consisting mostly of conventional activities such as attendance at school and related functions, household duties, and employment responsibilities. They have not yet developed the connections and hustling skills that afford a high level of drug availability. These initiates are, quite literally, occasional users, typically using heroin only on weekends or sporadically in response to unforeseen opportunities.

This career phase may last days, weeks, months, or even years, as Zinberg (1984) and others have demonstrated. All of the individuals who participated in this study eventually progressed to stable-addict status. Contrary to popular belief, however, this sort of progression is not an inevitable result of the addictive properties of heroin. If pharmacology were the primary determinant of addict careers, we would expect a fair degree of uniformity in the amount of time these individuals spent as occasional users. This is not the case, however. While the average length of time spent as an occasional user was just under one year for the addicts in this study,[4] there is phenomenal variation among these individuals in the length of time they spent using drugs on an occasional basis. Some, such as Old Ray, began using on a regular stable-addict basis within days after they first tried heroin. Old Ray had grown up in an area where heroin was readily available. Moreover, he had been going to New York to cop marijuana for some time and had established contacts with New York heroin dealers. Consequently, the transition to stable-addict status was facilitated very quickly.

Other users in the study, however, maintained modest occasional-use levels for a much longer time before "graduating" to stable-addict levels. As Horace explained, "Dope don't just jump on you overnight like people say. A guy could go six months, maintain a bag now and then; but when it jumps on you it's like you've been shooting a quarter of dope every day." Ron had an especially prolonged occasional-use period of about eight years before his habit escalated appreciably. During this period he consumed an average of $10 to $15 of street heroin per day. Toward the end of this eight-year period, he became a tester for a local dealer, a role that considerably enhanced his access to quantities of heroin. At about this same time, he lost his job and moved out of his mother's house. Forfeiting the rigorous routine imposed by his job and living arrangements at the same time that he established a stable source of comparatively inexpensive heroin, Ron increased his consumption dramatically over a very short period of time.

These experiences suggest that the progression from occasional use to stable use involves more than pharmacology. During this early period of occasional use, initiates learn basic criminal skills that enhance their money-making potential. They learn how to inject themselves, eliminating their dependence on other, more experienced addicts. They are introduced to wholesale dealers. The early occasional-use phase is, in short, a training period that prepares initiates for more extensive drug-using and criminal careers. As I describe in chapter four, the skills and associations that are cultivated during this period enhance drug availability and provide an alternative basis for life structure that accommodates higher levels of heroin use.

# 4

# Maintaining the Life:
# Stable Addicts

████████████████████████ The stable-addict phase is characteristic of the mature, seasoned heroin user. As occasional users, initiates learn the basic skills necessary to maintain a drug-using life-style.
They learn how to cop, cook, and prepare heroin and acquire a certain
level of criminal expertise. While the socialization process will continue
throughout an addict's career, the basic knowledge necessary to function independently in the heroin subculture is acquired in the occasional-use phase. In contrast, the challenge of the stable-addict period is
to maintain a successful criminal-addict life-style. By most standards,
this is the most productive time in an addict's career. Criminal specialties are cultivated that provide the addict with an adequate income
for maintaining a heroin habit without shirking other financial responsibilities. As competent criminals able to finance their habit, stable addicts do not have to resort to behaviors that violate their sense of ethics
in order to secure drugs. Structured routines are also established that
provide a degree of stability not characteristic of other phases in a heroin user's career. The stable-addict phase is the phase most analogous to
the productive, established period in conventional careers.

## Contingencies of Heroin Use among Stable Addicts

━━━━━━━━━━━━━━━━━━━━━━   Maintaining stable levels of heroin consumption requires access to dependable supplies of the drug on a day-to-day basis. It is therefore mandatory that addicts have a reasonably dependable income and a reliable source of quality drugs. Various circumstances enhancing drug availability and life structure contribute to these conditions that help sustain a stable addict's life-style.

### Enhancing Drug Availability

Maintaining adequate supplies of heroin is more difficult than might be commonly perceived. The underground economy of which heroin is a part is inherently unstable, subject to fluctuation due to stepped-up efforts on the part of law enforcement agencies, wholesalers who decide to *hold the bag* (refrain from selling) for a period of days or weeks in order to create a *panic* (shortage) that allows them to raise their prices, or greedy retail street dealers who excessively *cut* (dilute) their dope to enhance their profits. Unlike consumers of legitimate products and services who have ready access to whatever quantities they want or need, often as conveniently available as their nearest drugstore, heroin addicts must consciously and rigorously cultivate dependable supplies of quality heroin.

Stable addicts are successful in maintaining access to supplies of heroin through the dual strategies of increasing income and reducing costs (see chapter two). While full- or part-time legitimate employment may be sufficient to sustain an experimental or occasional-use level of consumption, users who become stable addicts must have a more lucrative source of income than most legitimate employment can provide. All of the participants in this study reported that their heroin consumption escalated to levels characteristic of the stable addict only after becoming criminally involved on a reasonably sustained basis. Booter recalled that it was when he had the daily income provided by criminal hustling that his habit increased substantially: "When I was laid off I started really doing it, really chasing that bag. I started shooting more, because I was hustling more money and I was getting paid every day instead of getting paid every weekend. I was hustling every day, and that way I had money all day and I was getting them bags all day."

Stable addicts also enhance the availability of heroin by finding ways to lower its cost. Most commonly, they reduce cost by buying from a wholesale connection rather than purchasing retail street dope. This was one of several strategies employed by Bertha to lower the cost of the heroin she consumed: "I never had to buy nickel and dime bags off the street. That's a waste of money. If you're really going to get into something, I'm not going to waste my money like that. I'm not going to buy a nickel bag now and decide I need some later. . . . If I had to buy dope like [that] I'd never make enough money!"

Buying in quantity facilitates stable-addict consumption patterns in several ways. First and most obviously, it lowers the cost—from $10 or $20 a bag to about $3 per bag. Moreover, heroin sold in "bundles" is not as likely to have been "stepped on" as street heroin usually is, which means that less of the drug is required for the same effect. Finally, wholesale purchasing of heroin also provides an important source of income to users who sell a sufficient number of bags to friends at retail prices to cover the cost of the entire bundle.

But establishing wholesale connections is not easy. Volume dealers usually refuse to sell to unfamiliar faces, and for good reason. A standard strategy employed by law enforcement agencies is to employ undercover officers to make buys for purposes of gathering evidence to make a *good* (prosecutable) bust. Moreover, most agencies are interested primarily in "major dealers" (Manning, 1977). Establishing the trust of a volume dealer thus serves as an important rite of passage for the heroin user, signifying membership in a subterranean fraternity of established drug users and dealers. Pagie recalled this significant turning point in his career. He had been traveling to Philadelphia with his dealer friend Tim for several months to cop from a wholesale connection. After several visits, the Philadelphia connection took him aside and said, "You don't need Tim. I know Tim's charging you." This was the beginning of a relationship that assured Pagie a dependable supply of high-quality, relatively inexpensive heroin.

Most stable addicts have established relationships with several such connections in different cities, or even in the same city, to ensure drug availability. Belle explained the importance of maintaining a broad base of subcultural contacts: "You got to start associating with different people. You got to be in touch with different people for the simple reason that not just one person has it all the time. You got to go from one

person to the other, find out who's got the best bag and who hasn't. . . .
You want to go where the best bag is for your money, and especially
the money *you're* spending. You got to mingle with so many different
people."

Stable addicts use other strategies to maintain reliable sources of heroin. One tactic, which was quite common among the women I interviewed, is to establish a paramour relationship with dealers who are
willing to keep the addict supplied. Sandy was using heroin quite heavily before she ever became criminally involved.

[**Interviewer**] You started using heroin three years before you
started boosting heavily. Why?

[**Sandy**] I didn't have to go out stealing during that time because
my man, he was a dealer. . . . Whenever I needed it, he gave it
to me.

There is one final avenue to increased availability that was essential to
the transition to the stable-addict phase among the participants in this
study, namely, learning the skills and techniques required for self-
injection. Almost without exception participants reported dramatic increases in their heroin consumption once they had learned to "spike"
themselves. As Gloria recalled, "It wasn't hard for me to learn to spike
my own arm—so he [a friend] didn't have to do it anymore. I did it
myself. . . . I went on and on, and it got to be so big that it got to the
point I wasn't selling, I was just using."

While Gloria mastered self-injection with relative ease, this was not
the case for many of the respondents. Some of them had an aversion to
needles that had to be overcome. Moreover, it was necessary to learn to
"tie up" to expose a vein. Many addicts initially found it difficult to control *rolling* (moving) veins; and, having done that, to know at what
depth to insert the syringe to avoid extending the needle through both
walls of the vein. These addicts also had to learn what mixtures of water
to add to the powdered heroin, how long to cook the heroin, and how
to draw the mixture into the syringe, avoiding air bubbles and straining
impurities. All of this is a complex process, and most users do not become adept at it without considerable practice.

Learning to self-inject is an important milestone in an addict's career because it signifies an independence from older, more experienced addicts and gives users increased stature and respect in the subculture. Little Italy summarized how this rite of passage affected his relationships: "They came back, fixed me up with a shot. I hit. I was hitting myself, man. And they were smiling, 'Oh man, you know how to hit yourself too now, huh?' So I done graduated. I'm one of the big boys now."

*Expanded Life Structure*

Like occasional users, stable addicts enjoy a high level of life structure. Contrary to the stereotype that portrays heroin addicts as people who have lost all sense of time and space, simply living from one shot to the next, stable addicts actually maintain a comparatively routinized life-style. Drug-using activities are part of a daily schedule that is fairly consistent from one day to the next. Shannon recalled, "My shots were so spaced that there was no need for [me] . . . to have it right then and there. . . . When I woke up in the morning I always made sure I had some dope." Penny took a similar approach: "I made sure I got up before I got sick, [took a shot], go out there and make that money, and make enough so I can get enough so I don't have to go out there no more that night." These routines frequently became so highly structured that they can be viewed as rituals; one participant, Mona, described the life-style in precisely those terms: "It's a ritualistic thing, the routines that you go through and places you go to and the people that you see. The rigmarole that you have to go through with this guy or this guy and getting the drugs and having the drugs with you and going somewhere and fixing the drugs and getting off and all that stuff. Very ritualistic."

There are, however, important differences between the occasional user and the stable addict in terms of life structure. Whereas occasional users are usually involved primarily in conventional routines, stable addicts usually expand the structure of their daily routine to include criminal and other subcultural roles as well. Indeed, these roles often replace many of the conventional roles performed by occasional users, particularly school and employment activities. This is not to suggest that stable addicts relinquish all conventional roles. An examination of the daily routines of the addicts in this study reveals that even during periods of comparatively heavy use, the daily activities of heroin addicts are not all that different from those of nonusers. Several of the addicts I interviewed held down full- or part-time jobs, and most engaged in quite ordinary domestic and recreational activities.

Nonetheless, the transition to stable addict does involve an expansion of one's daily routine to incorporate criminal and subcultural roles. Shoplifters typically establish *runs,* more or less predictable sequences of stores and malls from which they boost material goods that they will later sell to a fence or other customers. These runs and the subsequent activities associated with fencing their goods provide a daily routine within which drug copping, cooking, and spiking take place. A possible scenario might go something like this: After boosting from Mall A, the shoplifter may connect with a dealer who lives between Mall A and Mall B. After successfully boosting in Mall B, the shoplifter may stop at a partner's house who lives nearby and shoot up some of the dope just scored. The two of them may then hit one more store before returning to the shoplifter's home, where they sort the stolen merchandise in preparation for selling it to various local fences. By now it is early to midafternoon. Before selling their goods, they connect with another dealer who lives near one of their fences. These *boosters* have probably not yet consumed all of their dope from the first connection, which they will finish off after fencing their goods. The second purchase is for a *nightcap* and a *wake-up shot* in the morning so that they won't wake up sick. The next day, the cycle begins again, only with a different run and perhaps with different fences and drug connections.

Other criminal hustles also have their routines that serve to structure daily activities. Prostitutes maintain a schedule that keeps them working on the streets and in bars from late afternoon to late at night. Many of these women also have domestic responsibilities during daylight hours, such as getting children off to school and husbands to work, doing laundry and grocery shopping, and being home when their children return from school. Burglars also typically work at night but spend their days casing residential or business establishments, often while on other legitimate business. Mario had a job working for a fuel oil company, which provided a perfect front for his casing residential properties. While repairing furnaces and water heaters, he could assess the layout of various homes and take stock of the goods within them. Mario, who was very socially adept, would strike up conversations with the home owners in order to learn their daily routines and when they were likely to leave the house vacated. The occupants would often talk to him about upcoming vacations, which was an open invitation for him to burglarize.

There is perhaps no criminal routine that is more familiar to stable addicts than dealing. All of the participants in this study reported that they played the role of dealer at one level or another. Indeed, becoming a dealer almost inevitably accompanies becoming a regular user. Not only will a stable addict be approached to cop for occasional users or other addicts whose supplies may be temporarily limited, but more enterprising stable addicts quickly recognize those occasions when especially *righteous dope* (potent heroin) can be purchased, cut, and resold to drug-using friends at a substantial profit.

Dealing has another advantage that makes it an attractive part of the stable addict's routine. Because dealing, at least on a small scale, does not require much more time or effort than that required for one's own personal consumption, it can easily be integrated into other criminal routines. This is especially true if, as described above, these other hustles regularly bring the stable addict in the vicinity of other sellers and users. In short, dealing is a good way of enhancing drug availability while maintaining the structure of daily criminal and conventional activities.

Criminal routines are important to the maintenance of stable-addict status for a number of reasons. First, these activities provide a more lucrative return than do most conventional sources of income available to addicts, thereby enhancing drug availability. Moreover, these routines provide greater flexibility than do many conventional roles, with built-in periods of time for which the addict is not accountable to others who might question unusual behavior. Criminal routines thus provide the addict with the freedom to take the time to cop, cook, and shoot up. Just as important, however, criminal routines serve to constrain these consumer behaviors within reasonable bounds. Criminal roles may provide more daily flexibility than do conventional jobs, but they are by no means devoid of structure, and they are quite demanding. Stable addicts plan their daily routines, including their drug use, around these activities. Thus, criminal routines not only serve to enhance drug use through greater flexibility and availability, but they also serve to set broad limits on the amount of heroin consumed, thereby keeping one's habit more or less under control.

## The Drugs-Crime Connection among Stable Addicts

The complexity of the drugs-crime connection is perhaps most fully apparent during the stable-addict phase. One clear feature is the role that criminal activity plays in facilitating drug use. The participants in this study strongly concurred that their level of heroin consumption was a function of their ability to afford it, which was usually enhanced by criminal activity. "The better I got at crime," remarked Stephanie, "the more money I made; the more money I made, the more drugs I used." She went on to explain, "I think that most people that get high, the reason it goes to the extent that it goes—that it becomes such a high degree of money—is because they make the money like that. I'm saying if the money wasn't available to them like that, they wouldn't be into drugs as deep as they were."

Contrary to the "drugs cause crime" hypothesis, which suggests that increases in the level of heroin consumption are necessarily followed by stepped-up criminal activity, the dynamics reported by the addicts in this study are quite the opposite: increased heroin consumption is *preceded* by increased criminal activity as measured by estimated criminal income. This does not necessarily imply a greater frequency of crime, for, as I shall highlight below, stable-addict status usually brings with it greater sophistication in skill and technique, often resulting in higher proceeds per criminal event.

These life history data also reveal, however, that the relationship between drug use and crime is much broader and more complex than simple causality. As I suggested earlier, increased criminal income not only enhances drug availability but also provides the basis for an expanded life structure, an alternative daily routine. Because these criminal routines usually provide greater flexibility than do most forms of legitimate employment, they free the addict from prohibitive roles and social contacts that may be imposed by more rigid schedules. Drug-using activities are certainly facilitated under these more flexible routines. Nevertheless, criminal routines do impose certain constraints on the addict life-style. Moreover, they provide an important structure to one's drug-using activity. It is in this respect that Old Ray likened the routine of dealing drugs to legitimate employment: "When you're working, the world has its rhythm, its time clock. You have your eight-to-five time clock. Well, it's the same way with dealing drugs." The result is a curious paradox. Criminal activity not only enhances availability, thereby providing for heavier drug consumption, but also places broad limits on the amount of heroin consumed by providing some semblance of structure and routine.

There is yet another paradox in the drugs-crime relationship for the stable addict. While it is true that crime facilitates heroin use, many of the addicts I interviewed indicated that heroin and other drugs played a utilitarian role in their commission of crime as well. While it is commonly assumed that addicts are most likely to commit crimes when they are sick and desperate for a fix, the addicts in this study reported quite the opposite.[1] The following comments from Joe and Belle highlight the importance of being *straight* (not experiencing withdrawal) when committing crimes:

> [Joe] It would be awful hard for me if I was sick to be able to hustle. A lot of times if you're sick you go in and grab stuff. And run without caution. But if I was high it was a different story. I could take my time and get what I wanted.

> [Belle] Most people say about drug addicts [that] when they're sick is when they do their most damage. But that's the lying-est thing in the world. When a dope addict is sick, he's sick. He can't raise his hand if he's a drug addict. . . . They say when a dope fiend's sick he'll do anything to get money, but how the hell is he going to do it if he can't even go on the street and do it?

The prostitutes I interviewed found heroin especially functional in their criminal activities. Never knowing if their next *trick* (client) might be a *freak* (one who enjoys violence or sadomasochistic acts), carry a disease, or simply have unpleasant body odor, prostitutes understandably approach many of their dates with a good deal of apprehension. They reported that heroin allows them to work under otherwise difficult conditions:

> [Belle] I think that a woman that tricks has to do something. If they wasn't an alcoholic, they had to be a dope fiend. 'Cause a woman in her right sense, you just can't sit up and do some of the things you do with a trick.

[Penny] If I didn't have no heroin in me, I couldn't trick, because it turns my stomach. . . . I didn't feel nothin' then, I just went on and do it. . . . I always was noddin' before I even get to the date. And then when I get to the date, I go to the bathroom and get off again.

[Helen] I could forget about what I was doing; I didn't give a damn about anything. I just felt good.

Heroin is not the only drug that addicts use for functional reasons in their commission of crimes. Amphetamines are also sometimes used to maintain necessary energy levels on particularly busy days. Boss, who was an armed robber among other things, reported that he would frequently use barbiturates before going out on a robbery. He found that they put him in the necessary belligerent mood to play the "tough guy" in order to pull off the robbery successfully. He also reported that he would frequently celebrate a successful robbery with heroin or cocaine or perhaps even a *speedball* (a heroin and cocaine combination): "They'd be like a toast. Maybe nine-thirty or ten o'clock we'd done pulled a good score off and we're sitting there and say, 'Hey man, let's go get us some good motherfucking dope.' And it would carry you until two o'clock. Nodding in the apartment, everybody feeling all right because they got away with the crime, planning what you're gonna do with your half of the money. So it'd be like the cap for you. It'd be like a toast for a job well done."

Finally, the data from these life histories suggest that both drug use and criminal behavior are interrelated elements of a broader subcultural experience that cannot be fully understood in terms of a simple causal relationship. Particularly as stable addicts, these respondents regarded both drug use and crime as important parts of a challenging life-style. On the one hand, it is true that drugs provide an important perceptual framework from which addicts interpret their behavior. Boss commented on the importance of drugs in defining the meaning that he attached to his activities: "The money is good, but I wouldn't want the money if I couldn't have what goes along with selling the money [for heroin]. . . . Like with the whores, I wouldn't want the whores if I couldn't spend the money on dope. . . . It's like a working man. A working man, he wants a home and nice family. Just like in the life of crime you got to have all those essential things that go with it or it's nothing. It would be nothing if I couldn't spend that money the way [I want to]."

But while heroin is an important component of the subjective experience of addicts, it is only part of a more general life-style the maintenance of which motivates the addict. Also part of that life-style for most addicts is a nice wardrobe, fancy cars (for men), a nice *crib* (home), and a reputation for generosity with friends. As Boss reflected: "See, my concern wasn't catching the habit. . . . My thing was being able to make enough money to supply that habit and make enough money to keep my thing up to par—you know, my clothes and my living standards . . . to stay up to par enough so if my mother or sister or brother needed some money, I could loan them some money, plus keep my habit, plus buy some shoes or something, you know, rent a car for the weekend and just hang out like the guy that didn't have the habit. And in the course of that, that called for more crime."

As important as drugs and the fast life-style are in motivating addict behavior, one important fact remains: crime is a way of life with stable addicts. These people take pride in their ability to hustle successfully. Criminal success is a mark of stature in the subculture, and the more lucrative or difficult the hustle, the greater the recognition one receives. "The type of criminal activity he engages in, and his success at it determine, to a large extent, the addict's status among fellow addicts and in the community at large. The appellation of *real hustling dope fiend* (a successful burglar, robber, con man, etc.) is a mark of respect and status" (Preble and Casey, 1969:20; italics in original). Crime is a challenge that most stable addicts find tremendously appealing. It provides a source of excitement and a sense of accomplishment, similar to the challenge of climbing formidable mountain peaks or rafting turbulent white water. Mario compared the excitement of burglarizing a house with the anticipation experienced by a young child at Christmastime. Each package (house) has its own surprises, its own challenges. Some are located in wealthy sections of the city and have fabulous exteriors (pretty wrappings). Some of these promising houses resulted in a valuable *take* (loot), while others did not. What kept Mario going was the anticipation he experienced with each crime.

Mario's feelings reflect those of many of the addicts who took part in this study. Their perceptions defy any attempt to characterize criminal behavior as somehow being "driven" by an overwhelming need for drugs, even though heroin and other drugs constitute an important feature of a stable addict's motivational structure. For these addicts, drugs and crime are mutually reinforcing elements of a broader life-style, both of which play an important role in defining one's position in the criminal-addict subculture. Harry expressed it this way: "It was never really the drug. It was the life-style I was trying to keep going. And the drug was a lot of that life-style. . . . Back then [before becoming a street junkie] . . . it was just that it was there and I had all this energy and no vent for it. And I had begun to vent it into getting drugs, knocking people in the head, taking their money, going into somebody's house, taking that stuff out, running into the fence, going to get the drugs—a full-time job. It was more than your basic forty hours a week. And that's what it was about, sustaining that life-style."

By way of summary, in contrast to the occasional-user period of addict careers where drug use and crime are independent, parallel activities, the stable-addict phase is marked by a close interdependence between these two sets of activities. This relationship is more complex than can be captured in the empiricist language of cause and effect, however. The transition to the status of stable addict is a function of increased drug availability and expanded life structure, which, in most instances, result from increased systematic criminal activity. In this respect, we might characterize the stable-addict period as one in which "crime causes drugs" or, at least, crime facilitates drug use. Having attained the status of stable addict, the user has succeeded in jockeying for position in the criminal-addict subculture. The stable addict is, at least by minimal definition, a successful participant in the subculture. Success in the subculture is defined by drug-using and criminal activity, both of which are motivating factors in the behavior of stable addicts. In this respect, the drugs-crime relationship is not so much causal as it is reciprocal, itself contributing to one's stature in the subculture.

## Criminal Specialization among Stable Addicts

The career transition to stable addict usually entails an increasing reliance on a small number of criminal hustles or, in some cases, on a single type of crime. I pointed out in chapter three that early occasional use is a time of experimentation, not only with various types of drugs, but also with a variety of criminal roles. As in other careers, this trial period usually gives way to more focused activity as developing addicts discover what criminal skills and penchants they may have by experimenting with different criminal routines. In short, assumption of the stable-addict role usually implies the development of one or more main hustles.[2]

Developing a main hustle implies not only the achievement of increased specialization but also of increased skill and sophistication as a criminal. Stable addicts go beyond learning the nuts and bolts of their chosen trade(s) to master the subtleties of these criminal enterprises with a finesse more characteristic of a craftsman than of a stereotyped common criminal. Old Ray may have stated it most succinctly when he remarked, "You got to have a Ph.D. in streetology." There are three broad types of skills that the successful criminal addict acquires: technical, social, and intuitive skills (Faupel, 1986).[3]

*Technical Skills*

This category of criminal skills entails both the knowledge of how to perform the task as well as the physical adeptness for carrying it out successfully. Shoplifters stress the importance of being able to *roll* clothing items tightly with one hand with the clothes still on the hanger. Rolling loosely will not allow as many clothes to be packed in the bag, and keeping clothes on the hanger is important because empty hangers arouse suspicion. This must all be done with one hand because the other hand is used to finger through items on the rack, thereby creating the impression that the shoplifter is a legitimate customer. A slip in any one of the maneuvers involved in the complex process may mean failure to reach a quota for the day or, even more seriously, possible detection and arrest. Moreover, shoplifters must continually keep abreast of technological innovations designed to detect theft, including cameras, one-way mirrors, and alarm devices attached inside expensive clothing items.

Prostitutes also report the importance of developing technical skills, particularly streetwalkers who regularly *beat their johns* (rob their clients) out of credit cards and cash. Belle described her strategy for successfully stealing from her clients: "The car was sweeter than anything else as far as getting money. Because once you get a dude's pants down, you got him where you want him. He just automatically forgets about he's got money in his pocket. . . . All she's thinking about is getting him in a position to get his mind off his pocket long enough for her to get in there. . . . She might take his pants with her and leave him stripped for nothing—cause I've done it." A prostitute must also be able to determine where her trick keeps his wallet, take the wallet from his pocket, and then return it—all in a matter of minutes and without the client's being aware that this activity is taking place. These are skills not readily acquired; developing them takes time and practice, as Penny described: "When I started off I was scared. It took a little longer. . . . It might take four or five hours [on an all-night date] to get his wallet. . . . [Later] it didn't take me but a minute to get it and put it back in."

The acquisition of technical skills is critical to the success of other hustles as well. The technical skills required by burglars have been extensively discussed in the literature on professional crime (Letkeman, 1973; Sutherland, 1937). These same skills were also reported by the burglar-addicts who participated in this study. An intimate knowledge of alarm systems is part of the seasoned burglar's stock-in-trade. Moreover, because most burglars prefer to enter unoccupied homes, they commonly case a residential area for days or even weeks, meticulously noting the mobility patterns of the residents. Burglars working business districts also case their working areas to determine patterns of police surveillance. Pagie recalled "staying up all night watching the pattern of the police officers and seeing how regularly he made his rounds of the establishment—and charting all that stuff down and trying to get a fix on when's the best time for me to rip that store off."

Stable addicts are also involved in many other types of criminal offenses. The addicts in this study reported engaging in main hustles such as armed robbery, pickpocketing, forgery, fencing stolen goods, pimping, and drug dealing at one time or another during their careers. Each of these criminal enterprises involves its own modus operandi and requires the acquisition of specialized technical skills if one is to be a reasonably successful hustler.

### Social Skills

Most criminal hustles require the addict to be verbally and socially skilled as well as technically adept. These social skills involve verbally and nonverbally manipulating the setting to the criminal's advantage such that the offense can be carried out smoothly and without risk of apprehension or arrest.

Social skills, like technical skills, are quite specialized. Shoplifters who work in pairs, for example, frequently find it necessary to engage in small talk with salespersons, thereby diverting attention from the actions of their partners. Moreover, when they are detected, good boosters are often successful in talking their way out of an arrest. Gloria found that she could intimidate lower-level sales personnel from referring her to management by taking on the persona of an indignant, falsely accused customer. Some shoplifters, such as Slick, used a modus operandi that relied primarily on verbal agility. In contrast to the surreptitious strategies employed by many shoplifters, such as hiding stolen goods in garbage bags and false-bottom boxes or underneath one's own clothing, Slick opted for the bold strategy of walking out of the store with his stolen merchandise in full view of store personnel, as if he had paid for it: "I would take McCullough chain saws. . . . I would just pick up the big box, set it up on my shoulders, and even get the store security guard at the door to open the door for me. I just got bold." Then, rather than sell the chain saw to a fence for about one-third the retail value, Slick would rely on his verbal skills once again by returning the item the next day to the very store he had stolen it from (or bring it to another store in the chain) for a full refund.

Needless to say, this sort of strategy requires a unique ability to play the role of a legitimate customer. A shoplifter with highly developed social skills tends to assume this role so completely that he or she takes on the attitudes, feelings, and perspective of the customer. To use Mead's (1934) term, the shoplifter quite literally "takes the role of the other." Socially skilled shoplifters do not take the role of just any customer, however; they assume the role of an assertive customer who takes complete command of the situation. Indeed, they must do so. A legitimate customer can perhaps afford not to be assertive, but a timorous shoplifter may well forfeit his or her career by failing to command credibility as a legitimate customer.

Check forgers make use of some of the same social skills employed by shoplifters. Indeed, social agility can probably be said to constitute the principal stock-in-trade of the check forger. The entire act revolves around successfully convincing a bank employee that the signature on the check is in fact that of the individual whose name it bears, and that the forger is that individual and therefore the rightful recipient of the amount of the check. All of this involves the ability to assume the role of

an assertive individual with a legitimate claim, an ability Old Ray cultivated to his advantage: "I found the hardest teller I could find and she
sent me to the manager's office. . . . I went in there telling about this
godsent check—a tragedy in my life. It was all acting. . . . You got to
story-tell. But it was my check. It became my check the minute I walked
into the bank. . . . Once I packed up that type attitude, I became the
role. And it's easier to go to the top than the bottom. It's easier at the
top to get to anybody. . . . The guy at the bottom, he's gonna give you
hell . . . but the man at the top, he can afford to be benevolent."

Other criminal hustles require social skills of a slightly different nature. Prostitutes point out the importance of maintaining a position of
dominance in the interaction between them and their tricks. Rose advised: "Always try to keep control of the conversation. Never let them
see that you're soft. . . . They see one time that you stutter or aren't in
control, they're gonna try to take advantage of you." By maintaining
such control, the prostitute is also able to direct and focus her client's
attention, which allows her to engage in acts of theft. Penny was so successful at this strategy that she was frequently able to rob her clients
without even having to *turn the trick* (engage in sexual acts).

Drug dealing entails social skills with still another focus. Here the
primary task is to maintain a relatively stable clientele. This involves
advertising one's drugs and establishing a reputation as having "righteous" dope. Harry, who was heavily involved in burglary as well as selling drugs, understood successful dealing to be little more than hype
and good salesmanship: "Conning was part of everything. The whole
thing is an image. Believe it or not, it's the American way! . . . So you
learn how to hype. . . . One of my favorite lines was 'You better do only
half of one of these.' And that just made them get all that much more
motivation to do three or four of them. And they'd do three or four and
they'd come back and say, 'Hey, that shit was good!' Of course, if they
did three or four of them, they did get fucked up."

Inevitably, however, drug dealers are confronted with dissatisfied
customers who have reason to believe that they have been ripped off
with poor-quality dope. There was no consensus among the dealers I
interviewed regarding how they respond to discontented clients. Some
would play it tough, on the theory that to give in to a client's demands
sets a bad precedent and may serve as a signal to others that here is a
dealer who can easily be taken. Others saw themselves as conscientious

businesspeople and would quite readily supply a dissatisfied customer with more dope, urging them to spread the word that they were treated fairly. In either event, to borrow a phrase from the subculture of pick-pockets, dealers must "cool the mark out," employing all of the social skills they have at their disposal to maintain a stable clientele.

### Intuitive Skills

This last category of hustling skills entails an acute sensitivity to one's environment. Sutherland (1937) describes this characteristic as *larceny sense*, a term that Dressler also employs to describe the professional criminal: "Larceny sense, it seems, is the ability to smell out good hauls, to sense the exact moment for the kill, and to know when it is wiser to desist" (1951:255). Maurer (1955) applies the term *grift sense* to describe intuitive skills in his classic analysis of the professional pickpocket. But these skills are by no means limited to professional criminals. Gould et al. observe this ability among active heroin users: "Most successful dope fiends show an ability to size up people they meet in terms of trustworthiness and motivation, and have a good memory for people" (1974:45–46).

The addicts I interviewed also emphasized the importance of intuitive skills. Like technical and social skills, intuitive skills are manifested differently in various criminal contexts, but their general purpose is to help facilitate the commission of a crime or to help the criminal avoid detection and arrest.

Intuitive skills can facilitate the commission of crime by providing the addict with the ability to sense a profitable and reasonably safe opportunity. "I could see money. I could smell money," claimed Old Ray. "I could walk by a store and see if it was vulnerable. . . . I could sense the whole setup." These are the skills that contribute to larceny (or grift) sense, and many of the participants in this study explicitly acknowledged their importance. Representative observations of a prostitute, a pickpocket, and a shoplifter illustrate how these skills are applied in various hustles:

> [**Rose—a prostitute**] Look for the nice dates. When you spot a man with the raggediest car and the oldest clothes, he's probably got the money. Because he's cheap, he don't wanna spend all of that

money. It's usually the man that's got all this and that [who] ain't got a dime because he's paying out so many bills. [Rose went on to point out that she would probably have to steal his money because he is unlikely to be generous with her either.]

[Boss—a pickpocket] As I got better, I could spot people with decent money, and you play them. Whereas in the beginning, on the amateur thing, I might play anywhere from ten to fifteen wallets. But when I got professional, I might just play one or two wallets.

[Booter—a shoplifter] All days aren't the same for boosting. . . . If there's no situation where you can make some money, you just don't go in and make a situation. You understand what I'm saying? The situation has to be laid out for you. And to be really good at it, you got to be the type of person that can recognize a laid-out situation. If you get in there and try to make a situation, then you're rearranging the whole thing and it could be detrimental.

Intuitive skills are also instrumental in avoiding detection and arrest. The addict criminals in this study repeatedly stressed the importance of being able to detect and avoid undercover police officers, floorwalkers, and potential informants. This ability was regarded as absolutely crucial to their success in criminal roles:

[Harry—regarding drug dealing] I learned the ropes . . . how you spot cops. He [a friend] pointed out . . . those undercover detectives with the bee stingers on their cars, little teeny antennae on top; and how you could pick those cars out; and how two detectives in a car, how there were certain characteristics about them that were always the same. You could smell them a mile away. He really schooled me criminally, you know.

[Stephanie—a check forger] When she [the bank teller] sees the check, if she has to look up [or] if she has to call another teller or something like that, it ain't no good. . . . If the teller has to pick up the phone, then you tell her, "That's all right, there's something I have to do."

**[Penny—on shoplifting]** I can tell [who the floorwalkers are]. They constantly keep walking the floor looking at me. . . . They're still in that same department and ain't bought nothing.

**[Fred—a drug dealer]** Never take a deal that sounds too good to be true. . . . This guy came by and wanted to buy fifteen bags for $10 apiece—no shorts. Now any kind of a hustler junkie coming off the street and he's got $150, he's not gonna come to you wanting fifteen bags. He's gonna come to you wanting twenty-five or thirty. You know what I'm saying? The deal was too good to be true.

These observations illustrate the diffuse qualities characteristic of intuitive skills—it was difficult even for the study respondents to articulate their precise nature. Pagie recalled: "I always had a knack for sensing the police. I don't know why. I don't know if it's an ESP thing or what, but I always could sense when the police was there." It is because of their rather imperceptible quality that I have used the term *intuitive skills* to refer to this important set of abilities. It is important to understand, however, that they are not hereditary talents. These are skills that are acquired through the same process of socialization as are technical and social skills. Together, these three sets of skills distinguish successful stable addicts from beginning occasional users.

I have attempted in this discussion to demonstrate that contrary to stereotyped depictions of addict criminality, stable addicts are skilled criminal entrepreneurs. The level of criminal sophistication required to sustain a livelihood of the magnitude reported by these hard-core addicts is acquired only after spending considerable time in the subculture. Such skills are simply not part of the beginning occasional user's stock-in-trade. In the process of becoming stable addicts, however, most users narrow the range of their criminal activity considerably. I certainly do not wish to represent the stable addict as a professional in the tradition of a Chic Conwell (Sutherland, 1937) or a Vincent Swaggi (Klockars, 1974) nor necessarily as specialized as Preble and Casey (1969) imply in their watershed study of addict criminals. The addicts I interviewed, however, do favor a small number of crimes among the vast variety they could be committing. I am suggesting that as stable addicts, these hard-core users are sufficiently successful at their main hustles such that they seldom find it necessary to deviate from their preferred crimes. They attain a level of specialization not characteristic of amateurs nor even of their own criminal patterns during other periods of their careers. Indeed, I contend that it is only by such specialization that these addicts are able to develop the requisite skills for a successful career. There is thus a mutually reinforcing relationship between the development of a main hustle and the acquisition of technical, social, and intuitive skills that correspond to this specialization. The acquisition of these skills is, in the first place, dependent upon some level of specialization; at the same time, these skills provide the very foundation for stable addicts to maintain their main hustles.

These main hustles, which constitute more or less full-time criminal roles, also have other important consequences. As I suggested earlier, they provide an alternative basis for life structure that is capable of accommodating higher levels of drug use and consumer activity generally. At the same time, however, the routine nature of the main hustle prevents one's habit from getting out of hand. The stable addict's heroin use still takes place within a rather well defined, though modified, life structure. Moreover, full-time hustler roles provide addicts with increased dependable income. Unlike the marginal criminality of occasional users, the main hustle is both a primary means of income and a source of identity and prestige in the subculture. The study respondents were quick to distinguish between a main hustle typical of stable addicts and the more amateur or impulsive *flat-footed hustling* style characteristic of less criminally routine life-styles. Gloria emphasized her distinctive status as a booster: "I'm not a thief—I'm a booster. There's a difference between a thief and a booster. A thief . . . takes anything and everything from anywhere." Booter understood his role as a pimp in entrepreneurial terms, viewing his *who's* (prostitutes) as an investment: "You try not to spend too much money, unless it's important. You're playing economics here. Like I got some stock. . . . In order for her to collect the capital, she has to be a product. You have to have something that you can sell. You don't try to give up too much, but say you are into a new girl. . . . You have to put some clothes on her, put some capital into that to make her look presentable. . . . You're expecting her to get that money back."

Thus, the stable-addict phase is characterized by a comparatively high degree of criminal specialization, complete with the technical, social, and intuitive skills that contribute to success in the criminal role. As shown by this research and in previous studies, stable addicts are successful and sophisticated criminal entrepreneurs.

### Ethics among Stable Addicts
———————————————————— Becoming a stable addict almost always implies a relatively strict adherence to the dominant standards of behavior in the heroin-using subculture. In addition to developing sophisticated criminal skills that allow for a successful main hustle, the stable addict is also socialized with respect to the mores and folkways of the subculture. The normative code of the criminal-addict subculture is, to be sure, unfamiliar and often quite disturbing to the sensibilities of conventional citizens. That these addicts readily engage in acts of theft, prostitution, drug dealing, and the like—and do so with increasing frequency as they progress through their careers—should not be interpreted to mean that they are without a sense of morality. Rather, because these behaviors are normatively acceptable and even encouraged in the subculture, the stable addict is simply responding to an alternative set of normative expectations. The so-called moral degeneracy caused by increased addiction is, from the stable addict's point of view, neither degenerate nor caused by addiction. What is taking place is normative conformity, which is learned through a process of social interaction with other members of the subculture.

While drug use and crime are positively sanctioned in the subculture of hard-core heroin use, there are rules about how these activities are to be carried out. The life history data gathered in this study revealed a very complex code of ethics, much of which revolved around two themes: rules for drug-use participation and rules for choice of victim.

*Rules for Drug-Use Participation*

There is perhaps no normative proscription as pervasive in the heroin-using subculture as that against turning young children on to drugs. Old Ray contended: "Now I don't be sellin' nothin' to high school kids. I'm not into that. I don't sell nobody drugs the first time. That's one of my moral codes." This normative proscription extends beyond selling or sharing drugs with children, however. The study participants were nearly unanimous in their contention that turning anyone on who had not used drugs before, regardless of that person's age, constituted a violation of their code of ethics. According to Horace: "Dope fiends are not interested in making people dope fiends. A whole lot of people got the idea that dope fiends entice other people to shoot dope. But that ain't true. Most dope fiends don't want 'em to shoot dope." John provided some insights into the rationale behind this proscription:

> [Interviewer] Would you turn somebody on to drugs that had never done them before?
>
> [John] Not to heroin, no way, because that's something I don't think they want to get in. After me being in and experiencing it, I don't think that would be right to do that to 'em, especially if you don't know how they are. Some people are weak-minded, weak system. . . . Somebody that I don't know nothin' about, I wouldn't do it and would get mad if one of my friends did, 'cause I figure the cat got a nice job or something like that doing pretty good. I wouldn't want to mess him up like that. But someone that's already messing around and stopped for awhile and just decided to come on back to it, then I might go ahead and do to them because they know what they're doing. It ain't like they don't know.

John's rationale reveals some of the complexities of this normative ethic. He makes a fine distinction between someone who has never used heroin before and someone who is coming back to heroin use after a period of abstinence, because, as he put it, "they know what they're doing." He went on to suggest that someone he knew to be involved in other expensive addictive drugs, such as cocaine or *crank* (methamphetamines), he might consider turning on because that person should be cognizant of the potentially addictive nature of heroin.

The theme regarding rules for drug-use participation extends to yet another feature of the stable addict's normative code: the company with whom it is acceptable to use drugs. Getting off is often a solitary activity for stable addicts, as they are self-sufficient in the techniques of cooking, *drawing* (taking the drug into the syringe through a cotton filter), tying up, and spiking themselves. There are times, however, when heroin is used on a social basis: on weekends, for celebrating a difficult score or events such as weddings and birthdays, or on other occasions that may draw heroin-using friends together. It is generally understood that it is not appropriate to invite to such occasions friends who are strangers to the rest of the group. Little Italy provided some indication of the seriousness of this normative proscription: "And believe me, they [friends who brought a stranger] would get a verbal reprimand. 'What's wrong with you guys bringing this cracker in here like this?' They would get it. I would blow them away verbally." Belle and Slick explained why this normative taboo is so strong:

[Belle] You don't just take off in front of total strangers. Even though the man say, "This man is cool," like, he can be cool with him but he's not cool with me.

[Slick] I'd be uneasy about it [shooting up in the presence of a stranger]. Like if me and you were sitting here, I'd be afraid you were a cop or afraid you would tell a whole bunch of people, "Hey, that guy shoots dope," and put the word on me and it would eventually get to the man [police].

Hence, while these strangers may indeed be bona fide addicts, because they are not known by the rest of the group there is the realistic fear that they may be informants or, even worse, undercover police officers.

Neither will stable addicts generally shoot up in the presence of children or other adults known to be nonusers. Shooting up is an occasion that can only be fully enjoyed and appreciated by other heroin users. *Squares*, those who do not use drugs, are mere onlookers, not participants, and stable addicts are not willing for nonusers to become participants by offering to turn them on. Using heroin in the presence of children is especially avoided because stable addicts recognize that youngsters may look to them as role models. On those occasions when children are present, shooting up does not usually take place until after they are put to bed, or, alternatively, individual addicts may go to the bathroom and shoot up privately. Getting off is, in short, an activity that is accomplished either alone or in the presence of other known addicts.

The ethical considerations of stable addicts parallel those of alcohol users in many ways. Young teenagers experimenting with alcohol are eager to share this experience with their friends. Using alcohol is considered an enjoyable activity that provides a measure of prestige in one's peer group. Older drinkers are usually much more cautious about introducing youngsters to alcohol, for they are aware of the potential problems that can develop as a result of misusing the drug. Similarly, in contrast to occasional users who are eager to proselytize by sharing their newly discovered euphoria with less-experienced friends, stable addicts have been sobered by the realities of the user life-style. These sobering experiences translate into strong normative proscriptions against introducing neophytes to the drug-using life-style and make stable addicts much more cautious about who they will allow to participate in the drug-using experience.

*Rules for Choice of Victim*

Most addict-criminals make at least part of their living from the misfortunes they impose on others. They do not apologize for this. Such criminal exploitation is regarded as "taking care of business," what one must do to make a living. But contrary to what is commonly believed regarding the criminality of heroin users, stable addicts are not random in their choice of victim but are governed by fairly clear normative guidelines. As Belle explained: "You've got to have a set of rules. It comes to a point where you do things, but you don't do them to this person or that person. There's things I've done that I've been ashamed of. But there's things that I know I could have done that I didn't do."

The overriding principle that informs these normative guidelines is social distance. That is, those potential victims who are less socially familiar to addicts are more likely to be victimized than are those who are familiar actors in the social world of heroin use.

The most obvious application of this principle is the distinction between those who are *in the life* (part of the heroin-using subculture) and outsiders. Generally, fellow addict-criminals are not regarded as fair prey. Indeed, stable addicts express a strong sense of loyalty to comrades in the life-style. Shoplifters in this study reported that one of their cardinal rules when working in pairs is never to leave a store with a partner inside—even if lingering means risking detection and arrest. Stephanie described the rule this way: "If the security person grabs [your partner], then you just drop everything to get them away. If you can't get them out of their hands and pick up your bags [at the same time], then drop your bags. You never just leave nobody there to get busted."

Similarly, prostitutes who otherwise compete for potential business will not proposition a trick known to be another prostitute's *regular* (steady client). These women also warn each other of undercover vice officers and of potential *nuts* and *freaks* (tricks whose sexual fantasies run along sadistic lines). The prostitutes I interviewed also reported fidelity to their pimps, boyfriends, or husbands insofar as they guarded against becoming emotionally involved with their johns. Indeed, these women were careful not to allow themselves to experience orgasm with their johns because to do so suggests at least a modicum of emotional involvement that would betray the trust of their husband, pimp, or lover.

Drug dealers report that they express a mutual respect for other dealers by not infringing on their clientele. As John explained, there is, in effect, an informal franchise system that is generally honored by other dealers in the area: "We didn't mess with each other's customers. You have a set amount of people that always buy your drugs, right? If you have ten good people, you don't have to sell it to anybody else. They are the people that you do business with, you can give credit to, let 'em go short. . . . But when you start branching out taking your friend's customers, it causes hard feelings between you."

Generally speaking, individuals outside the subculture are more likely to be regarded as potential victims. They are frequently described in language that betrays an element of contempt: they are *squares, suckers,* or *marks* who exist to be victimized.

There are frequent exceptions to this "in-group/out-group" distinction, but even these adhere to the same principle of social distance. Heroin users, even as stable addicts, may on occasion victimize subcultural comrades. Unlike the street junkie, however, who may rip off dealers or steal from friends out of desperation for heroin (see chapter six), stable addicts engage in such acts only in retaliation against those who have previously wronged them. For example, a dealer who has a customer who continually comes up *short* (of cash) may eventually sell that customer a large quantity of *cut* (diluting substance with no heroin content). Similarly, a customer who has been *beat* (ripped off) by a dealer in the past for no cause may scheme to steal a quantity of drugs from the unscrupulous dealer. These are examples of normative behaviors that are fully sanctioned in the subculture. The offending party is viewed as deserving of this treatment and is not, in this instance, regarded as a loyal comrade.

There is also a social-distance scale applied to those who are not in the subculture. Generally, the more impersonal the target, the more it is

regarded as a legitimate object of criminal victimization. Almost universally, the addicts in this study considered it unethical to steal from family and close friends. As Belle remarked: "We always had another code
of ethics—there's some people you beat it from and some you don't.
You don't hit home." Booter emphasized how seriously this normative
proscription is regarded: "I had one scene where my mother-in-law accused me . . . of stealing her money. And I don't steal no money from
my people. A lot of people say junkies are like that. Now some junkies
are like that. And I'm saying, 'Hey, I did not steal money from my
people.' She would give me the money . . . and I didn't have to steal it
from her. And it hurt me real bad for her to think I stole that money
from her."

Relationships that extend beyond the family and a close circle of
friends are less clear, however. Most addicts report that they are hesitant
to steal from neighborhood stores and businesses. To be sure, these establishments are not as lucrative for shoplifters as are larger chains. The
normative proscription appears to be more deeply rooted than mere
monetary expediency, however. These proprietors are people with
whom the addict must interact on a regular basis. It is difficult to regard
these individuals as mere marks or suckers, as Joe explained: "I tried to
avoid people in my neighborhood, because I figure they're doing as bad
as I am. And I would probably run into them again. . . . Everybody
knows everybody in the neighborhood."

Similarly, prostitutes report that while much of their income derives
from stealing cash and credit cards from their tricks, most will not victimize their regulars in this way. Indeed, while these women are careful
not to develop romantic attachments to their regulars, they do frequently come to regard them as special friends. Penny, who would not
hesitate to rip off her johns even while propositioning them, regarded
her regulars very differently. She was flexible with them regarding payment and on a number of occasions actually lent them grocery money.
She would also occasionally throw parties for them. Although she
maintained a business relationship with these men, it was of such a nature that precluded any thought of stealing from them as she would
from other tricks.

More impersonal targets are almost always defined as fair game.
Whether it is a prostitute stealing credit cards from a trick that she will
never see again or a shoplifter boosting from a large department store,
it is always easier to deny the reality of the deprivation imposed if one's

victim is a faceless stranger. As social distance increases, addicts more readily and successfully neutralize any normative proscriptions that may prevent them from victimizing more personal targets.

More than three decades ago, Sykes and Matza (1957) identified five verbal techniques commonly used by delinquents to neutralize conventional proscriptions against illegal behavior. These are denial of responsibility (for delinquent behavior), denial of injury (to victim), denial of victim (this is someone who deserved to be harmed), condemnation of condemners (those who make judgments engage in equally unethical behavior), and appeal to higher loyalties (there are more important principles than abiding by the law). Sykes and Matza argue that while delinquents become immersed in the delinquent subculture, they are not immune from the influence and expectations of the broader culture. Hence, delinquents find it necessary to neutralize these conventional expectations by justifying their actions. Most of the addicts I interviewed also employed such verbal justifications for victimizing these more socially distant targets. Two of these strategies, denial of injury and denial of victim, were the most frequently employed by the study respondents.

Shoplifters often refuse to recognize their victims, claiming that expensive department stores have been ripping the public off for years and deserve whatever losses they incur. Slick recalled how he felt about taking advantage of a young female bank teller who cashed hot checks for him not once but twice—the second time after she had been warned that she would lose her job if she were so careless again: "I had no respect for her because she was so stupid. She had no business working there. It was almost like I felt like I had an obligation to burn her, to get rid of her because she was so stupid. I kind of felt bad about it, but in a way I didn't. I thought, 'That dumb bitch.'"

Many of the study respondents believed their victims somehow deserved the plight imposed on them. Indeed, Pagie saw himself as playing the role of a hero: "I looked at myself as being like a Robin Hood. I'm not taking from my peers. I'm taking from the stores. It made it easier for me to deal with." Speaking of some of the household larcenies she committed, Stephanie stated flatly, "If you would leave a check around—if you allow yourself to be that careless—then you should be ripped off." When asked if she would take a check that her friend may have carelessly left around, Stephanie replied that this was unthinkable because the dynamics of social distance implied a level of trust on the part of her friend that she would not betray.

I also heard in these accounts a denial of injury to victims. This was especially true of shoplifters who justified their actions on this basis in various ways. One common theme justifies these criminal actions because stores are insured for their losses. George expressed it this way: "Then I started realizing . . . all those cats gotta do is write it off—get insurance for it and all that stuff. I really went off then, man, [because] that's how I cleared my conscience."

Another common theme might be called the "drop in the bucket" rationale: the stores aren't really victimized because they have such a large stock that they will never miss it. As Stephanie claimed, they can afford to be victimized: "A company has got it to spare. They got all that money. If you can get it, then get it. Then too, if you rip off a person, they never get theirs back. . . . Those companies . . . they can stand the loss."

Slick successfully integrated both of these themes in his denial of injury to those banks and accounts against which he forged checks: "I even used to rationalize that it wasn't bad to be bustin' banks because the banks had it. I would be taking from you as an individual in a way, but all I was doing is I was depriving them for a little while. But you didn't lose anything unless you were stupid and couldn't balance your checkbook. . . . Your money is automatically put back into your account by FDIC. I never hit a bank that wasn't under FDIC."

It is important to understand that these themes are learned in the socialization process the heroin user undergoes in the transition from occasional user to stable addict. Indeed, the principle of social distance itself is acquired and internalized through participation in the social life of the subculture. Only by spending time with other criminal addicts, observing their behavior and the sanctions applied to those who misbehave, and by experiencing the school of hard knocks for oneself does the addict develop an ethical code in keeping with the standards of the subculture.

The ethical responsibility of stable addicts also derives from their success as criminals. Because they have become effective at one or more main hustles and maintain a relatively structured daily routine, there is no need to use the more unscrupulous tactics of some down-and-out junkies. Ready availability of heroin affords stable addicts the luxury of maintaining a comfortable level of consumption without engaging in many of the low-down or desperate acts characteristic of less-fortunate users. Little Italy reported that his ready access to dependable supplies of heroin was crucial in maintaining ethical respectability: "I just kept right at it [using heroin] every day because . . . I had it in my possession every day. . . . I could go get it and that's just the way it was. With that in order, I didn't have to go out and burglarize. No one had to worry about me stealing from them. . . . I had money. I didn't have to beat anybody." Rosenbaum (1981) explains the stable addict's ability to maintain ethical respectability in terms of his or her favorable position in the economic structure of the subculture: "The addict who occupies the top of the stratification system—the successful dealer or hustler—does not have to resort to those activities more characteristic of poorer addicts. Such addicts do not have to become unscrupulous and without values or morals. However, those addicts who are sick from withdrawal and penniless find themselves in a situation that forces them to get money by *whatever* means possible" (1981:77; italics in original).

Stable addicts are, from the perspective of the social world in which they participate, morally scrupulous. The extended period of subcultural socialization in which most have participated effectively reinforces the normative code of the subculture. Just as important, the contingencies that define the stable addict are most conducive to normative fidelity. The high level of drug availability combined with a stable life structure allows stable addicts the luxury of maintaining a satisfactory consumer life-style without violating principles of ethical integrity.

The stable addict is, in a word, successful. During this career phase, wholesale copping connections are established and maintained. Stable addicts hone criminal skills and usually develop particular expertise in one or two main hustles. Such criminal expertise is important for several reasons. First, it affords a level of prestige in the subculture not shared by the more amateur flat-footed hustlers, who are viewed as unskilled opportunists who respond impulsively to the circumstances of the moment. Second, the criminal sophistication of stable addicts provides an income capable of sustaining at least a moderate level of conspicuous consumption that further enhances their standing in the subculture. Third, the comparatively lucrative nature of stable-addict criminality affords a level of drug availability not characteristic of other career phases, particularly the occasional-user and street-junkie phases. Fourth, highly developed criminal routines serve to structure daily activity, including drug use. Finally, because of the stable addict's favorable position in the subcultural stratification system, addicts in this career phase do not find it difficult to maintain ethical respectability in the subculture. In short, criminal roles tend to play a predominant part in shaping the experiences of stable addicts.

While this is a dominant career phase for many addicts, it is by no means permanent. Any number of factors may undermine an addict's drug availability or disrupt established routines. When such changes occur, addicts may resume the role of occasional user. Alternatively, depending on the nature of these shifting external conditions, stable addicts may become either street junkies or freewheeling addicts.

# 5

# On a Binge:
# Freewheeling Addicts

████████████████████████████ The freewheeling addict phase of a heroin-using career is characterized by unprecedented levels of heroin consumption. During this phase the use of heroin escalates dramatically, beyond the ability of the addict to control it. This period contrasts sharply with the stable-addict phase in which drug consumption, while often extensive, is bounded by structured routines that limit heroin use to manageable amounts. The loss of control over heroin consumption can be attributed in part to the pharmacological properties of the drug itself. Heroin is a drug for which users can develop a tolerance very quickly. When this occurs, especially in extreme forms, users find it increasingly difficult to maintain control over their drug-using behavior. It is important to understand, however, that just as the social setting places limitations and constraints on heroin-using behavior, it is also the social setting of heroin use that facilitates this tolerance in the first place. Zinberg (1984) and other researchers (Blackwell, 1983; Powell, 1973; Zinberg and Jacobson, 1976) have demonstrated that many addicts are successful in controlling their heroin use and avoid becoming chronically dependent. Moreover, I pointed out in earlier chapters that numerous features in the social setting keep heroin consumption within controllable limits. Work routines, domestic responsibilities, and even criminal and other subcultural roles all serve to constrain heroin consumption.

It is in the absence of such external structures of constraint that users lose the ability to control their consumption. Losing a job, experiencing a divorce, or being apprehended by the police are but a few examples of events in the lives of addicts that may disrupt their daily routine. When these disruptions occur, the normal "times" for copping and shooting heroin no longer exist. Until life structure is reestablished with alternative routines, there is no mechanism in place to gauge drug consumption. Addicts will use heroin whenever and wherever they can, limited only by the availability of the drug.

A critical feature of the criminal-addict life-style that affects both availability and life structure is the highly variable income that criminal hustles provide. I suggested in chapter four that criminal routines are extremely important in structuring the daily routines of stable addicts. Unlike legitimate employment, however, which usually provides a highly predictable income, criminal income may vacillate considerably, subject to a multitude of constraints and opportunities. Ron described this characteristic feature of criminal income: "I think there are spurts. There are some people—say they're shoplifters. They'll go out and have three good days and they'll do pretty good stealing. . . . He will be extravagant. He will go to a dealer and spend $50 during the course of a day. . . . He may do this for three or four weeks. And then he'll go out and the best he can make is $40—that's a bad day. . . . The following day he may not make anything. That may go on for a couple of weeks." Insofar as these lean periods persist, stable addicts may be forced to resume the status of occasional user, or, even worse, if life structure is undermined as well, they may become street junkies. This phase is discussed in chapter six.

While difficulties in hustling are problematic because they limit availability, it is not so much the lean times that tend to undermine the stability of heroin-using life-styles. As Belle pointed out, "You can adjust yourself to a certain amount of drugs a day that you don't have to have but just that much." Addicts who find themselves in this situation of reduced availability have a number of alternative strategies available to them. Many of these individuals work longer and harder at their criminal routines and, in some cases, alter their hustles as a means of maintaining availability. It is also common for addicts to substitute more inexpensive functional alternatives—that is, different drugs with similar chemical and pharmacological properties—for short periods of time to get them through temporary lean periods. Methadone is most commonly substituted for heroin, primarily because it is readily accessible from nearby maintenance programs for little or no cost to the addict. Other addicts have access to Dilaudid or other "drugstore" narcotics that allow them to maintain their dosage level temporarily. Because these drugs are taken much more infrequently (since their effect lasts longer), they impose fewer demands on scarce monetary resources. Similarly, heavy cocaine users often turn to more inexpensive amphetamines or methamphetamines (*speed* or *crank*) when cocaine is less available. Fred described still another strategy for managing periods of low availability. Understanding that criminal income is subject to fluctuation, Fred would plan for these eventualities: "In this business you always got an up-and-down spell. It's never always up. So I learned that early when you got the up spell, get all you can, because eventually there's gonna be a slow period. And if you got a little nest egg stashed away from that up period, get enough to carry you through the slow period till your next up period. So if I'm sniffing up all the profits, when I get that next down period, I'm gonna be broke. I didn't wanna be broke. So I had that as a priority."

In sum, while the elasticity of the criminal marketplace is an omnipresent threat to the stability of criminal and drug-using routines, reduced criminal incomes do not necessarily result in an abandonment of these routines. Most stable addicts expect these lean times and prepare for them. While periodic doldrums pose real problems for stable addicts, they rarely destabilize life structure so severely that addicts are left without some semblance of routine that helps them gauge their drug-using behavior. Quite to the contrary, it is the sudden expansion of criminal income—commonly known as the *big sting*—that is more likely to be destructive of life structure.

### Enhanced Availability
### and Diminished Life Structure
———————————— The freewheeling phase results from sharply increased drug availability combined with a temporary erosion of life structure. It is the unusual success at crime—not the difficulties of hustling—that tends to undermine the stable routines of heroin addicts. According to Ron, one of the older addicts in this study, criminal success often leads to increased tolerance:

[Ron] People who come into large sums of money . . . they can buy excess. So instead of having a morning shot, he goes out, sells his goods, and comes home and gets off on it. And he wakes up in the night and shoots it. And so he increases his tolerance. And so that's the other way he increases by excess if he doesn't put some restraint on himself.

[Interviewer] So a lack of money acts as a restraint?

[Ron] Yeah. There's some people who put restraint on themselves even if they have money. They keep to some sort of schedule. But that's a different kind of guy than the "easy come, easy go." They get it and then they blow it.

One of the unintended and often unforeseen consequences of dramatically increased drug availability is an abandonment of all those daily routines that constitute life structure. The good fortune of unexpected windfall profits often results in an abandonment, or at least a temporary suspension, of normal daily activities. But because these routines are the very basis for maintaining a stable heroin-using life-style, abandoning that structure under conditions of high drug availability is almost always a sure recipe for an uncontrolled spiral of addiction.

The windfalls that enhance availability take many forms. One respondent was *fronted* several thousand dollars worth of drugs *on consignment* (given drugs by a wholesale dealer who is to be paid when they are sold). Instead of selling the drugs as he had agreed to do, he absconded with them, keeping a large amount as his personal stash and giving the rest away. Another precipitating event for several of the women in this study was their involvement with a live-in dealer boyfriend. Sometimes called *bag bitches*, women in this situation find themselves confronted with a seemingly unlimited supply of drugs 24 hours a day. Unless they are criminally involved themselves or are otherwise occupied during major portions of their waking hours, there is nothing to curb their heroin appetite. A number of the women I interviewed looked back on this period in their lives as the commencement of their hard-core addiction. Rose found herself in a similar situation, living with a girlfriend who had an exceptionally heavy habit: "I had a girlfriend . . . who was out there hustling. . . . And she came to stay with me . . . and she had an elephant on her back. . . . She would come in and get off and say, 'Here, Rose, do you wanna get off?' . . . Every time she got high, I got high. . . . This went on for two or three months."

These vignettes highlight the unique character of the freewheeling career phase with respect to drug availability and life structure. First, transition to the status of freewheeling addict usually corresponds to a sudden increase in drug availability. Stable addicts encountering seemingly limitless supplies of heroin or the resources to obtain them have no reason to keep their consumption in check. Booter recalled, "Then I had it. Then I'd shoot it—it seemed like every time I felt like it. I didn't have to go out and get it. I didn't have to do nothin'. . . . I just shot dope and shot dope and shot dope. . . . I had it and I shot it."

It is just this situation that many addicts encounter when they begin dealing drugs. Rather than buying their drugs every day, these addicts-turned-dealers now cop bundles for retail distribution. The temptation to appropriate these drugs for personal consumption is very strong, and lacking other external constraints on consumption patterns, beginning dealers often find themselves increasing their heroin use dramatically. Shannon recalled what happened when she began dealing: "I started dealing. I was around it, and it seems like I wanted to get higher and higher. Where before I was buying it myself. When you get it like that, you do it like that. I'm not realizing how much dope I'm gonna shoot when I just pour it in the cooker like that." Little Italy also found that his habit began to get out of control when he began dealing, but for a different reason. His problem was not so much a matter of shooting up his profits as it was friends and clients wanting to repay previously incurred debts by sharing their drugs with him: "I can remember, man, I wouldn't be sick. I wouldn't need a shot. . . . And some of the guys might come around, get a few bags, but they say, 'Man, like I don't have enough money—why don't you come get down with me?' I'm saying, 'Oh-oh, here I go!' And I would shoot drugs I didn't even need to shoot. So I let it get out of control."

*The Big Sting and Extravagant Life-styles*

While there are many conditions that precipitate the freewheeling-addict phase, it is the big sting that most dramatically increases availability of heroin. When addicts successfully pull off scores large enough to keep them supplied with dope for days or even weeks, it is not uncommon for them to abandon the usual criminal routines that brought them their windfall in the first place. Consequently, by virtue of the lucrative income it provides, the big sting is especially destructive of life structure.

Commonly, the big sting takes the form of a single large *take*, which sometimes amounts to thousands of dollars. In other instances a series of lucrative scores over a short period of time constitutes the big sting. Harry's experience is typical of what happens when a criminal addict suddenly confronts huge windfall profits. His usual hustle was burglary, a criminal enterprise that provided him with a reliable income and allowed him to maintain a stable-addict life-style. One momentous day Harry's longtime friend Bart made him a proposition that he found too good to refuse: "He had on him $30,000. He just was throwing it up in the air, and rolling it and smelling it and going crazy, kissing it and just flying it all over the room and everything. . . . So then I got hooked up with these people that Bart was hanging around with, and they were into this [armed robbery of grocery stores]. It was a very sophisticated thing. This is where he had been when I had not run into him. . . . This guy was, I don't know, he got hooked up with some organized crime, and it was a ten-percent fee, for him, to get the job. . . . So there was a string of those that went down, and we went hog-wild." Harry readily abandoned his burglary routine for this more lucrative line of work. His profits increased dramatically, but just as important, the robberies represented a critical disruption of his stable life-style. He no longer had to maintain a rigorous daily criminal routine but could secure a much more sizable income working only two or three hours per day in a three-day workweek.

This sudden increase in drug availability combined with the abandonment of his rigorous daily schedule gave rise to a life-style that was totally out of control. Harry's heroin use increased dramatically, and he began using substantial amounts of cocaine as well. His life-style also expanded in other ways. His was a life-style of conspicuous consumption: fast cars, fast women—indeed, a fast track:

> We went out and bought . . . this Austin Healey. Oh man, that fucking car was beautiful. It would do a hundred before you hit the overdrive switch, and then it would drop down like into a first gear, and then wind back up and you'd be up to about one-fifty and the damn thing wouldn't be shaking, you could just go right on. So we paid cash for that. We went in and told the guy we wanted to look

at that car and take it for a drive. He looked at us—you know, we were hippie-looking type persons. Expensive clothes on, but we were still hippie-looking. So we got back and the guy said, "How do you guys propose to pay for this?" And we said, "How's cash?" He said, "Oh, sure!" And that was fun, like making people who wouldn't waste the time of day on you, or would probably spit on you if they had the chance, making [them] jump with these bucks. . . . So anyway, we bought the car and we wrecked that. Then we bought a Thunderbird, brand-new Thunderbird. It had everything, the car was loaded. It was nondescript, other than that it was a Thunderbird. Like, it didn't have spoke wheels on it or anything, but it was just a nice, classy car. And that kind of fit what we were going through at the time. We had a lot of money, and things were rolling along. I don't know how much dope I was shooting at that time. I think when you knew how much you were shooting was when the amount of money that it cost you was hard to get. You follow me? And, like, when things are rolling like that, you didn't have to count how many dollars you got together. You would have plenty of dope, you know?

This life-style of conspicuous consumption is extremely important for the symbolic role it plays in establishing a person's status in the sub-culture. Harry understood this and used it to his advantage:

Oh yeah, and the girls. We were knocking them dead. You could just screw any girl that you wanted to when you had those kind of things. To have big money just opened up all these doors. . . . We used to go through there [old hangouts] in the T-bird, zapped the electric windows down and say hi to somebody, and, like, five or six girls come walking over to the car. Maybe buy some dope, and while you're buying the dope, pull out a $100 bill. Nothing where you pulled out a big stocking wad or anything like that, 'cause that was stupid. But to pull out a $100 bill was fairly impressive.

Harry's freewheeling life-style lasted for nearly eight months while he continued his armed-robbery binge. He marveled that he was not even aware of the extensiveness of his drug habit—or for that matter, of the robustness of his life-style generally—until he ended his armed-robbery spree and returned to burglary. The dramatic increase in his income provided him with seemingly unlimited resources for buying drugs, wining and dining women, driving high-priced sports cars, and generally living a lavish life-style. Moreover, Harry now had the luxury of a less-structured routine, which actually rendered him powerless to control his conspicuous consumption.

Harry's biography testifies to the powerful impact of sudden windfalls on heroin-using life-styles. Ironically, criminal routines are a source of stability for stable addicts, but the extraordinary profits that occasionally result from these crimes may actually erode life structure. When this happens, users truly lose control over their heroin consumption. It is during this time of freewheeling use that addicts develop an unprecedented tolerance for heroin. This is the time in their careers when many addicts, including Harry, remember becoming strung out.

The dynamics of the big sting differentiate drug-using criminal careers from respectable occupational careers. Most legitimate careers do not have as variable an income as do criminal careers. Pay raises and occasional bonuses are granted, to be sure, but these are not analogous to the phenomenal windfalls of the big sting. Nonetheless, the dynamics of the big sting can impact respectable routines; consider the potentially disruptive effect of an extraoccupational windfall such as a sizable inheritance, a major lottery win, or even a large settlement in a personal-injury suit. Many of those who encounter such good fortune not only expand their consumer life-style but may also quit their job, take early retirement, temporarily leave their job, or otherwise abandon their basis for life structure.

## The Drugs-Crime Connection among Freewheeling Addicts

Insofar as it is possible to establish a causal relationship between drugs and crime, the freewheeling period of drug-using careers can be characterized as one in which "crime causes drugs." I suggested earlier that the freewheeling-addict phase is typically initiated by the big sting. While many variants exist, these windfalls usually result from criminal activity and affect freewheeling drug-use levels in two ways. First, they increase the addict's ability to afford large quantities of drugs. Second, because of the extraordinary amount of money that the big sting represents, these criminal proceeds often undermine life structure. In short, the dramatic criminal windfalls that launch the freewheeling phase remove the two constraints to uncontrolled drug use, namely, limited availability and rigorous daily routines.

The causal relationship of crime to freewheeling drug use is exemplified by the experience of addicts in this study. For example, Richard was an armed robber who normally limited his criminal activities to street muggings and holding up gas stations and other small businesses. He had just started holding up banks when he *hit* (stole from) a bank for a take of over $65,000—a score that surprised even him. Because of the high visibility of this crime, Richard was *on the run* (hiding from the law) for the next year. Consequently, his normal routines were totally abandoned. Moreover, because of the unusually large quantity of money at his disposal, it was not necessary for him to maintain the rigorous hustling routine that he had previously pursued. In the absence of this familiar life structure, Richard found that his *shot* (habit) increased dramatically over a relatively short period of time.

Booter's big sting came in the form of a cash take of nearly $10,000 from a residential burglary. He took his earnings to New York where he intended to cop a *big piece* (an unusually large amount) to bring back to Wilmington to sell for a handsome profit. Instead of selling it, however, he kept it for his personal use. The impact of this big sting on his consumption pattern was dramatic. Booter increased his shot from a mere three bags per day to nearly a bundle (25 bags) daily within a very short period of time.

> [**Interviewer**] It's interesting that you made the big sting, but you didn't do anything else. So average, overall, you're not making nearly as much money as you did before when you were making a lot of little stings. But you're shooting a lot more dope.
>
> [**Booter**] I guess that's because I had all that money at one time. See, it makes a difference when you got all that money and you go to New York. And my whole intention was, I can sell it. . . . But I just shot mine all up. . . . I didn't even recognize I had a jones until I didn't have no more dope because I didn't hesitate to shoot it.

Booter recalled that after making his $10,000 sting and going to New York to cop his big piece, he virtually abandoned his usual criminal routine for five months. He had a seemingly endless supply of heroin and nothing else to do but sit around and shoot it: "I didn't have to worry about nothin', man. It was like I didn't have to go out and make no money, and I could shoot all the dope I wanted. . . . And when I came off that [New York] dope, I had my regular money—back to my $10 bags. . . . And I went into town to cop some dope and when I came off that [New York] dope, man, I couldn't make it. . . . Within six months I went through $5,000 worth of [more costly, less pure, local] dope."

Insofar as the freewheeling phase is a function of the big sting, this phase of heroin-using careers is most clearly characterized by the "crime causes drugs" model. There is, however, an important caveat to this characterization: the increased availability and decreased life structure typifying this phase are not necessarily the result of criminal windfalls. The participants in this study reported a number of noncriminal and quasi-criminal avenues to freewheeling addiction. Earlier I described an addict who was fronted thousands of dollars worth of drugs by a wholesale dealer to retail on the street. Instead, the addict left town and used the drugs himself. During this time he virtually abandoned all of his usual criminal and drug-using routines and lived a life of leisure. Although this was a relatively brief period of time, it was sufficient for him to develop a powerful addiction. Similarly, female addicts may sometimes develop a relationship with a dealer, which affords them a constant supply of heroin without their having to hustle for it. The effect of these arrangements is nearly as debilitating to self-control as the big sting because these users are not limited by a lack of availability and often relinquish familiar daily routines that have served to pace their drug-using behavior effectively. Mona experienced freewheeling dynamics immediately after she and her boyfriend Ike were married. Most of their friends were drug users who gave them quantities of drugs for wedding gifts. She described the period following her wedding as a drug binge: "We started getting high periodically [before the wedding], like maybe two or three times a week because we really didn't have any money. Ike had just gotten a job. We had to put [aside] money for food . . . so we really didn't get high a lot. We didn't lose control. Then we got married and everybody gave us drugs. . . . We had so much hash and heroin that what else could we do with it? We would get high with it. We started getting into it then."

These are all situations promoting the freewheeling-addict phase that are not necessarily criminally induced. Consequently, while this rather erratic period is characterized by the "crime causes drugs" hypothesis as epitomized by the big sting, the windfalls that are so debilitating to life structure and to self-control over drug-using behavior may come in a number of ways that are not directly related to one's criminal hustle.

### Criminal Specialization among Freewheeling Addicts

—————————————————— The sudden successes encountered in the course of hustling undermine the very routines that made these windfalls possible. For this reason it is inappropriate to speak of the freewheeling addict as engaging in a *main hustle*. This street term implies, among other things, a regularity of criminal routine relative to other types of hustles such that the addict depends on the main hustle as a primary source of income. The main hustle constitutes an occupation, a characterization that I have explained at length in chapter four. The freewheeling addict, in contrast, does not rely on the daily occupational routines of the main hustle. During this career phase addicts experience the rare luxury of being independently wealthy.

But neither are freewheeling addicts indiscriminate opportunists. Indeed, insofar as they are criminally involved at all, these addicts have the luxury of being even more particular about what crimes they will commit. Even freewheeling addicts find it difficult to pass up an opportunity when their larceny sense tells them that this is a sure score. They do not need this score, however, and may well pass it up if they detect even the slightest level of risk or if they are not in the mood to pull off such a hustle that day. Other freewheeling addicts may engage in daring ventures precisely because of the risk. For these addicts, hustling resembles a sport more than it does an occupation, a leisure-time activity rather than work. As Slick explained: "It got to be a game, it got to be fun. Something neat—to try on a new bank manager or a new bank teller. Pretty young girls was my favorite; compliment the hell out of them. I'm no ugly dude. I'd get all dressed up. I was all right. I'd go up there and talk some shit. I could get a date if I wanted! . . . You just get into a little Academy-Award-winning role and it's no problem." During her freewheeling phase, Stephanie was involved in forging checks but not in the disciplined manner of a stable addict. She enjoyed the hustle for the challenge and at one point was netting nearly double the amount she was shooting in drugs. When I asked her why she continued her check-forging spree, she replied: "Just for the fun of gettin' over. When I realized you could do it like that, I just hit all those banks."

The criminality of freewheeling addiction is neither indiscriminate nor disciplined. Addicts in this career phase do not maintain a rigorous hustling routine or cultivate a main hustle. Insofar as they are criminally involved, they are much more free-spirited during this period than they are as stable addicts. Freewheeling crime does not, however, resemble the commonly depicted indiscriminate behavior of the desperate down-and-out addict. Crimes committed during the freewheeling phase are of a highly selective nature, chosen much as one would choose a rewarding pastime.

### Ethics among Freewheeling Addicts

Despite the erratic nature of the freewheeling phase of addict careers, this period is characterized by a high level of conformity to normative standards in the subculture. I have described the freewheeling addict as on a binge, as one whose lifestyle is out of control. The critical feature of this period of addiction that allows ethical integrity is the high level of drug availability. The windfalls that catapult addicts to this type of heroin use and to conspicuous consumption generally allow them the luxury of avoiding the humiliation of having to violate the ethical standards of the subculture. Little Italy explained the importance of having ready availability: "So I'm a junkie now. But I'm not one of those scrub junkies, where I got to steal from my family. . . . I'm dealing. And I'm paying for my habit thataway."

The freewheeling addict often resembles the sometimes stereotypical "flashy" junkie, an image frequently associated with pimps. In addition to increasing their drug consumption, these addicts also buy expensive cars, expand their wardrobes, and extend extreme generosity to associates in the subculture, all of which serve to enhance their reputations as successful addicts. Indeed, so freely did some of these addicts pursue this pattern of conspicuous consumerism that they found their very identity being reshaped. Little Italy recalled the freewheeling period of his career: "Being in that scenery . . . I could change my clothes three times a day and not wear the same things a month later. . . . The things that I didn't have as a child . . . I got them as I came into the drug world. . . . And man, listen here, don't you know that everybody that didn't know me knew me now. Because I'm uptown on the Market Street Strip. You can drive by in your pretty car, blow at the girls. I had flashy clothes and the whole bit. Boom! Little Italy was born."

This binge period might be described as *anomic*, a term referring to the state of normative limbo that results during periods of social disruption or sudden social change (Durkheim, 1951; Merton, 1938). In effect, the constraints normally imposed by life structure become ineffective when daily routines are disrupted. These conditions make it difficult to maintain self-control. The anomie of the freewheeling addict appears to relate specifically to consumption patterns, however. That is, freewheeling addicts do not suffer from an inability to maintain subcultural ethical standards governing drug-use participation or choice of victim. Despite erratic, out-of-control consumerism, the freewheeling addict is able to maintain normative respectability.

Inherent to the dynamics of freewheeling addiction is a fundamental dilemma. On the one hand, the big sting in all its varied expressions eliminates an important source of constraint by affording a greatly expanded level of drug availability. Drugs are readily available to freewheeling addicts, with little effort required to obtain them. This situation of seemingly unlimited availability is enough to transform the most disciplined of addicts into short-term hedonists. Moreover, the sudden windfalls that launch this career phase also undermine stability and life structure by disrupting daily routines or, more likely, by making it possible for addicts to abandon voluntarily their pattern of daily activities. Hence, not only are the limits of availability neutralized, but the familiar routines used to gauge and pace the frequency of drug-using episodes are eliminated as well.

The impact of these dynamics on drug consumption is profound. The amount of heroin consumed in a given period tends to increase to the point where addicts lose control over their habit. Several of the addicts I interviewed remember this period as a time when they developed a *monkey on their back*, a phrase suggesting that their heroin use had escalated to levels beyond their control. Rose explained how she lost control of her habit, which she maintains was the beginning of her addiction: "I didn't get the addiction until the drug was there for me—when I didn't have to hustle for it. It was just there. That's when the addiction came." This tendency is certainly not limited to heroin use. Any behavior that is psychologically reinforcing is susceptible to this sort of uncontrollable escalation under conditions where opportunities for engaging in such behaviors are freely available and where daily routines are relatively lacking or so flexible and erratic that they are incapable of structuring the frequency of these behaviors. Smokers, alcohol drinkers, coffee drinkers, and those prone to overeating all indulge in their respective vices with more frequency during such times. Heroin addicts are particularly vulnerable to increased availability and decreased life structure because heroin is not only psychologically reinforcing but physiologically addicting as well. Hence, the addict is prone to using heroin more frequently under these conditions and in greater quantity with each use because of the tolerance that develops.

Yet the binge cannot last forever. The freewheeling phase of heroin addiction is nearly always temporary, for the money and drugs eventually run out. If the addict is going to be able to maintain even moderate levels of heroin consumption, it will be necessary to return to the workaday world of stable-addict hustling. Furthermore, without the rhythm of a scheduled routine, it is difficult to maintain such an erratic life-style over a long period of time. Despite the thrills and excitement that freewheeling dynamics provide, most addicts are much more comfortable with a scheduled daily routine that provides them with a measure of stability. Harry found that his freewheeling life-style as an armed robber became increasingly uncomfortable as it got further out of control. After several months he voluntarily quit that hustle and returned to burglary, the income from which was incapable of sustaining the sizable habit he had developed as a freewheeling addict.

Provided that the freewheeling addict has not severed connections or otherwise alienated himself or herself from the subculture, it may be possible to rebuild the necessary life structure to accommodate new (and often lower) levels of drug availability. Insofar as this can be accomplished, the freewheeling addict may resume a stable-addict life-style. In many cases, however, the big sting has the effect of isolating the freewheeling addict from the subculture by decreasing the need to participate in its copping and hustling routines. Those who manage to regain a standing in the subculture frequently find that their addiction has increased so dramatically that the routine hustling that had previously been sufficient to maintain their habit is now incapable of even keeping the edge off their "jones." When this occurs, the freewheeling-addict phase is likely to give way to the fourth and final street-junkie career phase.

# 6

# Hitting the Skids:
# Street Junkies

This last career phase, characterized by low drug availability and diminished life structure, most closely approximates the stereotyped image that most people have of heroin addicts: that of down-and-out junkies who are desperate for drugs they do not have the means to obtain. The street-junkie career phase also most closely resembles the image of the pathetically unkempt addict, unable to maintain even the most rudimentary hygienic standards. The life situation of street junkies is truly a difficult and perplexing one, consisting of the most meager hand-to-mouth—or perhaps more likely, hand-to-arm—existence. Gloria recalled her visit with a New York *junkie broad,* a woman who was obviously experiencing the hardships of street-junkie life: "The baby was all pissy and messy laying in a rag all over the floor. . . . It was ridiculous for anybody to live like that . . . because her being a woman, she could have got some kind of money some kind of way—if she had to whore, steal it, take it, or rob it— either way, she was supposed to feed those babies she had. But then she wanted me to bring her daughter back here [to Wilmington]. No, I wouldn't do that. I would take her clothes or whatever else." This scene had a profound impact on Gloria, for she realized that despite her rather harsh judgments about this young woman, she herself was vulnerable to similar conditions and hardships.

Among those who find themselves in the position of street junkie, the fall from grace occurs for one of two reasons. Either drug availability has been sharply curtailed or life structure has been seriously jeopardized. The manner in which particular addicts are affected by these changing contingencies depends largely on their career status at the time these conditions are imposed.

Freewheeling addicts are especially affected by sharply reduced availability. These addicts have usually developed such a high tolerance for heroin that curtailed drug supplies impose a major hardship. Moreover, because they have abandoned stable routines, they find it much more difficult to adjust to suddenly reduced availability and quickly find themselves living the life of desperate street junkies.

Because of the relative stability they enjoy in their drug-using and other routines, stable addicts can usually adapt to lower levels of availability by substituting other drugs, checking into a methadone clinic for temporary maintenance, or using less of what heroin they do obtain until they reestablish connections. They are, however, vulnerable to conditions that disrupt the conventional and subcultural routines they have developed. Divorce, loss of a job, defection of a hustling partner, hassles from the police—such occurrences may seriously threaten the stability of their daily routine. Unless stable addicts have been fortunate enough to score a substantial windfall that assures them of adequate drug availability, the loss of life structure will leave them vulnerable to chaotic street-junkie conditions. The following sections examine the way in which these changing contingencies may facilitate the transition to the street-junkie life-style.

### The Erosion of Life Structure
——————————————— Addicts tend to assume the street-junkie role when they lose the source of life structure that had stabilized their daily routine. Although disorganization can occur in a number of ways, two sources of disruption were particularly common among the addicts in this study: breakdown of family relationships and the loss of legitimate employment.

A breakdown of domestic life is perhaps the most frequent source of disruption to life structure. The fast-paced and at times frenetic lifestyle of heroin addiction and crime, combined with the risks and anxieties associated with these illegal activities, often places a severe strain on conjugal relationships. This strain can be particularly acute if one's partner does not participate in these activities. Little Italy described how he was affected when his fiancée broke up with him: "February eighteenth is when I started everything [drugs]. Yvonne had kept giving me a lot of rejection. I couldn't take it no longer. I just said, 'Well, fuck it.' . . . . I say, 'Well, what do I have to lose?' . . . I said, 'I don't have her so I don't need nothin' else.'" George had a similar reaction when the woman that he was dating died: "That's when I didn't care too much about myself. The woman that dated me died. . . . I got no sense of direction. I just don't care if I got no job. I'm gonna take now."

The second major source of disruption to daily routine is the loss of conventional employment. Many of the participants in this study worked at legitimate jobs. The heroin-using life-style is not always compatible with this sort of work, however, for several reasons. Most of these addict employees moonlight by engaging in criminal or quasi-criminal income-enhancing activities. After a period of time, they often find themselves exhausted by trying to maintain such a hectic pace, which forces them to miss work with increasing frequency. Even if they make it to work, those addicts who have not had an opportunity to shoot up in the morning will likely be sick and ineffective on the job until they are able to cop and get off. Moreover, especially if they are working in a large, impersonal firm, employee addicts probably have no compunction about stealing from their place of employment.

These job-related misbehaviors, cumulatively at least, are sufficient grounds for termination of employment, and this frequently occurs. On average, the participants in this study worked less than one year at each of the legitimate jobs they held since they began using heroin. Most were not fired. They left their jobs for any number of reasons, including not liking the work or the hours, not getting along with fellow employees, conflicts at home, and the like. Obviously, however, these persons did not have the stability that accompanies long-term legitimate employment.

Moreover, for many of these individuals, losing a job was destructive to life structure. The workday occupies a large part of most people's waking hours, and when this work is terminated they find time hanging heavily on their hands. Under these conditions, it is very easy to lose control over one's addiction. Pagie recalled: "After I lost the job with the county, everything escalated then. . . . Things went crazy. After

I lost the job, that's when the family breakdown started happening too. . . . Everything was accelerated. I had nothing but time on my hands."

There are other factors that may attenuate life structure as well. Several of the addicts in this study found their very success in crime a potential liability because once the police had ascertained their criminal routines, they become regular suspects and were forced to abandon their usual modus operandi or even to take up an entirely different hustle for a period of time. This change too is disruptive, for the routines that normally structure daily activity, including drug consumption, have been abandoned or at least replaced with less-familiar ones. Normal drug-using patterns can no longer be sustained because of this more general life-style disruption, with the consequence that destabilized street junkies will consume whatever heroin they can make available. But the dilemma for street junkies is that because of the unstable nature of their life-style, heroin is not usually available in the quantities to which they have grown accustomed.

## Inadequate Drug Availability

——————————————— Sharply reduced availability most dramatically affects addicts in the freewheeling phase. I suggested in chapter five that stable addicts are quite capable of responding to periods of reduced availability by altering their routines accordingly. They may work longer and harder at hustling to raise money for retail street heroin or switch temporarily to more inexpensive functional alternatives. All this is accomplished quite comfortably, provided that life structure is sufficiently viable to sustain a semblance of stability through these otherwise difficult times. Addicts who maintain rigorous criminal routines, work regularly at legitimate employment, or maintain demanding social and domestic schedules can usually adjust to lean times without undue hardship.

Freewheeling addicts, however, have already abandoned normal daily routines, and in many cases they have neglected to maintain the social relationships necessary for sustaining a stable criminal and drug-using routine. Consequently, when supplies run out—and they eventually will—freewheeling addicts lack the resources to rebuild the kind of daily routine capable of sustaining their customary levels of heroin use. These addicts have typically given up their usual criminal routines for a period of time, and it is often difficult to resume them. Detection technologies may have changed in the meantime, or patterns of police surveillance may have intensified, making resumption of old criminal hustles more difficult than expected. Furthermore, freewheeling addicts attempting to return to former criminal routines may find that their hustling skills have become dulled over time, which may erode self-confidence, a critical factor in successful hustling.

Drug availability is also reduced because *big dealers* (major distributors of high-quality heroin) often refuse to sell to street junkies. There are several reasons for this. First, wholesale dealers can expect only minimal profits from street-junkie patronage. Street junkies can never be certain when and for how much they will *get over* (obtain by criminal or quasi-criminal means); hence they are frequently unable to afford to buy enough drugs to make them worthwhile customers to wholesale dealers. Under these conditions, and because of their high tolerance, street junkies frequently find it necessary to beg drugs from anyone they know who might have access to them. Second, because of their financial difficulties, street junkies often attempt to *cop short* (get heroin for less than the going rate) or try to strike a deal to get drugs loaned or fronted to them on a short-term basis. These strategies only serve to discredit them further. Third, because their hustling degenerates into desperate and impulsive acts, street junkies are the type of addict most vulnerable to arrest, which means they are also most vulnerable to being *flipped* (manipulated) by police into becoming informants. Usually they will be promised immunity from prosecution on the charge for which they have been arrested if they *give up* (inform on) somebody *big* (a major dealer). Hence, doing business with street junkies poses considerable risk for wholesale dealers, most of whom are not willing to put up with all of the hassles that dealing with street junkies usually involves.

Thus, street junkies are limited primarily to retail street heroin, which has been repeatedly stepped on as it is passed from the highest level of dealer down to the retail street connection. One study (Leveson and Weiss, 1976:119) has shown that as much as 7% of street dope may have no heroin in it at all, while other studies (Smith, 1973) find a street-dope heroin concentration ranging from 3% to 10% compared with an average concentration of nearly 30% in bags seized from wholesale dealers. The irony is that as consumers of street dope, street junkies pay a higher unit price for heroin than any other person in the distribution hierarchy, which further reduces their drug availability. As Belle pointed out: "That street copping cost a lot more. . . . I might not have been shooting as much as I was [before], but I was spending a hell of a lot more money." Moreover, this very low and often unpredictable quality of heroin available to street junkies further destabilizes life structure, because of the increased demands placed on addicts to maintain their habit. Ironically, these demands affect the street junkie's ability to hustle successfully. Eddie described this irony in more general terms: "It was getting more difficult for me to gain access to a lot of places. People didn't treat me like they had so it was getting more difficult to hustle up money and stuff like that. . . . You kind of wear out your sources of credit."

The street-junkie phase is extremely troublesome regardless of the circumstances that precipitate it, but it is an especially difficult time for those who must make the transition directly from a freewheeling period in their heroin-using careers. These individuals have most likely developed unprecedented tolerance levels. Some of the respondents I interviewed described their dependence during this period as having an "elephant on my back." Moreover, freewheeling addicts have become accustomed to a hedonistic life-style and a privileged position in the social hierarchy of the criminal-addict subculture. Therefore, a sudden loss of access to all sources of drug availability not only throws addicts into a state of excruciating withdrawal but brings their easy life-style to a screeching halt. These addicts experience a rapid downward spiral that dramatically affects the nature and extent of their criminal hustling activity as well as their ability to adhere to normative subcultural codes. Harry vividly recalled this rather horrifying experience: "All of a sudden you're in the armpit of the earth, and you're wondering how it happened, where did it all disappear? I had all this money, I had all those people around me all the time when I had money, and I had plenty of drugs. . . . I had a lot of girls . . . something like showpieces, notches on my gun. I screwed such and such, and such and such. . . . I wouldn't mess around with anybody—on a scale from one to ten, anybody below an eight. Then all of a sudden I'm either not with any girls or I'm with the ones and twos, catching clap and crabs and everything else from them. It was so degrading."

In sum, the road to street-junkie status represents a degrading and often calamitous downward spiral in the social stratification of the heroin-using subculture. But while most addicts who have spent a substantial length of time in the subculture have experienced the street-junkie phase at one or more times during their careers, this downward social mobility is not an intrinsic and inevitable consequence of increased heroin use. The "inevitability hypothesis," however it takes expression, is not a sufficient explanation for the deterioration of addict life-styles over time. There are addicts who have been successful operatives in the subculture for months and even years and who have learned to control their habit so that sudden lack of drug availability does not have serious adverse consequences. Others have learned how to detoxify gradually through such periods by enrolling in methadone clinics before they find themselves in such desperate straits. Moreover, this hypothesis is not sufficient because it ignores the complexity of the environment within which addicts live. These persons are subject to a host of counteractive pressures, many of which are caused by the illegality of heroin itself. These conditions affect addicts very differently depending on their career status at the time they experience them.

Those who do assume the status of street junkie, however, find this the most chaotic period in their careers. Street junkies have neither sufficient drug supplies to ease their withdrawal symptoms nor a life structure capable of stabilizing and controlling the needs and impulses imposed by withdrawal sickness. For this reason, they are in an extremely vulnerable position, subject to being exploited by others and forced to resort to desperate actions that would have been unthinkable earlier. Such behavior, however, only exacerbates the situation, leaving street junkies vulnerable to arrest, alienated from others in the subculture, and unable to maintain even the most meager existence. Booter described the precarious position he found himself in as a street junkie: "You aren't cautious at all. From where I sit from here viewing the whole scene, it's nothing about being cautious at all. 'Cause when you're sick you want a bag of dope. There's many times when I've dumped it in the cooker and I don't know who gave me the dope at all." The street addict is said to have *hit the skids*, occupying the lowest position in the heroin subculture. This situation poses conditions that have direct and profound implications for the drugs-crime nexus, the nature of addict criminality, and for the ability of the addict to maintain ethical integrity.

## The Drugs-Crime Connection
## among Street Junkies

———————————————— Street junkies exemplify many of the stereotypical notions people have of heroin addicts, including the belief that addicts are the helpless victims of their own drug habits. Their level of addiction is no longer commensurate with their ability to support it, and they find themselves driven to engage in any action that might alleviate withdrawal symptoms. Mona described how her boyfriend Ike became more impulsive and less calculating during this period of his career: "He would . . . do something . . . just to get something for that day, drugs for that day. He didn't really think ahead that much. . . . He didn't plan ahead for the week. . . . When you're a junkie you don't think about how much everything is worth. You just think about how much you need right now to get over the feeling that you have."

The street junkies' plight is that heroin and other drugs are not available in the quantities and concentrations to which they have become accustomed as stable and freewheeling addicts. Street junkies typically find it difficult to cop from their usual wholesale connections. These persons may know or believe that the street junkie is under surveillance by the police and is consequently an especially risky client. Addicts in this difficult situation, perhaps already experiencing withdrawal symptoms, are easily "flipped" as informants and may "give up" their connection.

But an addict's reputation may suffer for other reasons as well. When a drug user begins to cop short or when a street-level dealer starts shortchanging customers by excessively cutting drugs with quinine and other substances, word gets around that this addict is in difficulty and is probably not trustworthy. This dilemma further exacerbates the street junkie's problems, for as the options for obtaining drugs and the money to buy them narrow, he or she must pay exorbitant street prices for poor-quality dope. Hence, while it was possible for stable or freewheeling addicts to purchase heroin in quantity from wholesalers for $3 per bag ($75 for a 25-bag bundle), street junkies may have to pay $10 or even $20 per bag for much lower quality heroin. Street junkies thus become even more desperate in their quest to relieve withdrawal pains.

Further complicating this situation is the fact that street junkies lack a stable life structure that was so instrumental in maintaining constraints on their heroin use as stable addicts. The loss of important daily routines undermines supports that street junkies depend on to limit voluntarily their appetite for heroin to quantities commensurate with available means. Indeed, with such large amounts of unstructured time and with no fixed routines providing a constraining rhythm to drug-using behavior, street junkies have no time during their waking hours when they are not thinking about getting high. Old Ray described the situation of the street junkie as one of a lack of involvement: "Usually the person that gets involved in drugs is not totally involved in anything else. I was on the street at the time [I started using more]. I just got laid off. . . . I had encountered a situation of economic castration—prejudice. . . . This made me susceptible to the street. . . . A man would become involved in anything—negative or positive—as long as he's involved. You must have some activity. Drugs is a commitment."

While the physiological responses of street junkies to a temporary lack of heroin may be no different than those of stable addicts, the experience, or "set" (Zinberg, 1984), is much more severe for street junkies because of a lack of other involvements to occupy their attention. Hence, street junkies find themselves almost continually *chasing the bag* (searching for drugs), looking for any opportunity to "get over," to hustle up enough money for their next fix.

Under these conditions the claims of many treatment specialists and others that "drug use causes crime" makes sense. Implied in this position is the notion that criminal acts are a direct response to a felt need for heroin or other expensive drugs. Only during this career phase does the relationship between drug use and crime appear to be so clearly a causal one among the addicts who participated in this study. During this difficult period in their careers, the motivation for continued criminality becomes more narrowly experienced as needing a fix. Whereas stable and freewheeling addicts view their criminality as necessary to sustain a broad-based life-style that includes drugs as well as a more general conspicuous consumption, street-junkie status does not allow for the luxuries of a fast life-style associated with these earlier career phases. The lives of these down-and-out addicts totally revolve around scraping up enough money to get their next fix. Crime is no longer the entrepreneurial challenge that it was previously, and the addicts' consuming interest lies in getting their next shot.

I have until now rejected the conventional wisdom that heroin use causes crime. Occasional users are criminally involved, but much like their heroin use, their criminal hustling is usually done on an experimental basis, and it is usually unrelated to their drug-using behavior.

Stable addicts are more heavily involved in heroin use and in crime, but it is incorrect to characterize these activities in causal terms. Quite to the contrary, criminal activity in this phase serves to facilitate drug use because of the increased income that results. The freewheeling phase is often precipitated by a major criminal event. After this, however, freewheeling addicts are often only minimally involved in crime, and that involvement is not driven by an acute need for drugs.

The street-junkie's life, by way of contrast, is dominated by a powerful, sometimes incapacitating need for heroin. The excitement of the life-style that characterizes stable- and freewheeling-addict career phases gives way to a much more sober daily existence that is absolutely dependent on a drug that is becoming increasingly difficult to obtain. Under these conditions, the street junkie feels compelled to engage in otherwise unthinkable behaviors with respect to both choice of crime and maintaining the ethical codes of the subculture.

## Criminal Specialization among Street Junkies

───────────────────    The street-junkie role, because of the debilitating circumstances that it represents, precludes the kind of specialization implied in the main hustle. By the time addicts have become street junkies, they have already developed a sizable habit. In many cases, these individuals are careening off a rather carefree freewheeling phase marked by virtually unrestricted access to ample supplies of drugs. Consequently, often without their even being aware of it, their heroin habit has grown out of control. The problem, of course, is that the supplies eventually run out, leaving these freewheeling addicts with a massive habit but no ready means to support it. At this point, they are likely to engage in whatever behavior—criminal or otherwise—that might net enough money to cop another bag. Boss reflected on his street-junkie days: "Even now when I talk about dope I think about all the things I've done that I wouldn't normally do as a hustle. But it's at a time when you're sick and there's nothing else you can do 'cause you can't stand that sickness."

Perhaps the most visible indicator of the shift from stable or freewheeling addict to street junkie is this seemingly random pattern of hustling activity. In contrast to the rationally calculated, planned criminal routine of the stable-addict period, street-junkie crime is highly impulsive, a response to whatever opportunities may be present at the moment the addict feels the need for dope. The lack of specialization characteristic of street-junkie status means not only the commission of a greater variety of criminal hustles than would ordinarily be attempted but also a lack of planning, no calculation of strategy that is so crucial to criminal success as a stable addict. Consequently, street-junkie criminality smacks of reckless amateurism, more closely resembling the trial-and-error method of early occasional users than the tactics of experienced criminals, which in fact most street junkies are. The difference between the street junkie and the occasional user, however, is that the street junkie feels compelled to engage in foolish and ill-conceived behavior because of severe withdrawal symptoms. The result is that street junkies fail more often than they succeed in their criminal attempts. Fred explained it this way: "Whatever business you're in, while you're calm or high, it's better for you because you're doing what you do best. But if you're not high and you're nervous and you're pressured to keep from feeling bad, then you're gonna make mistakes." Little Italy described his failed attempts at armed robbery in a similar fashion: "I know today, I can say that if you don't have a plan you're gonna fuck up, man. . . . Now those robberies weren't no plan. They didn't fit in nowhere . . . just by the spur of the moment, you know what I mean? I had to find something to take that place so that income would stand off properly, 'cause I didn't have a plan or didn't know anything about robbery."

The consequences of such unwise behavior usually spell disaster for street junkies. Abandoned are all of the comfortable routines and the modus operandi that have been successfully developed over a period of months or even years. In some cases, these addicts are forced to abandon their criminal routines because local law enforcement officers have deciphered their pattern. Probably more commonly, these individuals are simply desperate for drugs; they panic and impulsively commit a crime in hopes of a quick buck. Regardless of the reason, departing from usual criminal routines poses considerable risk of arrest for street junkies. Belle was emphatic about the possibility of arrest when I asked her if she waited until she felt sick before she worried about hustling or copping dope: "Now that's what I call a lazy person. . . . No, I couldn't do that. . . . I have to [cop] while I'm still on my feet and slept enough. Before I start getting ill, I'd always try to have it. . . . Because once you get like that . . . you're not going to be able to do anything. Anybody says that a sick person can go out and hustle and stick up a person to make money, they can't because they'll end up being busted and put in jail. Because you cannot hustle when you're sick."

Old Ray learned this lesson the hard way when he was sick and desperate and departed from his usual criminal routine: "All those times I pulled robberies were at crucial points. . . . Like the police would let me go through everything I could burglarize, every other game. I would do a robbery and they would step down and find out who was with me and they would always give me up. I had no business back in '64 robbing no real estate office—but it was a fact that I was mentally disconnected, my nose was running, I was jones-ing and the safe was open, and I went in there and took it and disregarded the consequences. That's what I was talking about, the mitigating circumstances of drug addiction—the immediate need."

These observations by Little Italy, Belle, and Old Ray highlight why street junkies are more subject to detection and arrest than are addicts in other career phases. In the first place, trying to hustle when sick from withdrawal symptoms seriously impairs the ability of street junkies to pull off a crime with the same degree of finesse and professionalism. Sick and in need of immediate relief, street junkies are usually sloppy in their hustling, leaving obvious evidence linking them to their crime. There is, in short, a failure to apply the necessary technical skills that were developed and employed quite successfully in the stable-addict phase. Moreover, social and intuitive skills are also impaired when an addict is sick from withdrawal. Hustles such as check forgery, con games, and shoplifting that require social acumen are especially risky because the addict's attention is distracted. Moreover, it is extremely difficult for street junkies to attend to the intuitive cues that might signal that they are being watched by a floorwalker or observed by undercover vice officers. The need to alleviate the "jones" seriously impedes the ability of street junkies to attend to business as usual.

There is still another reason that addicts are more vulnerable to arrest as street junkies, one alluded to by both Little Italy and Old Ray. When street junkies abandon their main hustle, they usually turn to whatever money-making criminal opportunties are available. The problem for the street junkie is that the requisite skills for successfully committing these nonroutine crimes have not been developed. Prostitutes may know how to detect undercover police officers posing as johns, but they are not necessarily adept at spotting cameras, one-way mirrors, and floorwalkers employed by retail stores to detect shoplifters. Experienced shoplifters, on the other hand, will not necessarily be attuned to telltale mannerisms and body language of bank clerks who suspect that they may be trying to forge a check. While there may be some transference of knowledge and skills across different types of criminal hustles, many of the skills that must be carefully honed are quite unique to particular types of crime. Consequently, when addicts step out of their main hustles, as Little Italy and Old Ray did when they tried committing robberies, they are met with a much greater likelihood of detection and arrest.

In summary, the street junkie seems to fit Goldstein's depiction of the opportunistic hustler: "[If] any single word can describe the essence of how street opiate users 'get over,' that word is *opportunism*. Subjects were always alert to the smallest opportunities to earn a few dollars. The notion of opportunism is equally relevant to predatory criminality, non-predatory criminality, employment, and miscellaneous hustling activities" (1981:69; italics in original). Street-junkie opportunism is a function of the inability to establish a stable life structure that routinely produces sufficient income to sustain an addiction. Consequently, the hustling activities of street junkies consist of a series of short-term crimes as well as legitimate and quasi-legitimate money-making enterprises. For a price, or in exchange for heroin, street junkies may cop for an out-of-towner, taste for a dealer, rent their works to another junkie, or even sell their food stamps or the *meth* (methadone) that they obtained at a clinic. In addition, street junkies will impulsively respond to shoplifting, forgery, burglary, or other criminal opportunities with little regard for the risks involved. Indeed, if they are desperate enough they may recklessly create criminal opportunities, such as Little Italy and Old Ray did when they began committing robberies. Not only does such opportunistic hustling pay very little, but none of it is stable. While one or more of these activities may net enough income to cop for today, none of them can be counted on to do so tomorrow. Moreover, because these crimes pay so little, because they must be committed so frequently, and because they are often not crimes for which the addict has developed the necessary technical, social, and intuitive skills, it is almost inevitable that the street junkie will eventually be arrested.

### Ethics among Street Junkies

———————————————— The stratification system endemic to the heroin-using subculture affects not only addicts' ability to hustle successfully but also the likelihood that they will turn young children or novices on to drugs, victimize family and close friends, or any of a number of other acts that violate the normative code of the subculture. These moral dynamics are not, of course, limited to the experience of heroin addicts. Hughes (1971), for example, has observed a "moral division of labor" in the legal and medical professions where, because of their relative position in the professional hierarchy, some lawyers and physicians end up doing the "dirty work," enabling those of higher status to "stay clean."

Besides the moral dynamics operative in the stratification system of the drug-using subculture, the contingencies of drug availability and life structure have profound implications for the ethical behavior of heroin addicts. Ready availability of drugs allows heroin users to maintain a comfortable level of consumption without engaging in many of the desperate tactics characteristic of less-fortunate addicts. Similarly, life structure provides an important source of stability that allows addicts to maintain ethical integrity. When normal conventional and subcultural roles that serve to guide and constrain drug-using and criminal behavior are abandoned or suddenly altered, heroin addicts find themselves in normative limbo. Lacking a routinized life structure, these addicts find it extremely difficult to discipline their conduct in keeping with standards of respectability. The problems of adjustment entailed in the shift from heroin to methadone maintenance and other drugs, particularly as this change disrupts established routines, provided a recurrent theme in the life histories of the addicts in this study. Belle discovered the problems entailed in these shifts when she attempted to replace her use of heroin with the use of crank (methamphetamines): "It was just like day and night between the person I had been when I was using heroin and the person I was when I got on this meth and crank . . . doing things in my home I had never done before and taking things from my home that I had never done before. It was always a no-no touching my home in any way . . . and this last period—whew! It was really abominable." This brief behavioral aberration, which lasted several weeks, captures the anomie encountered by addicts who experience an abandonment or sudden alteration of normal daily routine. In this respect, life structure exercises an important stabilizing force that helps regulate an otherwise insatiable appetite and provides the addict with a meaningful normative context.

The problem for street junkies is that both drug availability and life structure are conspicuously absent. Having developed a sizable habit by this time and having abandoned familiar routines that serve to structure and control drug consumption, they are the most likely candidates to violate the code of the subculture if it means alleviating excruciating withdrawal pains. As Stephanie observed: "After the money is coming in like that . . . and it gets to the point where their habit is worked up like that, then they might do anything [if they are cut off] and they have to find a new way of making their money. They might do anything."

Among other violations, street junkies often find themselves victimizing individuals who were previously regarded as off-limits. I described in chapter four the important principle of social distance employed in the heroin-using subculture to define who is an appropriate victim of hustling behavior. Impersonal strangers or businesses are the addict's preferred choice of victim. Family and close friends are not acceptable candidates, even if they are not active in the subculture. There is, of course, a great deal of discretion in the application of this principle of social distance. What is regarded by one addict as an acceptable target may be rejected by another. All of the addicts I interviewed, however, agreed that "hitting" family and close personal friends constituted a major violation of their code. Nevertheless, most of them did violate this code when they had no other options. Indeed, Old Ray contended that even fellow addicts become potential victims if the street junkie gets desperate enough: "You get to the point where you might exhaust your existing funds. Then you go through a cycle where you abuse your credit. Then you go through a cycle of manipulation of friends and family for money. . . . Then after you wear that out, you hustle other drug addicts." Similarly, Boss admitted that there were times when he victimized older, handicapped, or otherwise defenseless people when the need for heroin was particularly urgent: "That's dope. That heroin will make you do a lot of things . . . that I wouldn't do unless it's the dope that made me do it. Suppose she had a heart attack and died. I get life in prison for $300."

Many of the addicts in this study also admitted they occasionally turned young neophytes on and sold drugs to nonusers and strangers during these difficult times. The proscription against introducing youngsters to heroin is possibly the most prominent feature of most heroin addicts' ethical code. One of the major reasons for the strong taboo is the fact that addicts recognize the risks associated with the drug. Operative here is a version of the "school of hard knocks," lessons learned only from the experience of being an addict, including the understanding that this life-style is not exclusively about exciting challenges and getting high. The other realities that are learned in this street school are the pain of withdrawal, the risk of arrest and incarceration, the hurt of a spouse leaving, and the complications in copping during the all-too-frequent heroin *panics* (shortages). These realities become salient in the consciousness of heroin addicts only after they have spent considerable time in the subculture, which explains why occasional users are not hesitant to turn their nonusing friends on to heroin.

Ironically, street junkies, who are experiencing this dark side of addiction at its worst, are also the most likely to violate this important code. Because of the difficulty encountered in other hustling attempts, street junkies frequently turn to street-level dealing to make their shot from one day to the next. The quality of this dope is often very poor, stepped on more than usual in order to eke out a greater profit. The problem with this strategy is that the unscrupulous street dealer quickly gains a reputation for having bad dope, a problem Harry was familiar with:

> [**Interviewer**] You had a reputation for having good drugs?
>
> [**Harry**] For a while, until I got really strung out. Then I was beating the hell out of everybody I came across. . . . And once you get a reputation of being a beat, whew! All your status and esteem, height, went down the tube. . . . Everybody would say it was a fucking rip-off.

The challenge that Harry then faced was securing and maintaining a stable clientele. When regular customers take their business elsewhere, street-junkie dealers may have no choice but to seduce novices and youngsters into heroin use just to survive.

Similarly, street junkies whose undependable reputations have resulted in loss of access to a stable network of copping connections are likely candidates to turn on strangers or even neophytes who may be willing to introduce them to dealers in return for dope. Circumstances such as this almost always create a dilemma for street junkies, as the compelling situation in which the addicts find themselves does not remove the stigma they experience in having to resort to these tactics. Rose had recently lost her copping connection and had to rely on a young non-drug-using teenager to cop for her. Unfortunately for Rose, the young girl was not willing to make the purchase without compensation in drugs. Rose explained how she attempted to resolve her ethical dilemma: "I gave her the least amount I figured she'd feel with a whole bunch of water so it would look like she had a lot. . . . It wasn't that I was trying to cheat her . . . it's just that I didn't want her to really get into it."

The ethical predicament for street junkies may be summarized as follows: On the one hand, their access to heroin has been seriously curtailed, making the appropriation of a daily supply of drugs an increasingly dominant focus of their energy. At the same time, however, the usual hustling routines that they have developed and perfected as stable addicts have been disrupted, which not only further reduces drug availability through decreased income but also destroys whatever semblance of stability and routine these addicts have developed. With no life structure to constrain the street junkie's appetite for heroin, the intensity of withdrawal experience is even greater. During these difficult times, street junkies do not have the luxury of maintaining a fidelity to ethical codes that have little relevance to those who scarcely have the means to scrape together a meager existence. Rosenbaum describes the dynamics of this situation for the female addict: "The woman addict's self-respect is at least temporarily damaged when, due to the fluidity of the money-stratification system, she finds herself down and out, with no way to earn money legally. It is at this point that she becomes temporarily unscrupulous and may rip off a personal friend, even family. It is important to note that this unscrupulousness is *temporary* and that in some way, most addicts become unscrupulous in some form, at some point in their careers" (1981:60; italics in original).

In line with commonly held perceptions of the addict life-style, street junkies are driven by the need for dope to criminal acts that they would otherwise not commit. Many of these crimes are opportunistic and fortuitous in nature, committed on impulse without regard to consequences. It is also the street junkie who embodies the stereotype of the unscrupulous addict, the moral degenerate who is willing to victimize anyone and spread the venom of addiction to unsuspecting neophytes in return for a bag of dope.

It is understandable why common perceptions of heroin addicts are shaped by this career phase. Lacking a daily routine and finding drugs difficult to obtain, the street junkie must take more chances than would otherwise be the case. Under these circumstances addicts will engage in criminal hustles at which they are not adept. Unless their life circumstances change, arrest is virtually inevitable. While not universally the case, it is street junkies who typically encounter the criminal justice system. As Fiddle has observed: "The police see junkies at their worst. They see them under the spur of need or pseudo-need. . . . They see them violating even their own negative codes. The police rarely see the addict engaging in a purely voluntary humane act" (1976:12–13). Moreover, that population of addicts most available to the media as well as to researchers are those who have been apprehended. For this reason, the image of the heroin addict generally available to the public is that of the stereotyped street junkie.

It is important to recognize, however, that this period represents but one phase in the addict's career. For substantial portions of their careers, most addicts lead relatively stable, albeit fast-paced, lives. Far from being an inevitable result of the physiological and pharmacological properties of heroin, the behavior of the street junkie emerges only in response to the career contingencies that limit accessibility to heroin and disrupt established patterns of behavior.

# 7

# Implications of a Career
# Perspective for Research

████████████████████████████ I have written this book
with one primary purpose in mind: to portray the lives of street heroin addicts in a manner that captures their subjective experience. In
addition, I have tried to depict this subjective reality in terms intuitively
understandable to those who are not part of the heroin-using subculture. I believe that these two goals are inextricably related. Failure to
appreciate the addict's worldview by imposing explanations and im-
puting motives that have little relevance to the actors we are trying
to understand makes the resulting conceptual scheme a mere exercise
that is neither serious nor fruitful. And because most readers are not
participants in the heroin-using subculture, the addict's experience
must also be made comprehensible if this book is to accomplish anything beyond providing either a titillating account of an exotic life-style
or an overwrought, abstract analysis of interest only to a small group of
academics.

Two strategies have been particularly helpful in pursuing these goals.
The first is the use of the career history as a "window" into the experiences of hard-core street addicts. This methodology allows the respondents to frame both questions and responses in terms that reflect the
reality of their experiences in the heroin-using subculture. These addicts are, in their way, letting us know them in a way not possible
through more structured data-collection methodologies. I have attempted to preserve the subjective quality of the data in a number of

ways: by quoting the respondents themselves in relation to relevant issues, by using the terminology of the subculture, and by relating particular experiences of the study respondents to illustrate general findings and conclusions.

The second strategy is the choice of a conceptual scheme that frames the data collection, analysis, and presentation of this study. Heroin addicts are frequently depicted as pathological misfits leading exotic life-styles, as different, somehow, from the rest of us, and therefore as objects to be "explained." I have chosen instead to portray them as individuals pursuing careers, similar to doctors, lawyers, factory workers, homemakers, and others who practice legitimate occupational and non-occupational careers. This construct is valuable because it renders the life-style dynamics of heroin use and addiction intuitively understandable to those who do not share that lifestyle. Understanding addiction as a career rather than as a pathology helps observers to identify with the actions and perceptions of the addict. Most careerists, for example, can recall having difficulty in choosing a major and deciding what sort of work in which they wanted to specialize. Heroin addicts also experience this dilemma. Similarly, those in conventional careers can point to any number of transitions in their lives, some reflecting conscious choice, others beyond their control. Thus, while there may be pathological or exotic elements associated with heroin-using careers, the addict life-style can best be understood by using the same occupational framework as is used for other occupational and nonoccupational work histories.

The career perspective is also valuable because it directs our attention to the developmental nature of addict life-styles. As Horace remarked, "Dope don't just jump on you overnight like people say." Heroin addiction is not something that suddenly "happens" with the first or second shot. Rather, it is part of a broader life-style that develops over time. Thus, to explain addiction merely in simple cause-effect terms is to fail to appreciate the qualities that it shares with other, more familiar careers.

This study is not the first attempt to understand addiction in terms of career. For example, Rubington (1967) rejected the conventional wisdom that addiction is a pathology, arguing instead that heroin users develop as addicts in the context of a drug culture that facilitates and encourages such behavior. Borrowing from the earlier work of Chein et al. (1964), Rubington identified four phases in an addiction career: experimental use, occasional use, regular use, and attempting to quit.

Later, Fiddle (1976) described addiction as a sequence of activities, identities, and occupations. Similarly, Coombs (1981) delineated five developmental stages in drug-abuse careers: initiation, escalation, maintenance, discontinuation, and renewal. Taken together these studies form a rather impressive tradition of drug-career research that has successfully redirected attention to the occupational and entrepreneurial character of drug-using behavior.

The research reported in this book falls squarely within this tradition and, it is hoped, contributes to it. The career contingencies of drug availability and life structure are particularly important in that addict careers never develop in a vacuum, free of external constraint. Rather, they are shaped by powerful forces in the addict's environment that affect drug availability and life structure. These contingencies, in turn, define one's career status. The typology developed here also departs from previous drug-career research in that addict careers are not presumed to follow a linear path. While these careers all have an identifiable beginning and eventually an end, their duration is characterized by a great deal of variation in quantities of drugs consumed and in the nature and extent of criminal behavior. While addicts almost always begin as occasional users, the subsequent direction of their careers is not predetermined. These careers may move in any of several directions and change course repeatedly depending on life structure and drug availability.

These dynamics have important implications for several recurring research issues that have been discussed throughout this book. The next section reviews these issues from the perspective of the total career of the heroin user. This summary is followed by a discussion of important methodological implications.

## Heroin Use, Crime, and Ethics: A Summary

The stages of heroin-using careers discussed in previous chapters demonstrate that some of the traditional controversies about the consequences of addiction stem, at least in part, from a failure to recognize the dynamic nature of addict careers. A brief review of these issues should be helpful not only to untangle some of the complexities of heroin addiction but also to suggest some fruitful avenues for future research.

*The Drugs-Crime Connection*

The relationship between drug use and crime is a particularly long-standing controversy, dating back to some of the early reformers of the nineteenth century such as Richard Pearson Hobson, who argued that narcotics are so destructive of the body's centers of control that users are incapable of controlling their behavior. This explanation for drug-related criminality is now generally rejected, at least with regard to narcotics. Today, those who argue that heroin use causes crime explain this causal relationship in economic terms: heroin is both expensive and addictive, and addicts have no choice but to engage in illegal behavior that is more profitable than restricting themselves to legitimate sources of income. With at least one notable exception (Kolb, 1925), most studies conducted prior to 1950 supported this explanation (Greenberg and Adler, 1974). In contrast, research since 1950, as well as Kolb's early study, has found that most addicts have an arrest record that precedes serious narcotics use. These findings suggest that addiction is more affected by crime than vice versa. Minimally, they imply that addiction alone cannot account for addict criminality. More recently, however, several researchers have reported that addiction does indeed lead to increased criminal behavior (Anglin and Speckart, 1984, 1986; Ball et al., 1981, 1983; Johnson et al., 1985). There is, in short, no definitive answer in the literature regarding the causal nexus between heroin use and crime.

This study offers a new view of the drugs-crime connection by examining this relationship in the broader context of addict careers. The career perspective offered here suggests that the relationship between heroin use and criminal behavior is a complex one and varies throughout an addict's career. During the early occasional-use phase, drug use and crime are pursued relatively independently of each other; neither is particularly affected by the other during this experimental period. While most occasional users have engaged in criminal and delinquent behaviors prior to first taking heroin, this is because the opportunity to take part in such acts usually precedes drug-using opportunities. This fact, however, does not imply that criminal behavior causes drug use during this experimental period.

In contrast, stable and freewheeling drug use seems to be largely a function of availability, which in turn is enhanced by systematic criminal behavior. Hence, while it may not be appropriate to articulate this relationship as one of crime causing drug use, criminal income facilitates drug use because of the increased availability it affords. Quite the reverse is the case during the street-junkie period, where availability through normal channels is lacking and addicts lack the necessary structure to regulate drug needs. Under these conditions, addiction does indeed appear to cause crime in the manner commonly depicted.

Moreover, the career histories collected in this study suggest that the relationship between drugs and crime is too dynamic and complex to permit phrasing the issue simply in terms of cause and effect. In addition to providing the necessary income for the purchase of heroin, criminal activity also serves to structure drug-using behavior during the stable-addict phase. Crime thus provides addicts with a daily routine that serves to actually limit or regulate their drug use. Among free-wheeling addicts, however, criminal success in the form of unusually large windfalls may lead to the abandonment of these criminal routines. It is clear from this study that the relationship between heroin use and crime is far more subtle than previous research has suggested. The data presented here suggest that any generalizations based on "snapshots" in time will fail to capture the changing nature of the drugs-crime connection throughout an addict's career.

This issue will continue to attract a great deal of research if only because addressing the criminality commonly associated with addiction constitutes a secure platform for any administration at any political level. But future research in this area must move beyond current trends in several ways. First, the "sequence" methodology that seeks to establish which comes first, drug use or criminal behavior, is clearly not adequate to address the complexities of the relationship between them. Insofar as the problem of causality is of interest, it will be necessary to establish when drug use and crime begin to escalate. Second, it is necessary to move beyond our preoccupation with "cause" and address the conditions under which addicts engage in particular crimes or increase or decrease the level of their heroin consumption. Similarly, we should be developing methodologies that allow an assessment of the relationship between drug use and criminal behavior at different points in one's career. Finally, we need to begin asking different questions with regard to the drugs-crime nexus. What role does crime play in facilitating drug use? How does it constrain drug use? How does drug use facilitate crime? How does the legal and social milieu affect drug use and crime? Questions such as these do not presuppose a simple causal relationship but instead open up new vistas of drugs-crime research.

### Criminal Specialization and the Main Hustle

The debate over criminal specialization among heroin users is related to the question of causality. Those who understand criminal behavior as being driven by addiction tend not to perceive addicts as criminal specialists. Rather, they see them as jacks-of-all-trades or, as Goldstein suggests, as "grabbing what they could" (1981:70). From this point of view, addicts do not have the wit, the skills, or the professional identity to sustain a criminal specialty. On the other hand, those viewing addiction and criminality in less causal terms tend to describe addict criminals as people who develop their identities as criminals, who hone hustling skills, and who retain verbal and social skills even though they use drugs. These researchers more often describe addict criminality in occupational terms (e.g., Biernacki, 1979, and Sackman et al., 1978).

I suggest that the nature of addict criminality lies somewhere between the image of the undisciplined, compulsive addict and that of the specialized professional criminal (Faupel, 1986, 1987a). This reality is captured in the street term *main hustle,* which implies that addicts repeatedly engage in one or two types of crime, developing important skills that facilitate the successful carrying out of these crimes (Biernacki, 1979). The main hustle also implies a greater degree of criminal flexibility than is usually supposed. While addicts tend to rely on a small number of criminal hustles to support their drug-using life-style, they also respond to "sweet" opportunities that may be encountered. Thus hard-core heroin addicts are, for the most part, criminal entrepreneurs who derive a great deal of satisfaction in "getting over" another individual for a lucrative monetary return.

Previous chapters have demonstrated that criminality among heroin users is not static but may alter dramatically over their careers. As occasional users, most have not yet had sufficient time to develop a main hustle. These individuals are usually just beginning their careers and are experimenting with a variety of hustles. By the time they become stable addicts, however, they are well on their way toward developing one or two main hustles. They have discovered their criminal proclivities and developed criminal skills in one or two areas that afford them a decent standard of living.

Freewheeling addicts are also quite circumspect as criminals. Although they do not have a structured daily routine, supplies of heroin are readily available, and freewheeling addicts do not find it necessary to engage in the desperate tactics of street junkies. Most freewheeling addicts are only minimally involved in crime and not usually on a systematic basis. The only exceptions to this generalization involve those offenses committed for their intrinsic enjoyment and perhaps those instances of selling heroin to less-fortunate acquaintances out of one's own personal stash.

Street junkies, on the other hand, are the epitome of down-and-out addicts who respond in desperation to whatever criminal opportunities come their way. Addicts experiencing the dynamics of the street-junkie phase have neither the capacity nor the predisposition to limit their criminal activity to a carefully planned, systematic main hustle, for their need for drugs is more immediate than this kind of specialization allows. Consequently, street junkies engage in virtually any and all crimes depending not on personal penchants, talents, or skills but on the opportunities of the moment.

It is no coincidence that criminal specialization is least developed during that career phase in which a causal connection between heroin use and criminal behavior is most apparent. Insofar as crime is an entrepreneurial activity, motivated by the challenge of "getting over" successfully rather than by an acute need to relieve withdrawal symptoms, it is likely to be more focused, planned, and systematic. Crime is a challenge, and success in one or two main hustles confers status in the heroin-using subculture.

### The Ethics of Heroin Addicts

Drug-using careers, like other careers, are subject to external conditions that affect one's ability to maintain ideal normative standards. Regardless of the specific turns that people's careers may take, ethical conduct in the heroin-using subculture is dependent upon and sustained by the constraints and opportunities imposed by drug availability and life structure. Occasional users frequently deviate from subcultural standards because they have not learned the normative expectations of the subculture. These indiscretions nearly always reflect insufficient socialization and should not be interpreted to represent an inevitable moral degeneration resulting directly from narcotics experimentation.

Subcultural ethics are probably most faithfully adhered to during the period of stable use. Stable addicts have spent sufficient time in the subculture to be aware of the ethical distinctions between proper and improper behavior. Moreover, because addicts in this career stage enjoy the advantage of easily accessible supplies of drugs and a life structure that regulates consumption, there is no reason to deviate from these ethical standards. Stable addicts can, in short, afford to be ethical. Freewheeling addicts can also afford to be ethical because supplies of heroin are so available that these users do not have to sacrifice ethical integrity to obtain a fix. Unfortunately, the lack of structure associated with this life-style allows drug consumption to escalate out of hand, resulting in an extremely high tolerance for the drug.

When supplies of heroin run out, freewheeling addicts typically "hit the skids" as street junkies. The need for heroin is particularly acute during this time, in large part because the ability to secure needed quantities of the drug is greatly reduced. Hence, street junkies must often violate their own ethical standards for a bag of heroin.

That the ethics of addict behavior are subject to external conditions is hardly remarkable. This characteristic of social behavior has been documented in other contexts as well, such as in the areas of racial attitudes and behavior (Deutscher, 1966; Kutner et al., 1952; LaPiere, 1934; Linn, 1965), classroom behavior (Freeman and Ataov, 1960; Henry, 1959), and drinking behavior (Warriner, 1958), among others. In all of these situations, researchers have found disparity between what people say they will do and how they actually behave under specific conditions. Nevertheless, unlike individuals in these contexts who fail to adhere to their stated principles, the inability of heroin addicts to maintain ethical integrity with consistency is commonly understood to be evidence for a state of moral degeneracy.

The career histories of the addicts I interviewed suggest otherwise. These street addicts readily articulated their ethical standards. Moreover, even when they failed to maintain these standards behaviorally, they acknowledged and asserted the legitimacy of the very norms they violated. Many, like Penny, expressed deep regret at their behavior during these desperate times: "I felt bad . . . doing the things I was doing. . . . I didn't want to take nobody's check that I know [they] only get once a month and they probably got kids—and I know they did have kids or else they wouldn't be on welfare."

At other times addicts use various sorts of excuses or rationalizations to mitigate their culpability (e.g., see Sykes and Matza, 1957). They sometimes attempt to lessen the impact of their indiscretion by pointing to even more serious violations of actual or hypothetical peers. As Belle pointed out, "There's things I've done that I've been ashamed of . . . but there's things that . . . I know I could have done that I didn't do."

In short, it is not appropriate to evaluate the credibility of the ethical system embraced by street addicts in terms of absolute behavioral conformity any more than the credibility of business ethics should be established only by the absolute absence of fraud. Rather, the legitimacy of these subcultural ethics is established by the addict's reaction to their violation. The regrets expressed and the very necessity of offering excuses, rationalizations, and moral comparisons all acknowledge the legitimacy of those norms that have been breached. Through reactions like this, addicts honor and reaffirm their own indigenous standards of conduct. In this way, the normative subculture is sustained and preserved, much like displays of embarrassment at times of incompetent performance serve to sustain the interactional order (Goffman, 1967). Future researchers addressing the ethical components of the heroin-using subculture are advised to focus not only on the substantive components of the normative system but also on the conditions promoting or hindering the addict's ability to maintain fidelity to those substantive norms.

## Methodological Implications
## of the Career Model
The career perspective elaborated here has important implications for how we go about researching various substantive issues related to drug use and crime. Three methodological issues are especially salient: (1) the limitations of official data as a measure of drug use and criminal behavior, (2) the contribution of longitudinal research designs, and (3) the choice of sample and sampling procedures.

*Limitations of Official Data*

Researchers in the drug field commonly use data that have been collected and recorded by official agencies of the federal and state governments, including police departments, treatment centers, and data from emergency rooms and crisis centers. Crime statistics are commonly taken directly from the *Uniform Crime Reports* (*UCR*) published each year by the Federal Bureau of Investigation (FBI). The *UCR* supply data on arrests and crimes from police records that are voluntarily submitted to the FBI by more than 10,000 participating police departments across the country. Researchers examining the criminality of specific individuals typically use individual arrest records, sometimes in conjunction with self-reported arrests. The *UCR* are divided into two parts. Part I offenses, commonly known as "index crimes," are usually considered the most serious and include homicide, aggravated assault, rape, robbery, burglary, auto theft, larceny, and arson. Part II offenses are considered less serious; they include prostitution, driving under the influence, and drug possession, among others. Studies of criminality among heroin addicts rely heavily on such official data (Austin and Lettieri, 1976, and Gandossy et al., 1980, for a review of this literature). Studies of treatment effectiveness are especially likely to rely on official arrest data as indicators of reduced or altered criminality (Faupel, 1981).

Drug-use statistics are drawn from several sources including treatment centers, many of which participate in the Client Oriented Data Acquisition Process (CODAP). This reporting system, instituted in 1973, is a required procedure of all treatment programs receiving funding from the National Institute on Drug Abuse or the Veterans Administration. Another frequently used source of drug-use data is the Drug Abuse Warning Network (DAWN), a reporting system jointly sponsored by the National Institute on Drug Abuse and the Drug Enforcement Administration (DEA). DAWN collects incident reports from participating emergency rooms, crisis centers, and medical examiners in 23 cities nationwide. Unlike crime data, these sources of information are rarely used to trace individual drug-using careers. Rather, they provide estimates of the prevalence of drug abuse in the United States (Person et al., 1977).

The largest official data source for *criminal* addicts is the DEA's Drug Abuse Statistics System, which collects data reported to the DEA by local police departments. More recently, the Drug Use Forecasting System (DUF) sponsored by the National Institute of Justice reports the results of urine tests of arrestees in more than 20 cities throughout the United States. Arrestees are tested for ten different drugs including heroin and are asked to submit a voluntary interview regarding drug-using patterns on a quarterly basis (Mieczkowski, 1989; National Institute of Justice, 1988; Wish and O'Neil, 1989).

Official sources for both crime and drug-prevalence data have serious limitations, many of which have been discussed at length in the literature. The career model discussed throughout this book confirms many of these shortcomings and suggests other limitations as well. I shall first discuss the problematic nature of official crime data, particularly information on arrest. This is followed by a brief discussion of the limitations of official drug-use data.

**Arrest Data.** Critiques of the *UCR* generally fall into several categories. First, the extent of crime is underrepresented (e.g., Cressey, 1957; Doleschal, 1970; Hartjen, 1978; Inciardi, 1978; and Shulman, 1966). Erikson and Empey (1963) and Williams and Gold (1972) further show that official data greatly understate the actual amount of crime committed by delinquent populations. Such underreporting is especially marked with addict populations. For example, Inciardi (1979) indicates that one arrest occurs for every 413 self-reported crimes committed, and one arrest takes place for every 292 self-reported index crimes committed.

Second, official data distort the types and social location of crime (Cressey, 1957; Glaser, 1967; Hartjen, 1978; Savitz, 1978; Shulman, 1966). Some offenses, such as violent crimes, are by nature more visible and hence more subject to detection and arrest. Other offenses, especially crimes without direct victims such as drug dealing, are much more difficult to detect and are grossly underreported. Studies have also found that blacks, lower socioeconomic groups, and men tend to be overrepresented in the *UCR*.

Third, there have been numerous criticisms of the phenomenal variation in official rates across state and other jurisdictional boundaries, suggesting that official crime rates are more a reflection of the nature of police enforcement and recording practices than a record of the crime in any given area (Beattie, 1960; Cressey, 1957; Hartjen, 1978; Savitz,

1978). Inciardi (1978) found that in 1976 the small university community of Newark, Delaware, with a population of 25,000, reported a crime rate of 10,000 per 100,000 population. This was a higher rate than that reported for any metropolitan area of the country except Las Vegas. Yet reported violent crimes included only 3 homicides, 5 rapes, 22 robberies, and 36 aggravated assaults. This community was hardly a major crime center. Inciardi explains that Newark was serviced by four highly trained police forces: municipal, university, county, and state. Simply put, compared to communities with less-effective police enforcement, a higher percentage of the crimes committed in Newark end in arrest.

The career dynamics elaborated in previous chapters suggest a fourth problem with official police data: namely, among addict populations at least, official crime records do not accurately reflect the nature of individual criminal histories. That is, criminal addicts are disproportionately arrested for crimes that are marginal to their overall pattern of illegal activities. I suggested earlier that stable heroin addicts tend to specialize in one or more main hustles. One of the advantages of such specialization is that valuable technical, social, and intuitive skills are developed that facilitate the successful commission of these crimes. More important, these skills provide the stable addict with the ability to avoid detection and arrest.

However, career histories collected for this study also reveal that addicts are not always able to sustain their main hustle throughout their criminal careers. Particularly as street junkies, often sick and experiencing intense withdrawal pains, these addicts tend to be much less discriminate in the criminal options they consider. Belle, who relied primarily on prostitution as her main hustle, recounted several incidents of shoplifting and forgery; neither crime was part of her usual routine, nor was she particularly skilled at them. When asked why she resorted to these crimes, she explained: "I think it's because it's during the time you're pressed for money. It was because I was uptight for some money and I had to do these things."

Under these circumstances, the addict is confronted with an increased probability of detection and arrest, a situation familiar to the respondents in this study:

[Interviewer] You were into drug dealing. That was your thing. You never got busted for drug dealing, did you?

[**Little Italy**] No. Pisses me off too. Not that I didn't get busted for them, but I got jammed for something that's not even my style [robberies and forgeries]. . . . You get busted for something that's out of your league, man.

Penny reported: "One day this dude brought me a check. I just decided to try [to cash it]. It wasn't no thing that I was into. And I got busted for it." Belle explained why arrest is more likely under these circumstances: "Wherein boosters and people that burglarize, they all had these things set up for them. They know how to go about doing those kinds of things, and I feel like a person that goes out of their own thing, that's an automatic bust if you don't know what you're doing."

Addicts who engage in aberrant criminal activities usually do so under street-junkie conditions, when their usual routine has been seriously disrupted and when the need for heroin is particularly pronounced due to its lack of availability. These contingencies leave the addict in a temporary state of anomie, lacking constraints and direction. In the words of Old Ray, things get "out of whack":

[**Interviewer**] You got busted on three of these [robberies].

[**Old Ray**] Yeah. They were at crucial times in my life.

[**Interviewer**] How were they crucial?

[**Old Ray**] Well, when things were getting out of whack and I needed money immediately . . . I disregarded the consequences to take care of the immediate need. . . . I wasn't on my main hustle. . . . [The things I'm arrested for] are never the things I'm into. I've never been caught on my main hustle.

It is important to remember that the street-junkie phase is usually temporary. During the greater part of their careers, the addicts that I interviewed led the more or less routine lives characteristic of the stable addict. As Biernacki observes: "The work of addicts, their hustles, the ways in which they manage to support themselves, is not a diffuse, unregulated activity. The addict under 'normal' conditions, when he is not desperate, is *not* like some marauder, aimlessly plundering the city" (1979:549; italics in original).

Indiscriminate criminal activities also played a minor role in the overall career spans of the addicts who participated in this study. These are, however, precisely the crimes that are most likely to be represented on any given addict's arrest record. Main-hustle criminality, those activities making up the greater share of an addict's illegal acts, tends to be greatly underrepresented on one's official record. All of this suggests that official records do not accurately depict the criminal biographies of heroin addicts. Ron summarized the nature of the problem most succinctly: "You have a large number of people who are busted based on the *theory* that he has a whole line of these. You have guys around here [who have been arrested] saying, 'Hey, man, that's not even my M-O!'" While self-report methodologies also have deficiencies, the career dynamics elaborated here suggest that this is the only appropriate method for accurately reconstructing the criminal careers of heroin addicts.

**Drug-use data.** Official drug-use data suffer from many of the same limitations as does the *UCR*. The DEA and DUF data, of course, reflect only those addicts who have had contact with the criminal justice system, and hence these sources suffer from those limitations discussed above. CODAP and the Drug Abuse Reporting Program (DARP) that preceded it rely exclusively on data from federally funded treatment programs. DAWN data, in contrast, are obtained from emergency rooms, crisis centers, and medical examiners but in only 23 cities throughout the United States.

Addicts represented in all of these official sources have one thing in common: they are in trouble. They may have a run-in with the police and find their way into the DEA or DUF records; they may be suffering a personal crisis and refer themselves to a crisis center; or they may have experienced overdose symptoms and been rushed to an emergency room. It has been shown, however, that most addicts do not normally find themselves in these sorts of predicaments. The desperate situations that addicts in official sources represent are characteristic of one particular career phase: the street-junkie period.

The criticism that official data are skewed toward street-junkie addicts is perhaps directed at a specially constructed straw man, since those who use these data do not usually depict them as representative of the addict population as a whole. Rather, official drug-use data are typically used to measure the prevalence and incidence of drug use in particular populations. It is difficult, however, to estimate total drug use from these data. There is no necessary relationship between the number of addicts in trouble and the total addict population in any given area. Numerous factors affect one's ability to maintain a stable drug-using life-style. Changes in law enforcement practices, for example, may force addicts to shift suddenly their usual criminal routines, thereby enhancing the likelihood of getting caught. Similarly, during heroin panics, when supplies are drastically limited in certain areas, street-level dealers will cut their bags more than usual. Street junkies who rely on these expensive street bags often cannot keep the edge off their "jones" with such diluted dope and may voluntarily enter drug treatment in order to lower their tolerance. All these factors bear no relationship whatsoever to the prevalence or incidence of drug use, but they do profoundly affect official drug-use statistics.

There are other problems associated with official drug-use data. It is impossible to know how representative the 23 cities participating in the DAWN program are of other metropolitan and especially more rural communities. Furthermore, any projections of how many addicts live in any given jurisdiction made on the basis of these data are purely arbitrary. No formula exists for calculating the percentage of the total user population represented in police reports, treatment programs, emergency rooms, and crisis centers that can be universally applied across jurisdictions.

Even more problematic are attempts to measure changes in the prevalence and incidence of drug use over time. It cannot be assumed that because any of these measures reports a higher or lower number of events or of clients receiving drug treatment from one given year to another that more or less drug use is occurring in the community. Because these data do not accurately assess the overall level of drug use in the broader population, they are profoundly influenced by factors that may or may not include a growing prevalence of drug use in a particular area. Increased federal funding for treatment programs, for example, will inevitably result in a greater number of clients treated, which will, in turn, be reflected in official CODAP data. More important, because these data are not representative of the total addict population in any given area, it is difficult to interpret the meaning of any changes in these statistics over time. That is, because it is addicts who are in some sort of trouble that make their way into these records, any changes over time in these data reflect only that there are either more or fewer addicts who are experiencing difficulty.

The inability of official statistics to represent adequately either the nature of addict criminality or the incidence and prevalence of drug use, particularly as these may change over time, requires the use of self-reported drug use and crime data in such research. The following two sections briefly raise two important considerations related to this line of research. The first addresses the importance of longitudinal research designs for untangling some of the complex substantive questions in this area. The second looks at the importance of sample selection and its impact on self-reported crime and drug-use data.

### The Contribution of Longitudinal Research Designs

The addict career histories reported throughout these chapters support Denzin's (1970) assertions about the importance of research methodologies that measure social reality as it unfolds over time. These biographies reveal that it is not possible to understand addiction, crime, and other features of the drug-using life-style in static relation to one another. The connections between drug use and criminal behavior change over the course of an addict's career. Similarly, the nature of addict criminality does not remain constant across career phases. Even the ethical system of the heroin using subculture is subject to changing conditions that affect an addict's ability to maintain these standards.

The research design used in this study—and to which Denzin specifically referred—is the life history. The life history is a particularly effective longitudinal design because it incorporates the subjective perspective of the actor in the interpretation of the events in one's biography. This methodology more than any other facilitates what Matza (1969) calls an "appreciative" understanding of deviance. It reveals social life as it is experienced by the actors who are being studied.

This methodology is not without drawbacks, however. Just as quantitative methodologies suffer from the myopic prejudices of researchers using predefined categories derived from their favorite theoretical traditions, the life history reflects a particular perspective as well: that of the actors being studied. This is not a point of apology, and Matza argues that it is precisely this perspective that we should be attempting to reflect. It is, however, a social construction, just as the perspective of the social worker, the criminal justice professional, or even the academic drug researcher is a socially constructed version of the same reality. The life history provides but one description (albeit a critical one) of the proverbial elephant.

The life history methodology is also limited by the fact that biographical accounts are provided retrospectively. Such accounts may vary considerably, depending on how much time has passed since the events occurred and the particular situation in which addicts find themselves when interviewed. Consequently, older addicts who have more or less "retired" from the life-style may reflect on their biographies very differently than they would if they were still active in the subculture. Similarly, those in prison or in treatment (as many of the addicts in this study were) may reflect more nostalgically on the street life than they would if they were still active.

These limitations notwithstanding, the life history remains a useful and provocative method for assessing the unfolding character of social reality. But there are also other strategies of a more quantitative nature that hold considerable potential for examining career dynamics, such as the cohort studies pioneered nearly 40 years ago by Wolfgang (1972). Applied to drug users, this approach entails identification of a set of heroin-using criminals with an initial interview to establish baseline information about levels of drug use, types of crimes committed, criminal justice system contacts, and other information that can be used as indicators of career stage. Follow-up interviews are then conducted periodically, perhaps monthly or quarterly, assessing the same information at later points in time. After a series of follow-up interviews, some assessment of changes in the dynamics of drug use and criminal behavior can be made. The research design that is perhaps most adaptable to such a cohort analysis is that by Johnson and his associates (1985) described in chapter one. Their particular methodology is limited in that weekly follow-up interviews are conducted over a single month. Theirs is essentially a cohort analysis, however, and expanding this schedule over a longer period of time could be a great contribution to empirical testing of some of the observations presented here.

Other approaches such as the "crime days" methodology pioneered by Ball and his associates (1981, 1983) and the chronological method used by Anglin and Speckart (1986) also represent innovative quantitative attempts at the reconstruction of career dynamics. It must be remembered, of course, that all of these strategies involve making inferences about process while relying on data representing different static points in an addict's career. Much like moving pictures, the portrayal of the dynamics of addict careers using any of these methods can be nothing more than a series of still pictures that create the illusion of motion. That which substantiates the processes alluded to in such research are the participant's own interpretations and explanations given for whatever changes occur in these static descriptions. Such explanations cannot be obtained in quantitative form. Hence, while these methodologies can be useful, explanations for the dynamics involved, if they are any good, must derive ultimately from research designs such as that employed here.

*The Importance of Sample Selection*

The career perspective also has profound implications for how the nature of one's sample might affect portrayals of addict careers. Because each phase in an addict's career represents different patterns in criminal and drug-using behavior, sampling decisions may critically affect findings. Sampling among drug-using delinquents, for example, will almost surely yield data that are vastly different from that gained by an examination of older, more experienced addicts. Most delinquent addicts are probably occasional users, not particularly focused in their criminality nor skilled at what they do. Veteran addicts, in contrast, have usually experienced all or most of the heroin-using career stages, and they have the benefit of a long career to provide a broader perspective from which to interpret their experiences. Such considerations directly affect findings regarding the relationship between drug use and crime, the nature of criminality, the ethical content of drug-using and criminal behavior, and other research questions that one might want to address.

Worthy of special consideration, however, are those samples composed of officially processed criminal addicts, whether arrestees, prisoners, or clients in treatment. These samples are unique because they usually consist of addicts who have experienced all four career phases. All of the addicts in this study had some sort of contact with the criminal justice system, all but one had been in treatment at one time or another, and most were in prison at the time they were interviewed. Their testimony suggests that most arrests occurred during the street-junkie period of their careers. Incarcerated addicts have probably been arrested several times by the time they receive a prison sentence. Furthermore, most of those addicts who entered treatment programs indicated that they enrolled because life was getting difficult and they either wanted to lower their tolerance to make it more manageable or wished to leave the drug-using life-style altogether. All of these scenarios suggest street-junkie dynamics.

Reliance on these samples poses both advantages and disadvantages. By the time most addicts become street junkies, they have usually experienced the other three career phases. Consequently, these samples can potentially provide an overview of the critical features of criminal-addict careers, which may not be the case with less-experienced samples. I am quite confident that the typology that forms the basis of this book would not have been so clear had the sample been restricted to addicts who have not been exposed to the criminal justice system. Street-junkie status came into particularly sharp focus as these respondents related the sequence of events leading to their arrest or treatment experiences.

There are also disadvantages to these samples that impose some limitations on the generalizability of findings. First, these respondents have not merely experienced street-junkie status but have also, in one respect at least, failed. They were caught, arrested, and perhaps incarcerated or forced into treatment programs, or the stresses of street-junkie life became more than they could handle and they voluntarily entered treatment. Thus, it is not clear whether the careers of these addicts are simply more complete versions of those who have not had such encounters with official agencies or whether there are substantially different career dynamics at work among those who have never been arrested or in treatment. Studies of controlled users by Zinberg (1984), Zinberg and Jacobsen (1971), and Blackwell (1983), for example, suggest that such addicts have various mechanisms of constraint (such as stable family situations and meaningful employment) not available to addicts who go on to use more heavily. Controlled users have not experienced, and perhaps never will experience, the instability of the freewheeling-addict or street-junkie phases. For this reason, it is not possible to make generalizations beyond that population of drug users that have encountered official processing agencies. As it turns out, this is quite a sizable group.

# 8

# Implications of a Career Perspective for Drug Legalization

Understanding addiction in terms of career prompts reexamination of a number of long-standing debates regarding drug use and the criminal behaviors associated with it. Throughout this book I have attempted to demonstrate that heroin-using careers, when examined over their temporal course, are far more complex than depicted in much of the literature. Unfortunately, many of our law enforcement and treatment policies and practices are based on simplistic causal models of drug use and criminal behavior. Intervention and other "supply-side" strategies are promoted because of the belief by policymakers and many treatment practitioners that heroin addicts are the hapless victims of greedy drug lords whose ostensible goal is to create an ever-expanding population of "walking dead." Methadone-maintenance programs continue to service clients on the assumption that heroin use causes crime. Local law enforcement efforts are often based on the same assumption; the prevailing belief is that if the streets are cleared of junkies, the crime problem will be ameliorated as well. Ironically, this same understanding of the relationship between drug use and criminal behavior is a recurring theme in the argument for legalization of heroin and other drugs. Believing that addicts commit crimes because of the high cost of illegal drugs to which they are enslaved, reformers would seek to bring these drugs into the legal marketplace, thereby reducing their cost and eliminating the need for predatory criminal behavior.

148

The career histories described here raise serious questions about the empirical foundation on which current law enforcement and treatment efforts are built. The remaining two chapters address some of the major policy implications suggested by the career experiences of heroin addicts: this chapter addresses various issues related to legalization of heroin; chapter nine focuses on the implications of a career perspective for drug treatment. I begin by briefly sketching the evolution of American drug policy, providing a sociohistorical context for the current debate. This discussion is followed by an overview of the broad policy options available. The final two sections of the chapter explore the contribution of the career perspective to the legalization debate by examining (1) the impact of legalization on drug-related crime and (2) the effectiveness of current law enforcement practices.

## A Brief History of Drug Policy in the United States

The history of narcotics use and policy in the United States has been well documented, and it is beyond the scope of this work to add anything new to that social history.[1] Any discussion of legalization must be informed by this history, however, regardless of one's stand on the issue.

Narcotic drugs have been used for millennia with virtually no prohibition (Ray, 1978). Indeed, it was not until the twentieth century that narcotics were systematically prohibited in this country as a matter of public policy. Nineteenth-century America has been dubbed a "dope fiend's paradise" because opium and morphine were so readily available through doctors' prescriptions, over the counter, and in many patent medicines. While many of these patent medicines were used as teething syrups for infants, the primary consumers of these conventionally prepared narcotics were middle-class and middle-aged women (Brecher, 1972; Duster, 1970; Terry and Pellens, 1970). Some of these women became addicted to narcotics as a result of using them in heavy doses for menstrual cramps and other medical ailments. Others, however, found narcotics an attractive recreational alternative to alcohol, which was taboo for women during this time. In addition, many Civil War veterans were addicted to morphine, which was used extensively during the war as an analgesic (Musto, 1973). Significantly, while many of these men and women did become addicted to opium and morphine, these nineteenth-century addicts did not experience the ill-health effects usually associated with narcotics today. Nor were these individuals dependent upon criminal means of income to support their habit. Indeed, Brecher (1972) contends that virtually all of the negative health and social consequences experienced by twentieth-century addicts are directly attributable to the illegal status of these drugs.

There was, in addition, one other group of narcotic addicts during this period. The nineteenth century witnessed the immigration of tens of thousands of Chinese for whom opium smoking was a long-standing custom. Originally recruited to work on the railroads, most of the Chinese eventually migrated to cities, where they worked for low wages and formed ethnic enclaves. Hostilities toward these immigrants intensified, and the white power structure quickly came to identify many of the problems in these cities with the Chinese. Particularly targeted was the Chinese practice of opium smoking, as it was reported that many white women and young girls in these cities frequented the opium dens (Brecher, 1972). San Francisco acted first, outlawing the smoking of opium in dens in 1875. Brecher reports that the law was a total failure because it was impossible to enforce it adequately. Similar ordinances were passed in other places, such as Virginia City, Nevada, with negligible effect.

When the United States won possession of the Philippines from Spain in 1898, it was discovered that the Spanish government had operated an international opium monopoly from the islands. The Spanish had contracted opium to merchants (who paid taxes on the product) and sold it to the Chinese, the only ethnic group allowed to purchase it (Musto, 1973). In addition, two opium wars between Britain and China had been fought over the shipping of Indian opium products into China. Chinese opium producers complained that they were being undercut, but American business also saw valuable trade going to the British that might otherwise have come to the United States. American missionaries were also concerned about the opium trade in China for moralistic reasons (Brecher, 1972).

These concerns were the basis for a strong American interest in international opium control. At the request of Anglican Bishop Charles Brent of the Philippines, the United States urged all nations with an interest in the Far East to come together to work out a viable solution to the opium problem. This resulted in the formation of the Shanghai Opium Commission, which met in 1909 and urged the United States to develop legislation that could be used as a model for other nations. A second conference convened at the Hague in 1911 with a similar mandate (Musto, 1973). Against this backdrop, the U.S. Congress passed the Harrison Narcotics Act in 1914. Brecher (1972) notes that in the congressional debates supporters of the bill said little about the evils commonly associated with narcotics addiction today. Rather, the debate focused on the international obligation that the United States had incurred at the Shanghai and Hague conferences.

The Harrison Act remained the major piece of defining legislation for drug use and trafficking in the United States until 1970. Yet the act was not overtly intended as prohibition legislation. Criminalization was, after all, the jurisdiction of state governments. The Harrison Act was written as a revenue measure, calling for all persons who manufacture, dispense, or otherwise deal in the products of opium or coca leaves to register with the federal government and pay a special tax. Particularly targeted were narcotic products with higher opium concentrations, which were allowed to be distributed only through medical prescriptions. These more concentrated narcotics were to be distributed only by physicians and other licensed health-care professionals. The Act reads: "Nothing contained in this section shall apply . . . to the dispensing or distribution of any of the aforesaid drugs to a patient by a physician, dentist, or veterinary surgeon registered under this Act in the course of his professional practice only" (Public Law No. 223, 63d Congress; approved December 17, 1914; quoted from Brecher, 1972).

The Harrison Act ostensibly allowed for the orderly marketing of narcotic drugs through physicians and others licensed to do so. There was a catch in the act, however, which went unnoticed by many physicians until it was too late. After several Supreme Court decisions, particularly *Webb* v. *United States* in 1919, the phrase "in the course of his professional practice only" was read to specifically exclude administering narcotics to addicts for maintenance purposes. Hence, the act came to be used as a major prohibition device, and many physicians were prosecuted for illegally dispensing narcotics to addicts.

The long-term result of this legislation was dramatic. Narcotics use was transformed from a relatively benign vice practiced by some of society's most respectable citizens to an openly disdained activity prohibited by law, relegating the narcotics user to pariah status in most communities. Not surprisingly, the demographic profile of the typical narcotics user changed from the white, middle-class, middle-aged woman of the nineteenth century to the young, lower-class, minority male heroin-user of the twentieth century (Duster, 1970). It is also understandable that those stigmatized by this legislation would form close-knit associations for purposes of moral support, self-protection, and greater accessibility to illegal supplies (Kaplan, 1983). Moreover, because narcotics use was now a marginal activity, other marginal citizens—especially criminals and delinquents—began using heroin and other drugs, and American society witnessed the emergence of a distinctive criminal-addict subculture. Although this forced marriage between drug use and crime was not readily apparent in the nineteenth century (Lindesmith, 1965), the stigma of criminalization has totally transformed the social reality of heroin use in the United States.

Several pieces of narcotics legislation have been enacted over the past 75 years, culminating in the Comprehensive Drug Abuse Prevention and Control Act of 1970. A major innovation of this legislation was the recognition of differing addiction potentials among various drugs. Drugs were "scheduled" in one of five categories depending primarily on the substance's potential for addiction. Control over production and maximum penalties for illegal manufacturing and possession were tied directly to this schedule. This legislation superseded all previous legislation, including the Harrison Act, but did not substantially alter law enforcement efforts to control drug use. The attorney general remained responsible for enforcing the control provisions of the act, although the secretary of the Department of Health, Education and Welfare was assigned the task of determining which drugs would be controlled (Ray, 1978).

### Drug Policy Options

―――――――――― Developing a workable drug policy will be a complex process, fraught with ideological differences, conflicting political agendas, and honest differences in interpretation of available empirical data. There are, however, but three broad policy options regarding the legal status of recreational drugs. The first is criminalization, or prohibition, which has characterized the American response to narcotics and many other recreational drugs throughout most of the twentieth century. This approach makes the possession and sale of specified drugs a violation of the criminal code. American prohibitionist policies are based, in part at least, on a moral ideology which stipulates that hedonistic behavior which has no apparent socially redeeming value is wrong (Duster, 1970; Eldridge, 1967). In this way, a policy of criminalization provides a basis for moral solidarity in society, buttressing long-standing traditional values such as hard work and frugality.

Proponents of criminalization also contend that this approach restricts the number of people who use these substances because illegal drugs are less readily accessible than are legal substances (Kaplan, 1983). Moreover, many people who might otherwise be inclined to experiment with drugs will probably be more hesitant because of the criminal penalties associated with their use. America's experience with alcohol prohibition is instructive in this regard. During the 13 years that alcohol was constitutionally prohibited, the prevalence of alcohol use declined significantly, only to increase when it became legal once again (Kaplan, 1983; Ray, 1978). Moreover, in response to advocates of legalization, Inciardi (1986) contends that legalization will not substantially reduce drug-related crime, for, as he claims, drug-using criminals are *criminals* who also use drugs. Hence, there is no reason to believe that legalization will significantly lower property crime. Inciardi further asserts that so far prohibitionist policies have failed simply because of the lack of resolve on the part of the American government. Rather than urging the abandonment of prohibitionist policies, Inciardi insists that what is needed is a renewed commitment to law enforcement and treatment efforts.

The second policy option is decriminalization, which has been tried on a limited basis in this country.[2] Currently, 11 states have removed marijuana possession from their criminal statutes. Decriminalization falls short of legalizing the drug, making possession equivalent to a minor traffic offense for which one could be cited but not accrue a criminal record. This policy option has the benefit, ostensibly at least, of removing the criminal stigma that can seriously damage one's social identity while stopping short of the symbolic moral affirmation of drug use that might arguably result from legalization. Opponents argue that decriminalization does, in fact, lift the moral stigma associated with drug use. Moreover, proponents of legalization argue that decriminalization does not provide a means for regulating the drug market, an advantage that legalization would allow.

Recently, there has been a great deal of public discussion surrounding legalization as a third policy option. Legalization may take different forms, ranging from modest proposals to make heroin available as an alternative treatment to methadone maintenance (Trebach, 1982), to more radical proposals for a laissez-faire market for opiate drugs (Nadelmann, 1989). This more radical form of legalization has been supported recently by such high-profile figures as Mayor Kurt Schmoke of Baltimore, conservative commentator William Buckley, and the economist Milton Friedman (Marshall, 1988). It is this form of legalization that I shall address in this chapter.

Proponents of legalization present a multifaceted argument. Libertarians, both civil and economic, argue that drug use is essentially a victimless crime and the government has no right to interfere unnecessarily with the private affairs and transactions of American citizens. Moreover, they argue that it is highly questionable whether prohibitionist policies can effectively reduce drug availability without seriously infringing on civil liberties (Packer, 1968; Wisotsky, 1988). These advocates are generally not willing to compromise this social cost in exchange for other possible benefits, as they articulate the issue strictly in terms of the protection of constitutionally guaranteed liberties.

A second rationale offered for legalization stems from a public health concern. Proponents argue that most of the health problems associated with heroin use are directly related to the drug's illegal status (Brecher, 1972). Legalization would introduce government regulation that ensures some level of quality control. Such regulation would eliminate the greatly varying concentrations of heroin available in the black market as well as the drug's adulteration by questionable inert ingredients that may be more harmful than the drug itself. Moreover, there would be clear labeling, warnings, and other consumer protections. Still another advantage of such regulation is that heroin users would not have to rely on unscrupulous dealers, as drugs would be made available through pharmacies and other legitimate outlets.

A third rationale for legalization is that this step will actually reduce the amount of criminal activity in society (Nadelmann, 1989). While there are several components to the drugs-crime nexus recognized by proponents of legalization (which I shall highlight below), the basic premise is that illegal drugs are more expensive precisely because they are illegal, and those addicted to these drugs must therefore rely on more lucrative illegal means to support their habit (Lindesmith, 1968).

Finally, a fourth argument maintains that prohibitionist policies are simply not working (Wisotsky, 1988). A policy of legalization would substantially reduce law enforcement and correctional expenditures and at the same time provide additional tax revenues. Nadelmann (1989) estimates a net benefit of at least $10 billion in reduced law enforcement expenditures and increased tax revenues. Drugs would thus become a source of government income rather than a burdensome liability, an argument that has gained appeal under recent economic conditions.

Such incentives, combined with the apparent lack of effectiveness on the part of law enforcement agencies to deal with the drug problem, have led many academicians, commentators, and, more recently, politicians to entertain legalization as a viable policy alternative. The life history data that I report here address two rationales that have frequently been used to justify a policy of legalization, namely, its potential for reducing drug-related crime and the ineffectiveness of law enforcement under a policy of prohibition. These data suggest that while legalization is not a panacea for the current dilemma, it is a compelling alternative that demands a hearing by serious-minded policymakers. The data also offer insights that might be helpful in articulating a responsible drug policy for the twenty-first century.

## The Impact of Legalization on Criminality

Advocates of legalization maintain that such a policy will significantly reduce criminal activity among the addict population, which constitutes a substantial portion of all crimes committed. The historical record seems to substantiate this claim, and indeed, a strong case can be made that prohibitionist policies are a major reason for the strong link between drugs and crime in the first place. The obverse question, however, is not so clear: Will repeal of these prohibitionist policies reverse this process and effectively dissolve the link between drug use and criminal behavior?

Nadelmann (1989) summarizes four "connections" between drugs and crime that should be appreciably attenuated under a policy of legalization: (1) the intrinsic illegality of drug use, (2) the violent nature of the illegal marketplace, (3) the subcultural connection, and (4) the costly nature of illegal drugs that necessitates property crime. The career history data from this study provide some support for these claims but qualify them as well. I shall discuss each of these connections briefly.

## The Illegality of Drug Use

The possession, production, and sale of drugs are by definition criminal in nature. Hence, a policy of legalization would virtually eliminate these crimes, Nadelmann claims, except for violation of special provisions such as selling to minors. Nadelmann is fundamentally correct in this assertion. Approximately 10% of the inmates housed in state prisons and over a third of federal inmates are drug-law violators (U.S. Department of Justice, 1988a, 1988b).

Our 25-year experience with methadone maintenance is testimony to an enduring demand for an illegal drug market, however, as is the British experience with legally available heroin. Despite the ready supply of legally available narcotics, a strong underground market exists in both the United States and Great Britain (Inciardi, 1987). The career history data are replete with reports and observations of creatively developed means of diverting methadone from clinics to an illegal street market. Many addicts do not wish to endure waiting in long lines, answering batteries of questions, and providing urine samples while being observed by staff workers on a daily basis in order to obtain a 24-hour dose of methadone. They would much rather pay a premium for diverted methadone. The model that Nadelmann proposes is, of course, a more laissez-faire market that would certainly limit, but probably not eliminate entirely, the illegal marketing of narcotics.

## The Violent Nature of the Drug Market

Recently much attention has been focused on violence among high-level drug traffickers, but this sort of behavior can also be observed at the street level (Goldstein, 1985). Wholesale dealers often supply drugs on consignment to street-level retailers, who repay the wholesalers after the drugs have been sold. Because street-level dealers are also users, they sometimes shoot up these drugs themselves, leaving them short when it comes time to pay their wholesaler. If this happens frequently enough, the court of last resort for the supplier is threatened or actual violence. Or, if a dealer has repeatedly shorted a customer or sold a customer bad dope, the most efficient avenue to justice is to "get over" on the dishonest dealer, either through conning or by sheer force.

The systematic violence associated with buying and selling illegal drugs is a direct result of the illegal nature of the enterprise. Participants in these transactions do not have access to the civil or criminal courts to avenge the wrongs they have suffered at the hands of others in the subculture. In the words of one veteran of the heroin subculture, retaliatory violence is "a quick and speedy trial by a jury of your peers." Therefore, insofar as legalization reduces the illegal market for drugs, there should be a corresponding decrease in the systematic violence of the drug market.

## The Subcultural Connection

The third connection between drug use and crime is the common subcultural setting within which these activities take place. That is, with the forced marriage between these activities brought about by prohibitionist policies, drug users find themselves immersed in social relationships that are supportive of other illegal activities. Similarly, those criminals who might not otherwise use drugs now find them readily available. Hence, while drug use may not "cause" crime in the manner commonly assumed, the criminalization of drugs does result in this subcultural link between drug use and crime.

The life history data in this study suggest that this link is particularly characteristic of the early occasional-use phase of addiction, when persons are just beginning to experiment with heroin. More commonly, however, occasional users are introduced to drug use through their criminal associations rather than vice versa. Self-report studies have consistently shown that criminal behavior begins substantially prior to heroin use (Greenberg and Adler, 1974). Most of the respondents I interviewed indicated that they were involved in delinquent acts before they ever tried heroin and that it was often their delinquent friends who first turned them on.

It is questionable whether legalizing heroin would substantially dissolve this link. Subcultural associations are not responsible for introducing drug users to crime so much as introducing criminals to drugs. These persons are thus introduced to crime through other attachments in the neighborhood, the school, the workplace, or perhaps even the family. Legalizing heroin will not alter these patterns of interaction.

There are, however, two special circumstances that would be affected by a policy of legalization. The first is the subcultural link between drug use and drug dealing. Legalizing heroin will reduce (though not eliminate) the demand for illegal drugs, thus making dealing less lucrative and hence less attractive. Moreover, dealing is a crime that most addicts learn as a result of their being drug users. Unlike other crimes, dealing is learned in the subcultural associations of illegal drug use. Under conditions of legal drug use, where most drug purchases are transacted in the legitimate marketplace, drug users will not be as readily exposed to illegal dealing.

Legalization may also reduce the exposure of middle-class drug users to a criminal life-style. Under current policies, experimenting teenagers are forced to turn to an illegal marketplace if they wish to obtain drugs. Drugs are not as accessible to them under these conditions, which has been a major argument against legalization. Those who are successful in penetrating the heroin subculture, however, are exposed to a criminal life-style, which would not be the case if these drugs were available through legitimate outlets.

### The Costly Nature of Illegal Drugs

An argument commonly used to support legalization contends that the high cost of black-market drugs forces addicts to engage in illegal acts to support their habit. The implication is that these users would not be inclined to commit such crimes if drugs were legal and cheap. The career history data in this study provide only partial support for this argument. I suggest that this rationale for legalization is premised on an incomplete understanding of why heroin users commit crime. The assumption that addicts commit crimes merely because they must support an expensive habit greatly oversimplifies a complex relationship. I pointed out in chapter three that beginning occasional users are typically experimenting with both heroin and crime. Indeed, in most cases, these young occasional users have been involved in crime and delinquency for months and even years prior to their experimentation with heroin. Furthermore, I also demonstrated that addict criminality is not generally driven by an escalating habit; rather, most heroin addicts are drawn by the challenges of a criminal life-style that, when successful, provides the necessary revenue to expand their heroin consumption. Almost without exception, the addicts in this study reported that an escalation of their heroin consumption was preceded either by a substantial increase in criminal income or by an opportunity to obtain greater quantities of drugs in other ways, such as moving in with a dealer boyfriend.

This does not mean, of course, that this increased criminal activity is not motivated by a desire to consume more drugs, but it is premature to generalize this motive to all or even most heroin addicts for the greater part of their careers. Occasional users who are young and not criminally experienced may begin committing penny-ante crimes to pay for their drugs. This is often a time when young teenagers who are in school and not working panhandle from friends or steal from parents in order to pay for their experimental drugs. This sort of crime does not constitute a serious component of the crime problem, however, and would not be much alleviated by legalizing heroin.

Stable addicts, in contrast, are systematically involved in criminal activities. Certainly a substantial portion (though not all) of the income derived from these activities is spent on heroin and other drugs. I do not believe, however, that obtaining drugs is the primary motivator for the crimes that stable addicts commit. In this study, respondents usually articulated their motivations as stable addicts in terms of the intrinsic satisfaction derived from criminal activity. For Eddie, it was the excitement and challenge that motivated him: "In a way it was exciting . . . developing a reputation for being able to get money, being able to hustle . . . being slick. I always tried to do things the soft-soap way, the slick way." Slick was motivated by the challenge of being able to talk a teller into cashing a forged check. Mario claimed that it was the curiosity that gripped him when contemplating and planning a burglary. He compared this feeling with the curiosity that grips a child getting ready to open gifts at Christmas, wondering what is in all of those boxes, or with the anticipation a bass fisherman experiences, daring to hope with each throw of the line that this time he will pull in a record catch.

When motives are expressed in terms like these, it is doubtful how much stable-addict crime would be eliminated through a policy of legalization. If heroin maintenance is not the major motivation for these crimes, these addicts can readily find something else on which to spend the proceeds of their hustling activity. Indeed, they already do. Successful stable addicts like to drive nice cars, maintain expensive wardrobes, and display their generosity, all in a manner that reflects a life-style of conspicuous consumption. Drugs are part of that life-style and, if legalized, would probably continue to be part of the stable addict's way of life. These data suggest, however, that reducing the cost of heroin through legalization will more likely encourage alternative consumer behaviors rather than seriously diminish income-producing criminal behaviors. These addicts are accustomed to a criminal life-style and are not likely to abandon it voluntarily simply because one component of their life-style has been made substantially cheaper. Like the rest of us, these consumers will find other good with which to enhance their life-style and will probably soon come to define them as necessities as well.

A policy of legalization would, however, substantially affect the opportunistic and impulsive crime committed by street junkies. During this period of heroin-using careers, the excitement and challenge of crime give way to drudgery and necessity as street addicts must literally live from minute to minute, not sure from where their next fix will come. This is a time when addicts will engage in crimes that are not part of their main hustle. These crimes, which are often committed while the addict is sick and "jones-ing," are hardly the exciting and challenging enterprise experienced during the stable-addict period. Street-junkie criminality is directly driven by the street junkie's need for heroin. Making heroin available at reduced cost through legitimate outlets will relieve the intense financial pressure experienced during this chaotic phase of drug-using careers. One testimony to the effectiveness of a legalization policy in reducing street-junkie criminality is the frequency with which persons in street-junkie circumstances enroll in methadone-maintenance programs. These decisions are made not to ultimately go drug-free but rather to escape the escalating spiral of costly heroin use and the frenetic, desperate activities required to support it.

It is also reasonable to expect that legalization will greatly improve the life chances of street junkies. Renting "dirty works," copping low-grade and impure drugs at premium prices, and forgoing proper nutrition and health care are just some of the ways in which a policy of prohibition leaves street junkies vulnerable. By increasing the availability of heroin through lowered cost, legalization would help to stabilize the life-style of street junkies, enhancing their life structure. Indeed, legalization may actually eliminate this difficult career phase entirely for many addicts.

To summarize, the contention by proponents of legalization that drug-related property crime should be substantially reduced with drug legalization is partially supported by the data in this study. Street-junkie criminality would certainly be greatly reduced. But it must be remembered that this stereotyped image of heroin addiction applies only to a comparatively short period of the careers of most addicts. More of their time is spent as stable addicts, a period that will be only minimally affected by a policy of legalization. Hence, while legalization will surely have a positive impact on drug-related property crime, it will not be the panacea prophesied by many proponents of legalization.

## The Effectiveness of Law Enforcement

While advocates of legalization may be overly optimistic regarding the policy's potential impact on criminality, they also challenge the effectiveness of prohibitionist law enforcement efforts. Indeed, even if it were the case that legalization made no impact whatsoever on drug-related criminality, the monumental social costs incurred by legal repression may justify legalization if these law enforcement efforts do not make a substantial dent in levels of drug use and crime.

Since the passage of the Harrison Act, official response to drug use in the United States has been dominated by a "criminal model" (Inciardi, 1974, 1987), though Tieman (1981) has suggested that strong voices have once again been heard for a treatment approach since the 1960s. Despite increased concern for treatment and rehabilitation, however, American society continues to understand drug use and addiction as primarily a criminal issue that should be addressed by imposing criminal sanctions against users and dealers and by engaging in interdiction strategies to prevent the importation of expensive drugs. Recently declared "wars" on drugs by just about every administration since Nixon's have allocated comparatively greater funds to law enforcement and interdiction efforts in combating drug use. These activities have always been the fundamental strategies of prohibitionist drug policies in this country.

Unfortunately, there is little evidence that these strategies have been effective in combating drug use, especially if effectiveness is defined in terms of reducing the number of drug users or the crimes that they commit. Attempts at interdiction have had dubious results whenever they have been attempted. Brecher (1972) describes "Operation Intercept," an attempt in 1969 to intercept marijuana coming into the United States from Mexico, as a total failure. Estimates are that about 150 pounds of marijuana were seized at the border during this short three-week experiment—about the same amount that had been seized daily throughout the prior year under normal customs patrol. Furthermore, it is likely that increased smuggling took place elsewhere because of the transfer of large numbers of customs officials to the Mexican border. Brecher's conclusion is poignant: "The conclusion seems inescapable: as in the case of heroin, cocaine, the amphetamines, the barbiturates, LSD, and other illicit drugs, law enforcement can raise the price and thus the profits of the black market. Indeed, availability is *increased* when rising prices attract additional entrepreneurs" (1972:450; italics in original).

Nevertheless, interdiction efforts continue, with negligible results. One of the more broad-sweeping indictments of interdiction strategies is Wisotsky's (1988) biting critique of American drug policy. He maintains that recently stepped-up border and harbor patrols have forced the international drug trade into the hands of an elite but powerful syndicate who have the means to compete with the high-power detection technology of U.S. customs and military units. Drugs continue to pour into this country, however, because the demand remains. Indeed, it seems that the most obvious effect of these interdiction strategies has been to enhance the profits of those involved in the international drug trade.

Street-level law enforcement has not been particularly effective either. While massive assaults on local dealers and users have netted hundreds, even thousands of arrests, the impact of these efforts on reduced drug use and crime is questionable (Chaiken, 1988). Kleinman (1988), for example, suggests that while stepped-up law enforcement may make it more difficult for beginning users to obtain drugs, more experienced users will probably not be affected, since they typically have several connections. Moreover, even if an entire area is cleaned up, experienced addicts may move into different neighborhoods or even to neighboring cities where they know wholesale dealers.

The data from the career history interviews shed further light on why these law enforcement efforts have failed to have their intended effect. There is no reason to believe that tough enforcement efforts will have any impact during early periods in addict careers. In the first place, these experimental users are not usually addicted to heroin anyway and can readily adjust to temporary "panics" that might be created by stepped-up law enforcement. Moreover, insofar as law enforcement is directed at reducing addict criminality, I have already demonstrated that the link between drug use and crime during this occasional-use phase is largely spurious. This is not to suggest that occasional users are not criminally involved; indeed, most of them already have a criminal history prior to their involvement with drugs. Many of them have an arrest record that also predates their initiation into heroin use. Pagie explained how he came to be arrested during this early period in his career: "For the most part they [three burglary arrests] were carelessness on my part. . . . The TV thing—I kept that TV too long. . . . It was the first burglary I did. I think maybe that had something to do with it, being a rookie, so to speak. I never kept that stuff like that again." Pagie's bust was due solely to his inexperience. He was not a systematic criminal at this time, nor was he targeted by the police for a bust. This arrest did, however, label him and conferred upon him a criminal identity: "Once I did that burglary . . . see, I had a number then. I had a police record. And it's like the police officer tells you, 'This is gonna follow you till the day you die.' Like, you're labeled, you know?"

Pagie's experience suggests that many times these early encounters with the criminal justice system have unintended consequences that are counterproductive to the overall intent of law enforcement efforts. Reflecting on his early confrontation with the criminal justice system, Harry recalled: "Going to court gave me a certain sense of importance. I've made it now. I've graduated." Similar experiences were echoed by many of the addicts who participated in this study. Hence, these data suggest that far from curbing crime and drug use among occasional users, the imposition of criminal sanctions may actually facilitate careers in drug use and crime.

With the attainment of stable-addict status, one has usually developed a sizable habit that is largely financed by criminal activity. The impact of law enforcement efforts on stable-addict criminality is also questionable, however, for several reasons. First, by the time addicts reach this career phase, they have begun to specialize in one or more main hustles. This sort of specialization allows them to acquire the many skills necessary for the successful accomplishment of the criminal act. Among these skills, discussed at length in chapter four, are the technical, social, and intuitive abilities that aid stable addicts in avoiding detection and arrest. Shoplifters learn to detect and avoid floorwalkers; prostitutes and drug dealers acquire the ability to recognize undercover law enforcement personnel; check forgers develop a verbal ability to convince bank personnel of their legitimacy and a sense that tells them when to make a hasty exit. The keenness of skill developed by stable addicts renders many law enforcement efforts ineffective.

The highly structured daily routine of stable addicts also insulates them from falling victim to the criminal justice system. These routines allow stable addicts to plan their criminal acts carefully, and there is no necessity for desperate or impulsive criminal attempts. Hence, stable addicts not only benefit from greater criminal skill but also enjoy a more comfortable routine that can adapt to intrusive law enforcement activity.

Neither does repressive police action seem to affect the overall level of heroin consumption by stable addicts. Getting drugs is not a problem during this period. By the time they have achieved this career phase, stable addicts have probably developed more than one connection, so that if a wholesale supplier is busted, stable addicts have alternative sources of the drug. During those times when heroin is more difficult to obtain, the high level of life structure provides stable addicts with greater control over their habit. The participants in this study reported that during this period of their careers, they readily adjusted to lowered levels of drug availability when stepped-up law enforcement made it necessary for wholesale dealers to "hold the bag" for a period of time. Several strategies were used, including using a lower amount of heroin each time they shot up; shooting up less frequently; or using alternative drugs, especially methadone, as a way of making their heroin supply last a little longer.

Neither is repressive law enforcement especially effective against addicts in the freewheeling phase of their careers. Particularly insofar as this period is initiated with the big sting, heralding a period of unlimited availability of drugs and short-term hedonism, law enforcement is already too late to curb consumption. The windfalls provided by the big sting allow the freewheeling addict to maintain a large stash of heroin without daily exposure to police surveillance strategies.

The street junkie, in contrast, is especially vulnerable to the efforts of law enforcement operatives. During this stage of heroin-using careers, characterized by a lack of a ready supply of heroin and by eroding sources of life structure, the activities of street junkies are especially visible. Because wholesale supplies of heroin have probably been cut off, addicts in this situation must cop from whatever street-level dealer is available. This strategy is risky, however, because the quality and content of these street drugs are questionable and because street junkies have not established a long relationship with these dealers. These buys are made impulsively by addicts who are feeling sick and desperate for drugs. The small-time dealer may even be an informant who turns in his or her customers. Street junkies who themselves turn to "juggling" by selling highly diluted drugs are also vulnerable because they are desperate to sell these drugs to make enough money to buy more for themselves. Under these conditions, street-junkie jugglers are apt to make a sale to an informant or an undercover narcotics officer. The usual precautions are disregarded when one is sick and in desperate need for more "re-up" money.

Regardless of their hustle, street junkies are also far more careless in their criminal activity than at any other time in their career, which makes them more vulnerable to law enforcement efforts. Belle talked about the risks associated with prostituting while in this condition: "If you're sick and not thinking straight, you go out there and you jump in one of those cars . . . just because you need that money. You automatically get busted." An even greater risk for street junkies, however, is getting out of their usual criminal routine, engaging in crimes that are not part of their main hustle. As I discussed at length in chapters six and seven, these are not crimes at which they are adept. The technical, social, and intuitive skills necessary for avoiding detection and arrest have not been developed for these crimes. When sick and desperate for drugs, however, street junkies often have no other option but to respond to whatever criminal opportunities come their way. Under these conditions, the job of law enforcement is made quite easy.

In sum, the data from the career histories in this study suggest that law enforcement effectiveness is currently limited primarily to this last, street-junkie phase of addict careers. Addicts in this situation face almost inevitable arrest or, alternatively, becoming informants. Either option has negative consequences in terms of continued drug-using and criminal routines. Arrest typically results in either incarceration or treatment, both of which terminate or at least disrupt participation in subcultural activities. Informing on other addicts will buy more time on the street; however, this too alienates the street junkie from the subculture. Hence, there is little doubt that sustained and conscientious law enforcement can make a dent in street-junkie criminality.

But the effect of repressive street-level law enforcement on reducing the level of heroin availability and drug-related crime is questionable. Street-junkie status comprises but a small part of overall addict careers and accounts for a comparatively minute proportion of drug-related crime. It is as stable addicts that heroin users are systematically involved in lucrative criminal routines. Stable-addict criminality is not nearly as vulnerable to detection and arrest as is street-junkie criminality. Only if law enforcement efforts are massive enough and protracted over a substantial period of time so as to force stable addicts to engage in non-routine criminal activity to supply an increasing need for heroin—in essence, forcing a change from stable addict to street junkie—will these efforts significantly affect stable addicts. All of this can only be accomplished at a staggering cost in the form of valuable public resources and deprived civil liberties.

Moreover, despite stated priorities to go after "major dealers" (Manning, 1977), local law enforcement strategies most effectively target smaller street dealers. The use of informants is a standard mechanism used to get to bigger dealers, but it is questionable how "big" these dealers will be since it is street junkies who are most vulnerable to police surveillance. By the time one reaches street-junkie status, connections to major-level dealers have often already been severed. Moreover, while "flipping" street junkie informants might prove helpful in locating some major dealers, its overall impact on reducing heroin availability would appear to be negligible unless all or most of these wholesale dealers were somehow "hit" simultaneously.

These data suggest, therefore, that while police surveillance and other law enforcement strategies may make small dents in the level of crime and heroin availability, these are not the tools with which to be waging a "war" on drugs. Particularly if those critics of interdiction efforts are correct, law enforcement strategies seem relegated to a marginal position in fighting the war on drug use. Indeed, these data lend substantial support to the criticisms of prohibitionist policies that law enforcement has not been an effective deterrent to drug use or crime. Other measures such as education and treatment (which will be discussed at length in the following chapter) should be advanced as policy priorities for the 1990s and beyond.

The issues surrounding legalization are far more numerous and complex than can possibly be addressed here. I have not, for example, attempted to assess the potential effect of legalization on those populations that do not currently use heroin or other drugs. Certainly the number of drug users would increase, probably dramatically, and this is a reality that must be taken seriously when considering such a policy. Other important issues that have been omitted include the health and economic consequences of a legalization policy. These would probably be beneficial. Inciardi's (1981) admonition to measure carefully all of the costs and benefits of marijuana decriminalization is certainly applicable as well to the issue of legalizing heroin and other expensive drugs. I strongly support his call for well-designed evaluation research assessing the overall potential impact of a legalization policy.

Meanwhile, the debate over legalization is beginning to take center stage in the arena of public discourse—as well it should. Legalization has a number of potential benefits over current policies that need to be assessed critically and openly. This can only be done if legalization is defined as a legitimate policy option by the media and other agencies responsible for shaping public opinion. It is only in the openness of public debate that the best information will be used by policymakers. Without an informed citizenry armed with information representing the various sides of complex issues such as this, policymakers too easily fall victim either to an unarticulated commitment to the status quo or to the pressures of special interest groups that are very skillful at managing the flow of information. Only by maintaining open and honest public discourse can we hope to establish intelligent policy. It is for this reason that I join the written discourse—not as a militant propagandist of legalization but rather to facilitate the development of a rational drug policy that can only occur in an atmosphere of open discussion and debate under the critical eye of public scrutiny.

Legalization is no panacea to the current drug crisis. But neither is it the major threat that opponents depict it to be. Contrary to public fear, there is no reason to believe that newcomers to the drug scene will become criminals under a policy of legalization. Under current policies, those who are most likely to be attracted to heroin tend to be marginal members of society who are more likely to be involved in other deviant behavior as well. Those attracted to legal heroin should be much more reflective of the general population and should not represent a threat to ongoing community life any more than users of alcohol, tobacco, caffeine, or a host of other legal drugs are criminal threats. There would, in short, likely be two distinct populations of heroin users under a policy of legalization, at least for some time to come: traditional heroin users who are part of the criminal-addict subculture and conventional users who obtain their drugs strictly through legal means and who are otherwise indistinguishable from the rest of the community.

Given that law enforcement efforts are not working, we need to be examining other policy options. We need to be developing sound educational programs that are serious about educating rather than merely propagandizing. Along with this, we need to be developing strategies for treatment that address the complex social basis for addiction, rather than merely treating the less-complicated physiological addiction. A policy of legalization may, in fact, be a critical beginning strategy for fighting the war on drugs in more effective ways than we are now doing.

# 9

# Implications of
# a Career Perspective
# for Drug Treatment

Regardless of the legal status of drugs, treatment for drug addiction will continue to be an important policy issue. The focus and goals of treatment will vary, of course, depending on whether these drugs remain prohibited or if they become decriminalized or even legalized. Currently, for example, the three major indicators of treatment success are remaining drug-free, cessation of criminal activity, and finding legitimate employment. The last two indicators are relatively unique to conditions of prohibition. While it is true that a small criminal-addict subculture will almost certainly continue to exist even under a policy of legalization, the primary focus of treatment will probably be those in the noncriminal population who are addicted and seeking to go drug-free. Most of these addicts will have legitimate, often professional employment. Hence, these indicators will be neither relevant nor helpful. Much like current treatment for alcoholism, addiction treatment foci under legalization will probably include abstinence and rebuilding family and other social relationships. Moreover, treatment for legal drug addiction will probably not emphasize severing relationships with an addict subculture as do residential therapeutic communities today, since many of those individuals seeking treatment will already be integrated into conventional social networks. Hence, while treatment will continue to be a part of any drug policy, its goals and strategies will vary considerably depending on the form that policy takes. But because it is less useful to deal with what might be than with what is, the discussion in this chapter pertains specifically to treatment under current prohibitionist policies.

Since the turn of the century, treatment for opiate addiction in the United States has been dominated by those in the medical profession. As a result, treatment has focused primarily on the physiological process of increased tolerance for heroin as the essence of addiction. Those who subscribe to this medical understanding of addiction contend that by eliminating the physiological craving for heroin, the addict will not only be able to live a drug-free life but will be more socially productive as well. Underlying this orientation is the assumption that the highly addictive quality of heroin combined with inflated black-market prices means that addicts cannot afford to feed their escalating habits on legitimate income and must therefore turn to crime. Hence, reducing the physiological need for the drug should reduce the necessity for crime and allow the addict to pursue lower-paying but legitimate income-producing activities. Pittell (1977) refers to this argument as the "myth of addiction as cause." The research reported here challenges this rather unidimensional portrayal of heroin addiction.

### The Lesson from Methadone Maintenance
The inadequacy of the myth of addiction as cause is perhaps best exemplified by the unsuccessful experience with methadone as a treatment alternative in the United States. The synthetic narcotic methadone was developed during the 1940s and it was not long before its value as a means of gradual withdrawal from heroin came to be recognized. Prior to this time morphine was used to withdraw addicts from heroin, but morphine is also addictive and it became increasingly unacceptable for treatment of heroin addiction (Terry and Pellens, 1970). Methadone produces physiological effects similar to those caused by heroin and morphine but was believed to lack the addictive potential of its predecessors. Methadone was perceived to have an added benefit in that its effects were much longer lasting (from 24 to 36 hours), making it possible to dispense the drug on a daily basis. Hence, methadone was promoted as an ideal means of gradually withdrawing addicts from heroin with minimal side effects.

The first outpatient methadone clinic in this country was established by Vincent Dole and Marie Nyswander in New York City in 1965. The principle upon which this and subsequent methadone programs were based is purely physiological. Methadone eliminates the need for heroin, mimicking its effects but presumably not its addictive potential. Furthermore, because the addict is maintained on an inexpensive legal drug, crime and other antisocial behaviors are presumably no longer necessary. Methadone maintenance was thus represented by its proponents as a panacea for the heroin problem in the United States (Dole et al., 1968).

But by most assessments, the promise of methadone maintenance proved to be more optimistic than its ability to deliver. Even Dole et al. (1982) are far more cautious in their assessment of methadone effectiveness some 15 years after their earlier report. In the first place, contrary to early reports, the effectiveness of these programs in reducing criminality is highly suspect (Faupel, 1981). While one study (Gearing, 1974) reports a 99.9% reduction in criminality following treatment, at least two studies have reported higher levels of criminality following admission to methadone treatment (Hayim, 1973; Lukoff and Quatrone, 1973). More recently, Ball and his associates (1988) found evidence that since the AIDS epidemic, 71% of those who remained in methadone maintenance for a year or more had ceased intravenous drug use. Nevertheless, the discrepancies between studies over the years render suspect any claims of success of methadone maintenance. If, as early advocates claim, the basis for the effectiveness of this modality is the pharmacology of the drug, we would expect much less variation in reporting results. Methadone is methadone, whether administered in New York or San Francisco! The discrepancies in reported results suggest that either the research studies have been poorly designed or addiction has a far more complex etiology than physiology and pharmacology can explain.

Perhaps even more problematic from a policy point of view is the extensive diversion of methadone to illegitimate markets. Only four years after Dole and Nyswander established their first outpatient clinic in New York, reports were filtering back that methadone was being marketed illegally (Inciardi, 1977b; Martin, 1978). By the early 1970s, enough evidence for diversion had accumulated that the National Institute on Drug Abuse contracted with Fordham University to conduct an extensive research examination in five cities. The results were staggering. Nearly half (46%) of the Fordham sample reported using illegal methadone during the week preceding the interview, and 70% had used it sometime during the preceding three months (Inciardi, 1977b:2). Virtually all the illicit methadone was obtained through patients who had received the drug from a clinic. Indeed, the respondents in my study indicated that methadone clinics often become secondary "copping areas" and favorite hangouts for addicts in the area. As Mona explained: "The meth clinic in Wilmington was always the place to buy drugs. You could go there at seven A.M. and you'd know that all the junkies would be there that were on meth. Half of them . . . were doing heroin also. So you could go there and you could get either meth or buy drugs. That was hysterical. I never did methadone, but I used to go there a lot [to buy drugs]."

Most of the addicts in the Fordham study did not rely on diverted methadone as their primary source of narcotics but used it to supplement regular supplies of heroin, as indicated by the fact that only 4% of the sample indicated that methadone was their primary drug. But neither did these addicts use the drug for the purpose for which it was intended. Nearly 58% of the methadone-using sample reported that they used the drug to keep from getting sick. Moreover, 37% reported "getting high" as a motivation for using methadone (Martin, 1978).

These were also the primary motives reported for enrolling in methadone clinics among the addicts I interviewed. For Belle, "drugs were just garbage . . . and the only choice was to join the methadone clinic." Belle was experiencing a chronic "jones," and the available street heroin was being diluted so much that it was incapable of relieving her withdrawal pains. She thus turned to methadone as a temporary solution to these poor market conditions. Pagie also found himself in an unfriendly market that motivated him to turn to the meth clinic:

> [Interviewer] Is that why you went [in the meth clinic], because of the panic?

> [Pagie] Oh, yeah. It gets a little monotonous when you're riding around in your car in Wilmington like four hours trying to find dope and you don't find it. People saying there's no dope on the streets and you know someone's shooting it. . . . You just get sick and tired of going through all the inconveniences that it brings about.

In Harry's case, using methadone was a way of temporarily slowing down his hectic life-style without his having to cut down substantially on his drug consumption:

[**Interviewer**] Why did you go into methadone treatment the second time?

[**Harry**] It was a shelter the second time. That was a place to get out of the rat race. . . . Chippy-ing was fun. It was a nice high. I could still function . . . but now I'm hot. The cops are after me. Every time I turn around, some kind of paranoia is going on about who's going to be busted or when the heat's going to come down. . . . You get so . . . burned out that you say, "I'm going to try something." I went back to the methadone clinic. I know it's a free high.

Despite the shortcomings—even failures—of methadone maintenance, our experience with this treatment modality has taught us a valuable lesson regarding the nature of drug addiction generally, with important implications for its treatment. Drug addiction is not merely a physiological phenomenon triggered by a pharmacological catalyst. Indeed, it is more than a behaviorally reinforced psychological dependence. To be sure, addiction has both a physiological and a psychological basis, but I have demonstrated throughout this book that it is also fundamentally social in its etiology and in its very character. Hence, effective treatment must also address the social basis of addiction.

### Synanon and the Therapeutic Community
The other major treatment modality for heroin addiction is the therapeutic community, or "TC." This treatment concept was introduced in 1958 when Charles Dederich, an ex-alcoholic, began a program in California that eventually came to be called Synanon.[1] The Synanon model, which actually predates methadone maintenance by over half a decade, is premised on the belief that drug addiction is part of a larger behavioral pattern. In this respect, the philosophy of Synanon and other subsequent therapeutic communities is simple but nevertheless perhaps more profound than any other treatment philosophy to date. Briefly, proponents of this

model hold that in order to modify behavioral patterns that have been developed and reinforced over a lifetime, a 24-hour community environment that encourages a constructive rather than destructive lifestyle is required.

The hallmark of the traditional therapeutic community is its extensive use of confrontational therapy. Commonly referred to as the "haircut," this type of therapy involves the use of harsh verbal attacks by fellow clients and counselors in order to encourage behavioral and lifestyle change.[2] According to Yablonsky: "This form of verbal attack employs ridicule, hyperbole, and direct verbal onslaught. . . . An important goal of the 'haircut' method is to change the criminal tough guy pose. The self-image held by newcomers is viciously attacked and punctured in the 'haircut'" (1965:241).

While therapeutic communities are most well-known for these confrontational techniques, other treatment strategies are employed as well, such as individual counseling and the development of interviewing and other job skills (DeLeon, 1984, 1985). Larger therapeutic communities provide extensive educational opportunities for clients. One such program is the "Miniversity" program established in 1979 by Daytop Village in New York. In conjunction with local colleges, the "Miniversity" provides the residents of Daytop Village the opportunity to earn matriculated credits toward an undergraduate degree.

The program is a relatively long-term one, often exceeding 18 months from initial entry to graduation, depending on the progress of the individual client. An increasingly important feature of most programs is the reentry phase, in which after demonstrating a readiness to function in the outside world, the resident is encouraged to find outside employment while remaining under program supervision. Initially, recovering addicts maintain a resident status within the program, working during the day and returning to the program in the evening. After a period of time, aftercare status is achieved whereby clients establish outside living arrangements while maintaining frequent contacts with the program.

While not as pervasive as methadone maintenance, the therapeutic community has met with varied but consistently positive results. System Sciences (1973) reported an 81% reduction in arrests after 12 months in treatment. Nash (1973) observed a 53% reduction in arrests after entering residential treatment. More recently, DeLeon (1984) found that indicators of drug use, crime, and employment all improved after treatment, and treatment success was directly related to length of time in treatment. Graduates of the program reported almost zero drug use and crime, and employment increased substantially. Those who dropped out of the program were less successful as a group, but those who were in the program at least 12 months before dropping out did much better than those who dropped out after less time.

Despite these successes, the therapeutic community has also met with substantial criticism, much of it centering on the lack of sufficient attention to community reintegration. While most therapeutic communities have some sort of aftercare program, this component has not traditionally been a central part of this form of treatment and continues to be the weakest link of the treatment process for most programs. As I shall point out below, this process is critical to the rebuilding of an alternative life structure capable of insulating the addict from future drug use and criminal behavior.

These shortcomings notwithstanding, the therapeutic community offers a model for treatment that is compatible with the social basis of drug use discussed throughout this book. For example, this treatment modality places a high priority on removing addicts from the social environment of heroin use. It recognizes the need to alter behavioral rituals that have been reinforced over a lifetime and to affirm alternative lifestyles through client and staff support. The discussion that follows draws heavily upon this treatment model while extending its principles in some important ways.

## A Career Model for Drug Treatment

In the context of the career framework developed here, the goal of treatment should be to reduce drug availability while at the same time establishing an alternative life structure consisting of conventional statuses and roles. Traditional therapeutic communities have generally done a very good job reducing availability; they have been less effective in facilitating conventional life structure.

### Reducing Drug Availability

I indicated earlier that drug availability implies much more than merely possessing a quantity of drugs. Getting these drugs in the first place entails establishing contacts with other users and dealers who have available supplies. Furthermore, it involves learning criminal and other entrepreneurial skills capable of generating an adequate income to purchase these drugs. Drug availability therefore depends upon an extensive socialization process whereby one establishes the necessary relationships and learns the intricacies of the social world in which drugs are sold and used.

Reducing availability is also a social process and must recognize the social basis of heroin addiction. It must take into account the normative structures that guide drug-using and criminal behavior. Most important, it must address peer pressures and group support systems that facilitate drug-using life-styles. In short, because availability is pervasively social in character, treatment efforts must be directed toward relinquishing those social ties that facilitate drug availability and encourage its use.

This bridge-burning process has long been recognized in other areas of social life, particularly religious conversion. Kanter's (1972) work is especially instructive for a socially based treatment model (see Faupel 1981, 1985). Kanter identifies two types of mechanisms that successful nineteenth-century utopian communities used to foster the commitment of adherents. "Dissociative" mechanisms facilitate the severing of previous relationships and life-styles that would interfere with commitment to the commune. "Associative" mechanisms secure loyalty and bond the new member to the commune.

These conversion mechanisms, which are nothing more than resocialization techniques, are particularly suited to a career-based model for drug treatment. Dissociative mechanisms involve the sacrifice of important aspects of one's biography. Many residential treatment programs impose a celibacy rule, even for married clients, and curtail all visitation rights for a period of time. Just as significant, incoming clients are stripped of all distinctive features that would set them apart from others in the program. Street names are forbidden, as are *war stories* (the recounting of drug-using and criminal exploits) and distinctive styles of dress. Rules like these are imposed to facilitate the renunciation of past relationships and life-styles. Mona reflected on her experience in treatment at East Coast House in contrast to the treatment program at the federal hospital in Lexington, Kentucky:

[At Lexington] we used to sit around at night and just bullshit about all this stuff—for hours! It just seemed to never end 'cause it was so exciting. . . . It's called, like, war stories. Everybody told them. That's the difference between there and East Coast House. In East Coast House you couldn't even talk about, "Hey, I used to do this." If you did, you got instantly yelled at. They stripped you of all that. You're not allowed to wear makeup. You're not allowed to cut your hair [men, however, must cut their hair]. You're not allowed to pluck your eyebrows. And you can't wear jewelry. I wasn't allowed to call my parents. . . . You weren't allowed cars either . . . and you couldn't talk about dope except in group. No war stories.

A key feature of these dissociative mechanisms is their irreversibility. While any addict in treatment has the option of returning to his or her former life-style, successful conversion-model treatment programs seek to make such reversions more difficult. The significance of the permanent renunciation of former relationships is captured by Harry's reflections: "Going to the program was like, ah, like going to church. . . . And then all the unsaid messages. Like you're giving up every friend you might call a friend that you've ever accumulated during the period of time. . . . So I'm cutting off with a whole period of my life—almost twenty-five years . . . and that's very difficult to face." Mona's experience is also illustrative: "They didn't want you to be into your husband or mother . . . to think about men all the time or meet a boyfriend. . . . This was called falling into a trap. . . . They were constantly on us about that 'cause a lot of the girls had crushes on the guys. For me, they wanted me to forget about Ike [her husband who was in the male unit]. You know, 'Fuck Ike, Ike's in Care House, but he'll take care of himself.'" Her renunciation of Ike was ultimately expressed when she divorced him as she saw their relationship inhibiting her goals in the treatment process.

These mechanisms, which are ultimately aimed at reducing opportunities to obtain drugs, recognize the complex social basis of drug availability. Simply detoxifying addicts so that they no longer have a physiological need for drugs does not address the problem of availability. Psychological approaches that stress individual and group therapy also fall short if they do not recognize that drug use is a function of availability and that availability is fundamentally social in character. An effective treatment strategy must employ mechanisms that have the effect of socially distancing addicts from the street life, which is the source of their drug availability.

*Altering Life Structure*

Unless addicts also develop an alternative life structure devoid of drug use and criminal routines, the treatment process is not complete. Addicts will inevitably be drawn back into the social world of drug use as they attempt to fill the void established by the bridge-burning acts described above. This world is, for many addicts, the only one they know.

Kanter (1972) suggests that successful nineteenth-century communes employed mechanisms of association that anchored the commitment of converts to the group. These techniques included communal sharing of property and work as well as extensive structured group contact. In addition, the communes provided a coherent and transcendent ideology that facilitated a bonding of the convert to the group. These mechanisms of association reinforce the initially tenuous commitment initiated by imposed dissociation and firmly establish the relationship between the individual and the community.

Traditional therapeutic communities incorporate these mechanisms in several ways. There is a strong basis for communal identity in these programs, as all of the members share a common experience. In addition, within the programs themselves, members share similar experiences that are often made highly visible: each is subjected to ritualized "degradation ceremonies" (Garfinkel, 1956); jobs are consciously rotated periodically; and group sessions are structured on a regular basis. Residential treatment programs employ numerous specific strategies to effect radical resocialization of their clientele. By imposing sanctions on unacceptable behavior while rewarding positive attitudes and behavior, by encouraging participants to examine their own feelings through group reflection and insights, and by making status within the program dependent on the behavioral and attitudinal espousal of program goals, these therapeutic communities provide an alternative basis for self-esteem and self-identity. Moreover, the participant is provided with a coherent, overarching value system that serves as a constant reference point for new experiences. Catchphrases such as "I'm a *recovering* addict" and "I'm really into myself now" keep salient the overarching ideology of drug-free living.

Most important, these programs seek to provide recovering addicts with an alternative basis for life structure—one that is devoid of drug use, crime, and other subcultural elements. These alternative routines are, however, constructed in the rather synthetic environment of the therapeutic community. One of the major criticisms of the therapeutic-community treatment model is that it fails to reintegrate the addict into the conventional community. From the career history perspective developed here, this last phase of treatment is the most critical to this social process of rebuilding a drug-free life structure.

## Community Reintegration

Unlike that of religious communes, the goal of drug treatment is not to foster loyalty and commitment to the group itself. The successful treatment program is one that ultimately facilitates a process of dissociation as addicts leave the program to live an independent life free of drugs. This is, however, the weakest feature of current residential treatment practice. As Hawkins notes: "We have created treatment enclaves where we seek to cure abusers in isolation from the larger community. Our treatment programs are taboo places reminiscent of TB sanatoriums visited only by patients, their families where permitted, and a handful of dedicated volunteers. These places are avoided by the unscathed" (1979:26).

Dissociation from the program to participate in conventional routines also requires association, or reintegration with conventional society. This is an extremely difficult challenge for reforming addicts who have spent much of their adult life in the drug-using subculture. Joe's experience is insightful regarding the importance of a structured reintegration: "They should show a dude the other side of life—the good things, the positive things. Take 'em out there. They have a tendency to say you need to go on your own. But if you ain't never been there, you don't know how to get there. . . . They always told me, 'You should try to get out and meet some new people, new ideas.' And I kept saying, 'I don't know them people. I get around them people and I get kind of leery, 'cause I don't know how they take me . . . square people.' They tell me, 'You got to break the ice yourself.' And that's kind of hard, man."

Even the common routines that most of us take for granted can be extremely difficult for the recovering addict. In one of his more candid moments, Boss shared his apprehension about getting out of prison:

"Eating, for instance. In here it takes you approximately five to six minutes to eat a meal. But now when you go out on the street, man, it takes an hour to eat, man. And the little period between the meal and the dessert—you'd be surprised at how uncomfortable you are. Just them little things like that."

The adjustments that Boss described are no less relevant to the recovering addict anticipating release from treatment. Like prison, a drug treatment program is a total institution that insulates individuals from the outside world to which they will eventually return. This adjustment is part of the overall treatment process, and community reintegration should be a central feature of any career-based treatment program. Three specific areas are critical for establishing an alternative basis for life structure: eliciting strong community participation, enhancing employment opportunities, and facilitating the formation of primary group contacts in the conventional community.

*Community Participation*

An essential precondition for successful community reintegration of recovering addicts is that host communities be receptive to them. Hawkins addresses this issue: "Reintegration requires building enduring bonds between former abusers and conventional members of society. These can be created only if members of the larger community actively reach out to reattach ex-abusers. Community members must come to view ex-abusers as part of the community, though they have violated its expectations, rather than as 'outsiders'" (1979:41).

Regardless of the quality of the treatment experience, it is extremely difficult for recovering addicts to function effectively in the conventional community if it has a bias against them. Unfortunately, most communities are extremely hesitant to accept treatment programs and the recovering addicts they graduate. Dembo et al. (1983) suggest that several factors contribute to this lack of support, including fear of crime, concern over deflated property values, and often a denial of the very existence of a drug problem in the community. This sort of resistance is based on legitimate fears that must be considered when deciding where to locate a treatment facility in the first place. Singh (1981) identifies several community variables that are conducive to posttreatment success. One of the most powerful predictors is the level of education in an area. Factors inhibiting posttreatment success include high unemployment and crime rates.

Unfortunately, those communities most conducive to posttreatment success are usually the most hesitant and able to resist locating recovering addicts in their neighborhoods. Community education programs are therefore essential. Numerous stereotypes, many of them unfounded, surround heroin addiction. Educating citizens in the community about the nature of drug addiction, the treatment process, and the potential benefits and risks involved should allay some of the unrealistic fears and misplaced resistance. Such education should, of course, be both realistic and truthful. Perhaps one of the most effective community education mechanisms is structured contact between recovering addicts and the host community. I will always remember the expression of delightful surprise vocalized by a former student after listening to a recovering addict relate his biography: "You're not at all like what I expected. You're just like us!" This encounter in the classroom resulted in yet another student becoming actively involved in establishing contact with potential employers on behalf of this individual.

*Employment*

It has long been recognized that an important predictor of posttreatment success is legitimate employment (National Institute of Law Enforcement and Criminal Justice, 1978; National Institute on Drug Abuse, 1977; Wolkstein, 1979). Employment must be meaningful if it is to be effective, however. Many addicts have considerable skills and experience that are readily marketable. It is illogical to put these individuals to work at menial jobs and expect them to remain interested in maintaining conventional employment. Harry recalled his first job after getting out of the program:

> My real bitch was, I walked out of the program and I went to work in a factory for $3.50 an hour. I was working in a lousy, stinking, smoky factory. I used to burn my hands on 450-degree liquid that they had heating in pans, working shift work which is a real dog— taking home maybe $125 a week. And I used to shit with $125. Back before the down-slide, I would recall that and whenever I would see one of them suckers that didn't get busted, and they

were still riding around in Cadillacs and they had girls out on the street, and now he has graduated—he's running a numbers ring, and he's got big drugs coming into the state. And I know he's . . . worth millions. I'm pitching a bitch to myself saying, "Man, wouldn't I love it. I know I could pull it off now." I just had to keep telling myself, "You can't do it, you can't do it." And eventually you find some things in life that will be worth more than that. . . . You keep telling yourself that's like stardust in your eyes. It's like, all that glitters ain't gold, and all that stuff. But you've really got to keep telling yourself that.

Harry's "bitch" was not so much that he was making a mere $125 a week but that the work didn't challenge him, and he constantly found himself lured back into the more challenging life of drugs and crime. He remained drug-free, however, largely due to the fact that he found more challenging employment in sales, where he could make use of his highly developed verbal skills: "The fascination doesn't stop. . . . Like I can wheel and deal in sales. I do it every day and I love it. I'm slinging shit all over the place. But it's OK. I'm not breaking any laws. I'm holding up my end of the bargain, I'm Basic U.S. Citizen. . . . It's the people that don't believe you can do that are the ones who go back. Because I just still . . . I've got to be where the action is. I've got to be someplace where I've got my finger on the pulse."

Promotion of this sort of meaningful employment for recovering addicts can only be accomplished within the context of a receptive host community. Treatment programs are therefore well-advised to establish meaningful relationships with dependable employers and employment agencies. Apprenticeship programs with local employers should be especially encouraged, as they not only teach recovering addicts marketable skills but also provide an opportunity for the addicts to develop positive work habits and attitudes. Boss reflected on some of these difficulties for recovering addicts: "The hardest [thing] I found out was how can you just put yourself to work for a solid week and budget that thing for a whole week? I don't want to get up in the morning and put on a hat, go to work at the plant . . . and come home at six o'clock with no money in my pocket."

Facilitating employment for recovering addicts entails far more than merely training clients in interview techniques and perhaps a few vocational skills. The recovering addict must be comfortable maneuvering in the conventional world of work. Because this is a foreign world to many of these individuals, prearranged relationships must be established with understanding employers who are willing to provide more supervision and guidance than usual. Efforts must be made to match the skills and penchants of individual addicts with employment opportunities. Employment is too critical a variable in treatment success to be left to chance. Required is a comprehensive employment program involving (1) community/employer education, (2) addict training, (3) a referral service insuring an appropriate match between addict and employer, and (4) structured contact between recovering addicts and potential employers.

### Primary Group Contacts

While recognizing the critical role of employment for the reinforcement of a positive self-image, I would further suggest that meaningful social networks in the conventional community are also critical to this social transformation process. People typically spend only eight to ten hours per day at work, leaving quantities of unscheduled time after work and on weekends. Without extraoccupational relationships in the conventional community, recovering addicts will most naturally drift toward those comrades with whom they are most comfortable. As Boss explained: "Now [on the street] . . . I'm with cats that's playing ball, other cats fuckin' chicks, there's partying over here. Things constantly going on that I like and that I'm familiar with 'cause I've been doing it all my life. So now peer pressure's pressuring me over here and peer pressure's putting me over there. . . . And that's got to be real tough. . . . You're playing both ends from the middle. You're fence-straddling at that time. In my case, the life of crime on this side is much stronger and outweighs this here [straight life]. I ain't balanced too tough no way, and it don't take much for me to sway this way."

Horace also found the streets to be a powerful enticement when he was released into aftercare. He was told to go out and find a job and to report back to the program if he had any problems. This was easier said than done when he found himself out of the protective environment of the program, however: "Then they start letting you out [of 24-hour care] to look for employment. But in the process of looking for employment, you're running around the streets and you can't find no jobs. So instead of going back to the program . . . you go to the corners. . . .

You go to corners where dope fiends is at. You don't go to corners where guys are playing checkers. You go to corners where dope fiends are at."

Quite in contrast to the experience of Boss and Horace, Harry understood that he had to establish meaningful contacts in the conventional community if he was to sustain a drug-free life-style. At the time of this interview, Harry had been clean some six years and attributed much of his success to the supportive network that he had developed in the straight community: "I went out and made enough friends who know what I'm into, so if that ever happens to me—if I have an anxiety attack now, I call my doctor. . . . She knows. And she's a sweetheart. I met other people through political campaigns that I did, that know me and know where I was at. . . . I burnt those bridges [with the treatment program] for that reason, because I said I'll never grow as a person if all I ever am is an ex-addict."

The experiences of these and other addicts in this study suggest two important features of successful reintegration. First, effective reintegration occurs within the broader community as opposed to specialized agencies established for the purpose of handling specific individuals. The goals of reintegration will not be accomplished if addicts are provided special make-work jobs with some government agency. Special employment programs will only have the effect of further ghettoizing these persons as an identifiable deviant group. They need to be put to work in local factories, retail outlets, and service agencies. Involvement in other community groups can also be extremely important for effective reintegration. Churches, YMCA groups, and the family are part of the ongoing life of the community and provide an important source of group support for maintaining a conventional life-style. Groups such as this provide a very different function than specially created support groups for ex-addicts that may play an important role in the ongoing recovery process but do not accomplish reintegration.

Second, while reintegration is often described merely as a final, aftercare phase in the treatment process, the ultimate goal of reintegration should be central to the treatment process from the beginning. In this respect, the resocialization that takes place within drug treatment programs is radically different from the model provided by religious communes. Whereas the ultimate goal of religious communes is to establish an unwavering commitment to the group, drug treatment must facilitate independence from the group if it is to be successful. Simply providing an "aftercare" component without preparing the addict for life in the outside world only invites frustration and failure. The "Miniversity" program at Daytop Village is but one example of how reintegration can be effectively introduced earlier in the treatment process.

An important principle in establishing an early reintegration focus is to connect the program itself as much as possible to ongoing community life, thereby minimizing the aura of institutionalization. I am not suggesting a total or even partial deinstitutionalization, as this would undermine the treatment process. The process of dissociation from the street subculture can work effectively only in a 24-hour total institution. This is especially true given that neighborhoods most receptive to community-based treatment facilities tend to be low-income central city areas (Davidson, 1982). While these neighborhoods contain important resources for reintegration (e.g., shopping centers, proximity to public transportation for employment, etc.), their proximity to the street environment precludes a totally deinstitutionalized program. Rather I am suggesting that treatment programs establish strong bonds with host communities—bonds that can be made a part of the resocialization experience of addicts even in the early phases of treatment. Even in the context of an institutionalized environment, neighborhood picnics, church functions, and even job and career fairs can be very helpful in preparing the addict to function in mainstream culture. These opportunities can only be made available if the treatment program has established a strong positive relationship with the host community.

In short, reintegration should not be an appendage to treatment. Rather, it needs to be incorporated throughout the treatment process with increasing emphasis, such that by the time the addict is ready to leave the protective care of the program, ideally he or she will find it as natural to function in conventional society as it was to function in the subculture.

The treatment model proposed here recognizes addiction—and withdrawal from addiction—as fundamentally social processes (Faupel, 1985). Moreover, this model recognizes the importance of drug availability and life structure in the addiction and treatment process. Removing the addict entirely from those situations that define drug use in positive terms by maintaining a closely monitored, 24-hour-care environment, therapeutic communities have quite effectively addressed drug availability. Furthermore, because these programs are highly structured and impose a rigorous daily routine, they do not allow recovering addicts unstructured, unsupervised time to drift back into drug use. Still needed, however, are better strategies to facilitate the development of a strong basis for life structure in conventional drug-free communities. These communities, which can meaningfully structure the daily routine of the recovering addict with non-drug-using and noncriminal activities, should be at the heart of an effective treatment policy.

# Notes

---

## Chapter 1

1. Mario and Harry were associates, and Mario actually referred me to Harry. Belle and Ron were very close friends in addition to being criminal partners at various points in their careers. They were both incarcerated at the time I interviewed them. I also have reason to believe that Mona had met and used heroin with Helen years earlier, but they did not know each other well.

## Chapter 2

1. See Glaser (1968) for descriptions and analyses of careers in other organizational contexts.

2. Deviant careers vary in their degree of predictability. Studies of occupational deviance (e.g., Inciardi, 1975; Letkeman, 1973; Miller, 1978) suggest a relatively highly structured career context more closely resembling organizational careers than nonoccupational deviant careers. This point is elaborated later in the text.

3. Some of these career types have been more extensively researched than others. There has been considerable research on Type I (respectable-occupational) careers. Most of this research has focused on professional careers, such as medical and dental careers (e.g., Hall, 1948; Sherlock and Cohen, 1966); academic and teaching careers (Becker, 1952; Caplow and McGee, 1958); and the careers of lawyers (Smigel, 1964). Blue-collar careers have received less atten-

tion, with some notable exceptions such as Chinoy's (1955) study of careers of automobile workers, Niederhoffer's (1969) work on police officers, and Harper and Emmert's (1963) study of postal carriers.

There has been less systematic research on Type II (respectable-nonoccupational) careers, although a number of recent studies have focused on the career dynamics of being a homemaker (e.g., Chenoweth and Maret, 1980; Miller, 1981; Olson, 1979; Rae, 1981; Rosenfeld, 1986; Taylor and Hartley, 1975; Townsend and Gurin, 1981). In addition, avocational pursuits, such as amateur archaeologists, artists, and actors (Becker, 1982; Stebbins, 1979), volunteer work (Boles, 1985; Daniels, 1988; Deegan and Nutt, 1975; Oldham, 1979), and leisure-time activities (Kaplan, 1960; Kelly, 1983; Roberts, 1978) have been researched, although not necessarily from a career perspective.

Type III (deviant-occupational) careers have been extensively studied by criminologists, beginning with Sutherland's (1937) classic work on the professional thief. Since that time, the careers of fences (Klockars, 1974; Steffensmeier, 1986), pickpockets (Inciardi, 1977a, 1983; Maurer, 1955), and armed robbers (Einstadter, 1969; Letkeman, 1973) have been systematically studied. In addition, sexually deviant occupations such as prostitution, stripping, and taxi-dancing have also been examined in this way (Best, 1982; Boles and Garbin, 1974; Bryan, 1965, 1966; Dressel and Petersen, 1982; Goldstein, 1979; Heyl, 1977; Hong and Duff, 1977; Luckenbill, 1986; Skipper and McCaghy, 1970).

Finally, Type IV (deviant-nonoccupational) careers refer to deviant activities that are not oriented to making a living. Research in this area includes Goffman's (1959) classic study of the moral careers of mental patients; Buckner's (1970) study of transvestites; and studies of nudists (Weinberg, 1966), homosexuals (Kelly, 1979; McCaghy and Skipper, 1969), skid row alcoholics (Wallace, 1965, 1968; Wiseman, 1970), and juvenile delinquents and status offenders (Kelley, 1983; Smith and Smith, 1984; Smith et al., 1984).

4. Users of expensive drugs who are not part of the drug-using subculture will not necessarily be involved in income-producing crime. This is one important way in which subcultural addicts may differ from occupationally related addicts such as physicians or even from more "conventional" middle-class addicts.

### Chapter 3

1. These six respondents had been working or in school, but they quit or dropped out around the time they began using heroin. It is not clear whether they were in these structured roles when they first tried heroin, but clearly they were having difficulty maintaining them adequately.

2. See Lemert (1951) and Matza (1964, 1969) for excellent discussions of the distinction between singular deviant acts and the development of deviant careers and identities.

3. The street-junkie phase is also a time when normative violation is common, but in this case it is motivated by the need for drugs. These dynamics are discussed in chapter six.

4. This figure was calculated by subtracting the mean age at which the sample used heroin the first time from the mean age at which the sample began using on a continual basis (more than once a week for at least a month). These ages were 19 and 20 years respectively. This is an imperfect measure, since continued use as defined here does not necessarily imply stable-addict career status. Any error, however, is likely to be on the conservative side, since stable-addict status is more likely to succeed rather than precede continued use as defined here.

## Chapter 4

1. This is not always the case. During the street-junkie phase of addict careers, criminal acts are typically committed out of desperation due to withdrawal sickness. I take up this issue in chapter six.

2. This is by no means universally true. Some addicts remain "flat-footed hustlers," engaging in any and all crimes as the opportunity arises. While most addict-criminals do go through periods of their careers when they are similarly opportunistic in their criminality, there appear to be some individuals who, even as successful stable addicts, sustain a broad base of criminal activity. Insofar as my observations are representative of hard-core street heroin users, however, I would contend that most hard-core addicts become successful at a restricted number of hustles on which they rely for virtually all of their criminal income during the stable-addict phase of their careers.

3. Letkeman (1973) provides a slightly different typology that includes mechanical skills, social skills, and organizational skills. Social skills have the same meaning for Letkeman as they do here. Mechanical and organizational skills are subsumed here under technical skills (although organizational skills as such were not especially salient among the addicts I interviewed). In addition, I found intuitive skills to be especially salient among the addicts in this study.

## Chapter 8

1. See Ashley (1972), Brecher (1972), Duster (1970), Eldridge (1967), Inciardi (1986), King (1972), Lindesmith (1965), and especially Musto (1973) for extensive discussions of the development of narcotics legislation in this country.

2. Some writers, such as Nadelmann (1989), do not differentiate between decriminalization and legalization. The differences between these two policies are substantial, and I maintain the distinction here in order to highlight the implications of each approach.

## Chapter 9

1. The word *synanon* originated with one of the early residents of the program. Attempting to say two words in the same breath—*symposium* and *seminar*—he managed to come out with "synanon." From that point forward, the organization was known as Synanon (capital S) and the group seminars were referred to as synanons. For further discussion see Yablonsky (1965:vii–viii).

2. The "haircut" is not restricted to verbal attack. The participants in this study who had enrolled in these programs reported that after repeated offenses the client is often given a physical haircut as a symbolic gesture of disapproval, an act in which fellow clients participate.

# Glossary

Heroin addicts use many terms and phrases that are not used in ordinary everyday language by most people. This specialized vocabulary, called *argot,* has been used quite extensively throughout this book in order to convey information about heroin-using careers as perceived by heroin users themselves. This glossary contains words and phrases that have been used in this book as well as other terms that have special relevance to the heroin subculture. Most of these terms are recognizable to anyone familiar with the heroin subculture, although some terms may not be as widely shared in their specific meanings as others.

**bag**–the most basic unit in which heroin is bought and sold on the street. Typically comes in a small glassine envelope and usually contains about 90 milligrams of substance, of which about 3–10 milligrams is heroin. The rest is *cut.*

**bag bitches**–female addicts who live with dealers or provide regular sexual services for dealers in exchange for heroin.

**beat a john**–to steal from a client; said of a prostitute. In addition to the fee they get for their services, lower-status prostitutes, commonly called "streetwalkers," often steal cash and credit cards from their clients.

**big dealers**–dealers in quantity, wholesale drugs.

**big piece**–a large quantity of heroin.

**big sting**–a particularly lucrative score from a criminal hustle.

**boost**–to shoplift. Shoplifters are referred to as *boosters*. Some boosters distinguish between themselves and more amateur shoplifters, who are commonly called "snitches."

**boot**–to mainline. Refers specifically to the procedure whereby one injects directly into the vein a little at a time, drawing the blood-heroin mixture back up into the syringe, then injecting a little more, etc. Addicts report that this technique enhances the *rush*.

**boy**–heroin. This is a term often used when *speedballing*. Heroin is referred to as the *boy* and cocaine as the *girl*.

**bundle**–the equivalent of about 25 bags of heroin. Bundles are not usually separated into bags, and are sold much more cheaply than bags.

**burning out**–tiring of the life-style of heroin addiction. Contrasts with Charles Winick's notion of "maturing out" which suggests that addicts eventually outgrow heroin addiction as part of a developmental process. *Burning out* suggests a retirement from the life-style due to fatigue factors.

**bust**–arrest.

**case**–the part of the act of burglary and shoplifting that involves carefully observing the physical layout, as well as the social patterns of potential residential or commercial victims. Synonymous with "staking out" an establishment.

**chasing the bag**–all of the activities involved in securing heroin for consumption, including *hustling*, locating *connections, copping,* etc.

**chippying**–an infrequent use of heroin, typically on weekends, that does not involve a strong addiction to the drug. Those who use drugs on this basis are called "chippers."

**cold turkey**–sudden withdrawal from heroin.

**connection**–source of drugs, usually a drug dealer. Often used to refer to a wholesale dealer from whom one can buy in quantity, such as by the bundle.

**consignment, selling on consignment**–usually done by wholesale dealers, who give drugs to street or middle-level dealers with the understanding that the wholesaler is to be paid when the drugs are sold.

**cook**–to prepare heroin for use. This is done by mixing the powdered heroin with water in a small container such as a spoon or soda bottle cap. The mixture is then heated, usually with a match or cigarette lighter, until it dissolves. It is then drawn into the syringe through a piece of cotton or sometimes a cigarette filter to strain out impurities.

**cop**–to purchase heroin.

**cop short**–to attempt to purchase heroin without enough money. Under these circumstances, addicts rely on the goodwill of dealers to sell the drug to them on the assurance that they will make up for it next time.

**cotton shot**–the residue left in the filter in the process of preparing heroin for use (after the substance is drawn into the syringe through a piece of cotton, or sometimes a cigarette filter). Addicts who are particularly hard up may resort to collecting this residue for their *fix*. The term is also used to refer to addicts who rely on this residue; when used in this way, it is usually a derogatory term.

**crank**–methamphetamines.

**crib**–one's home.

**cut**–to dilute heroin; or, the dilutant in heroin. Street heroin is only about 3 to 10% pure. The rest is made up of benign substances such as milk sugar or quinine.

**dirty works**–needle and syringe that have been used by other addicts who have an infectious disease such as hepatitis or AIDS.

**do time**–to spend time in prison.

**dope**–heroin. The term has this specific meaning in the heroin subculture, and does not refer to marijuana or illegal drugs generally.

**dope fiend**–a heroin addict. Sometimes implies a greater degree of respectability than a *junkie*.

**fix**–a shot of heroin.

**flat-footed hustler**–a criminal addict who does not specialize in one or more crimes, but rather engages in whatever criminal opportunities become available. His or her counterpart in the conventional work world is the "jack of all trades."

**flipped**–to be manipulated by law enforcement agencies to reveal the identity of drug dealers and/or fellow users.

**freak**–term used by prostitutes to refer to a client whose sexual preferences involve violence and sadomasochism or other bizarre sexual behavior.

**front**–to provide drugs and get paid for them at a later time. This is usually done by wholesale dealers who sell to street-level dealers. Payment is made to the wholesaler after the drugs are sold, similar to legal arrangements in the conventional work world. Also referred to as *consignment*.

**get off**–to shoot up. Refers to the *rush*, or sense of exhilaration, experienced when shooting directly into the vein.

**get over**–to take advantage of someone for monetary gain, often by guile or deceit.

**girl**–cocaine. See also *boy*.

**good bust**–an arrest that has followed all proper procedures so that it will hold up in court.

**good-guy bad-guy routine**–common strategy used by police officers for breaking the defenses of addicts in order to get them to talk. Typically, one officer will play the role of the "bad guy," acting harshly and perhaps threatening the addict with punitive actions; then a second officer, the "good guy" will step in and attempt to entice the addict into talking with promises of immunity, etc. This routine continues until an addict "breaks" and starts to talk.

**heat**–pressure and stress resulting from being under surveillance by the police. One who is under such surveillance is said to be *hot*.

**hit**–to shoot up; also, a successful injection into the vein; also, an act of theft, as when a shoplifter *hits* a department store.

**hold the bag**–to keep but not sell a supply of drugs in order to create a shortage, or *panic,* thereby driving up the price; said of a dealer.

**holder**–one who maintains possession of a dealer's drugs. Many dealers prefer to have someone else hold their drugs so that if a client informs on them, they will not have drugs in their possession. Clients purchase drugs from the dealer and are then directed to the holder to acquire the drugs. The holder is typically alerted to the sale through a series of hand signals.

**hooked**–addicted; denotes loss of control over one's heroin consumption.

**hustle**–criminal or quasi-criminal means of obtaining money for drugs.

**in the life**–to be part of the heroin-using subculture.

**john**–client of a prostitute.

**jones**–used by most of the addicts in this study to refer to the withdrawal symptoms they experience when they stop using heroin. Also used to refer to one's habit generally.

**juggling**–small-time dealing. User/dealers buy a wholesale quantity, divide it into bags, and sell just enough at retail prices to get back their original investment, keeping the rest for their own personal use.

**junk peddler**–derogatory term for drug dealer.

**junkie**–a heroin addict. Sometimes connotes a lower-status, down-and-out addict.

**junkie broad**–a heavily addicted female.

**main hustle**–one's primary *hustle* (see *hustle*). Criminal heroin users engage in many hustles, but often rely primarily on one or two as their primary means of income.

**mainline**–to inject directly into the vein—usually in the forearm, but may be just about anywhere a vein can be found.

**mark**–victim or potential victim of an addict's crime.

**meth**–usually refers to methadone, a substitute for heroin that is administered by clinics in most major American cities. Sometimes refers to methamphetamines, such as "crystal meth."

**monkey on the back**–a particularly powerful habit which the user recognizes is out of his or her control.

**nightcap**–the last heroin shot of the day, typically taken just before going to bed.

**nut**–see *freak*. Prostitutes also use this term to refer to a client's ejaculation. For example, when quoting prices a prostitute may say, "A nut and a quarter." This means that for $25 the john can "get off" (ejaculate) one time.

**on the nod**–a drowsy, dreamlike state usually resulting from highly concentrated heroin. This is an extremely desirable euphoric effect that most addicts seek to experience but seldom do.

**on the run**–hiding from the police, usually after committing a major crime or after escaping from prison.

**panic**–a shortage of heroin in an area, often intentionally created by major dealers by *holding their bag* for purposes of increasing their prices.

**quarter**–a wholesale quantity of heroin, slightly less than a *bundle*.

**regular**–a repeat customer of a prostitute.

**rent works**–to use another addict's works in exchange for money or drugs. Many addicts prefer not to maintain possession of their own set of works because in many jurisdictions such possession constitutes a criminal offense. Renting works thus reduces risk of arrest.

**re-up**–replenish one's drug supply.

**righteous dope**–good, high-quality heroin.

**roll**–the procedure by which shoplifters wrap clothing items tightly in order to get as many as possible into a container, typically a plastic garbage bag.

**run**–a sequence of stores targeted by shoplifters.

**runner**–a dependable individual hired by a major dealer to transport large quantities of drugs from one location to another.

**rush**–the initial sense of exhilaration and euphoria experienced when mainlining heroin. Sometimes compared to a sexual climax.

**score**–the proceeds from a criminal hustle; also, the act of purchasing drugs.

**shake the monkey**–to withdraw successfully from heroin addiction. This is typically done more than once throughout the course of an addict's career.

**shooting gallery**–a specified location, typically an abandoned building, where addicts can come to shoot their heroin out of easy view of police officers. More elaborate shooting galleries also sell heroin and rent works, often at highly inflated prices.

**shoot up**–to inject heroin.

**shot**–a dose of heroin.

**square**–one who is not a part of the heroin-using subculture.

**speed**–methamphetamines.

**speedball**–a combination of heroin and cocaine or heroin and methamphetamines, which is usually mainlined.

**spike**–hypodermic needle; also, the act of injecting.

**stash**–one's supply of heroin. Dealers often specially designate their "personal stash," which is what they keep aside for their own personal use.

**steer**–to promote a particular dealer's drugs; also, one who promotes a dealer's drugs. For this service, a steer is usually remunerated in drugs by the dealer. Same as *tout*.

**step on**–to cut, dilute. Each time a quantity of heroin is stepped on, its purity is typically reduced by 50%.

**straight**–the condition that results after one has injected heroin and is no longer experiencing withdrawal symptoms. Unless one injects too much heroin in too concentrated a form, which could leave them *on the nod,* heroin addicts function most normally after they have injected heroin. This term has a very different meaning in the heroin subculture than it does in the marijuana subculture, where it means *not* being high on the drug, and also refers to *squares,* individuals who are not part of the subculture.

**street dope**– heroin bought at retail prices by the individual bag.

**street price**–the retail price of heroin when sold by the bag, the smallest unit of sale.

**strung out**–to be totally out of control of one's heroin consumption. This is a time when heroin addicts often neglect other responsibilities because of their habit.

**sucker**–victim. Same as *mark*.

**taking care of business**–phrase used by heroin addicts to describe all of the activities involved in maintaining their heroin-using life-style. Especially connotes the criminal activities engaged in for purposes of paying for their habit.

**take**–the proceeds from a crime.

**taste**–a very small quantity of heroin.

**taste face**–a derogatory term, usually referring to down-and-out addicts who support their habit by renting out their works for a *taste* of heroin.

**test**–to assess the purity of a quantity of heroin, often by giving certain amounts to users with a small habit to gauge how it affects them. One who introduces heroin into the bloodstream for this purpose is called a *tester*.

**tie up**–to wrap one's arm tightly, usually with a rubber hose, so as to more clearly expose one's veins for purposes of injection.

**tout**–see *steer*.

**trick**–to prostitute; also referred to as *turning tricks*. Prostitutes also sometimes refer to their clients as tricks.

**turn on**–to experiment with heroin; also, to introduce someone else to heroin.

**wake-up shot**–first shot taken in the morning, immediately after getting out of bed.

**war stories**–reminiscences about one's exploits while on the street, often related in prison or in residential treatment programs.

**who'**–whore; prostitute. Pronounced "ho."

**works**–needle and syringe.

# Bibliography

Adler, Patricia A.
1985 *Wheeling and Dealing: An Ethnography of an Upper Level Drug Dealing and Smuggling Community.* New York: Columbia University Press.
Agar, Michael N.
1973 *Ripping and Running: A Formal Ethnography of Urban Heroin Addicts.* New York: Academic Press.
Akers, Ronald L., Robert L. Burgess, and Weldon T. Johnson
1968 "Opiate use, addiction and relapse." *Social Problems* 15, 4 (Spring): 459–69.
Anglin, M. Douglas, and Yih-Ing Hser
1987 "Addicted women and crime." *Criminology* 25, 2: 359–97.
Anglin, M. Douglas, and George Speckart
1984 "Narcotics use and crime: A confirmatory analysis." Unpublished report, University of California, Los Angeles.
1986 "Narcotics use, property crime and dealing: structural dynamics across the addiction career." *Journal of Quantitative Criminology* 2: 355–75.
1988 "Narcotics use and crime: a multisample, multimethod analysis." *Criminology* 26, 2: 197–233.
Anslinger, Harry J., and William F. Tompkins
1953 *The Traffic in Narcotics.* New York: Funk and Wagnalls.
Ashley, Richard
1972 *Heroin: The Myths and the Facts.* New York: St. Martin's Press.

Austin, Gregory A., and Dan J. Lettieri

1976 *Drugs and Crime: The Relationship between Drug Use and Concomitant Criminal Behavior.* National Institute on Drug Abuse, Research Issues Number 17. Washington, D.C.: U.S. Government Printing Office.

Ball, John C., W. Robert Lange, C. Patrick Myers, and Samuel R. Friedman

1988 "Reducing the risk of AIDS through Methadone Maintenance Treatment." *Journal of Health and Social Behavior* 29 (September): 214–26.

Ball, John C., Lawrence Rosen, John A. Flueck, and David Nurco

1981 "The criminality of heroin addicts when addicted and when off opiates." Pp. 39–65 in James A. Inciardi (ed.), *The Drugs-Crime Connection.* Beverly Hills, CA: Sage Publications.

1982 "Lifetime criminality of heroin addicts in the United States." *Journal of Drug Issues* 12 (Summer): 225–38.

Ball, John C., John W. Shaffer, and David Nurco

1983 "The day to day criminality of heroin addicts in Baltimore: a study of the continuity of offense rates." *Drug and Alcohol Dependence* 12:119–42.

Beattie, Ronald H.

1960 "Criminal statistics in the United States—1960." *Journal of Criminal Law, Criminology and Police Science* 51:49–65.

Becker, Howard S.

1952 "The career of the Chicago public school teacher." *American Journal of Sociology* 57, 5 (March): 470–77.

1953 "Becoming a marijuana user." *American Journal of Sociology* 59:235–42.

1963 *Outsiders: Studies in the Sociology of Deviance.* Glencoe, IL: Free Press.

1967 "History, culture and subjective experiences: an exploration of the social bases of drug induced experiences." *Journal of Health and Social Behavior* 8 (September): 163–76.

1982 *Art Worlds.* Berkeley, CA: University of California Press.

Beschner, George M., and William Brower

1985 "The scene." Pp. 19–29 in Bill Hanson, George Beschner, James M. Walters, and Elliot Bovelle (eds.), *Life with Heroin: Voices from the Inner City.* Lexington, MA: Lexington Books.

Best, Joel

1982 "Careers in brothel prostitution." *Journal of Interdisciplinary History* 12, 4 (Spring): 597–619.

Biernacki, Patrick

1979 "Junkie work, 'hustles' and social status among heroin addicts." *Journal of Drug Issues* 9:535–51.

Blackwell, Judith Stephenson

1983 "Drifting, controlling and overcoming: opiate users who avoid becoming chronically dependent." *Journal of Drug Issues* 13, 2 (Spring): 219–35.

Blankenship, Ralph
1973  "Organizational careers: an interactionist perspective." *Sociological Quarterly* 14: 88–98.

Blum, Richard
1972  *The Dream Sellers*. San Francisco: Jossey-Bass.

Blumer, Herbert, Alan Sutter, Roger Smith, and Samir Ahmed
1976  "Recruitment into drug use." Pp. 161–73 in Robert H. Coombs, Lincoln J. Fry, and Patricia G. Lewis (eds.), *Socialization in Drug Abuse*. Cambridge, MA: Schenkman Publishing Co.

Boles, Jaqueline M.
1985  "The administration of voluntary associations: a course for the '80's." *Teaching Sociology* 12, 2 (January): 193–207.

Boles, Jacqueline M., and Albeno P. Garbin
1974  "The choice of stripping for a living: an empirical and theoretical explanation." *Sociology of Work and Occupations* 1, 1 (February): 110–23.

Brecher, Edward
1972  *Licit and Illicit Drugs*. Boston: Little, Brown and Company.

Brown, Barry S., Susan K. Gauvey, Marilyn B. Meyers, and Steven D. Stark
1971  "In their own words: addicts' reasons for initiating and withdrawing from heroin." *International Journal of the Addictions* 6, 4 (December): 635–45.

Bryan, James H.
1965  "Apprenticeships in prostitution." *Social Problems* 12: 287–97.
1966  "Occupational ideologies and individual attitudes of call girls." *Social Problems* 13, 4 (Spring): 441–50.

Buckner, H. Taylor
1970  "The transvestic career path." *Psychiatry* 33: 381–89.

Caplow, Theodore, and Reece J. McGee
1958  *The Academic Marketplace*. New York: Basic Books.

Chaiken, Marcia R.
1988  *Street Level Drug Enforcement: Examining the Issues*. Washington, D.C.: National Institute of Justice.

Chein, Isidor
1956  "Narcotics use among juveniles." *Social Work* 1: 50–60.

Chein, Isidor, Donald L. Gerard, Robert S. Lee, and Eva Rosenfeld
1964  *The Road to H: Narcotics, Juvenile Delinquency and Social Policy*. New York: Basic Books.

Chenoweth, Lillian C., and Elizabeth Maret
1980  "The career patterns of mature American women." *Sociology of Work and Occupations* 7, 2 (May): 222–51.

Chinoy, Ely

1955 *Automobile Workers and the American Dream.* Boston: Beacon Press.

Cloward, Richard, and Lloyd Ohlin

1960 *Delinquency and Opportunity.* Glencoe, IL: Free Press.

Coombs, Robert H.

1981 "Drug abuse as career." *Journal of Drug Issues* 11 (Fall): 369–87.

Crawford, Gail A., Melvin C. Washington, and Edward C. Senay

1983 "Careers with heroin." *International Journal of the Addictions* 18: 701–15.

Cressey, Donald R.

1957 "The state of criminal statistics." *National Probation and Parole Association Journal* 3: 230–41.

Daniels, Arlene Kaplan

1988 *Invisible Careers: Women Civil Leaders from the Volunteer World.* Chicago: University of Chicago Press.

Davidson, Jeffrey L.

1982 "Balancing required resources and neighborhood opposition in community based treatment center neighborhoods." *Social Science Review* 56, 1: 55–71.

Deegan, Mary Jo, and Larry E. Nutt

1975 "The hospital volunteer: lay person in a bureaucratic setting." *Sociology of Work and Occupations* 2, 4 (November): 338–53.

DeLeon, George

1984 *The Therapeutic Community: Study of Effectiveness.* National Institute on Drug Abuse, Treatment Research Monograph Series. Washington, D.C.: U.S. Government Printing Office.

1985 "The therapeutic community: status and evolution." *International Journal of the Addictions* 20, 6–7: 823–44.

Dembo, Richard, James A. Ciarlo, and Robert W. Taylor

1983 "A model for assessing and improving drug abuse treatment resource use in inner city areas." *International Journal of the Addictions* 18, 7: 921–36.

Denzin, Norman

1970 *The Research Act.* Chicago: Aldine.

Deutscher, Irwin

1966 "Words and deeds: social science and social policy." *Social Problems* 13: 235–54.

Dole, Vincent P., Marie E. Nyswander, Don DesJarlais, and Herman Joseph

1982 "Performance-based rating of methadone maintenance programs." *New England Journal of Medicine* 306, 3 (January 21): 169–72.

Dole, Vincent P., Marie E. Nyswander, and Alan Warner

1968 "Successful treatment of 750 criminal addicts." *Journal of the American Medical Association* 206: 2708–11.

Doleschal, Eugene
1970 "Hidden Crime." *Crime and Delinquency Literature* 2 (October): 546–72.
Dressel, Paula L., and David M. Petersen
1982 "Becoming a male stripper: recruitment, socialization and ideological development." *Work and Occupations* 9, 3 (August): 387–406.
Dressler, David
1951 *Parole Chief.* New York: Viking Press.
Durkheim, Emile
1951 *Suicide: A Study in Sociology.* New York: Free Press.
Duster, Troy
1970 *The Legislation of Morality: Law, Drug, and Moral Judgement.* New York: Free Press.
Einstadter, Werner J.
1969 "The social organization of armed robbery." *Social Problems* 17, 1 (Summer): 64–83.
Eldridge, William Butler
1967 *Narcotics and the Law: A Critique of the American Experiment in Narcotic Drug Control.* Chicago: University of Chicago Press.
Epstein, Edward Jay
1977 *Agency of Fear: Opiates and Political Power in America.* New York: G. P. Putnam's Sons.
Erikson, Maynard L., and Lamar T. Empey
1963 "Court records, undetected delinquency and decision making." *Journal of Criminal Law, Criminology and Police Science* 54: 456–69.
Faupel, Charles E.
1981 "Drug treatment and criminality: methodological and theoretical considerations." Pp. 183–206 in James A. Inciardi (ed.), *The Drugs-Crime Connection.* Beverly Hills, CA: Sage Publications.
1985 "A theoretical model for a socially oriented drug treatment policy." *Journal of Drug Education* 15, 3: 189–203.
1986 "Heroin use, street crime and the 'main hustle': implications for the validity of official crime data." *Deviant Behavior* 7: 31–45.
1987a "Heroin use and criminal careers." *Qualitative Sociology* 10, 2 (Summer): 115–31.
1987b "Drug availability, life structure and situational ethics of heroin addicts." *Urban Life* 15, 3–4 (January): 395–419.
Faupel, Charles E., and Carl B. Klockars
1987 "Drugs-crime connections: elaborations from the life histories of hardcore heroin addicts." *Social Problems* 34, 1 (February): 54–68.

Feldman, Harvey W.

1968  "Ideological supports to becoming and remaining a heroin addict." *Journal of Health and Social Behavior* 9: 131–39.

Fiddle, Seymore

1976  "Sequences in addiction." *Addictive Diseases: An International Journal* 2, 4:553–68.

Fields, Allen, and James M. Walters

1985  "Hustling: supporting a heroin habit." Pp. 49–73 in Bill Hanson, George Beschner, James M. Walters, and Elliot Bovelle (eds.), *Life with Heroin: Voices from the Inner City*. Lexington, MA: Lexington Books.

Form, William

1968  "Occupations and careers." Pp. 245–54 in *International Encyclopedia of the Social Sciences*. New York: Free Press.

Freeman, Linton C., and Turkoz Ataov

1960  "Invalidity of indirect and direct measures toward cheating." *Journal of Personality* 28:443–47.

Gandossey, Robert P., Jay R. Williams, Jo Cohen, and Hendrick J. Harwood

1980  *Drugs and Crime: A Survey and Analysis of the Literature*. Washington, D.C.: U.S. Government Printing Office.

Garfinkel, Harold

1956  "Conditions of successful degradation ceremonies." *American Journal of Sociology* 61:410–24.

Gearing, Frances R.

1974  "Methadone maintenance treatment five years later—where are they now?" *American Journal of Public Health* 64 (December supplement): 44–50.

Ginzberg, Eli, Sol W. Ginsburg, Sidney Axelrad, and John L. Herma

1951  *Occupational Choice: An Approach to a General Theory*. New York: Columbia University Press.

Glaser, Barney G.

1968  *Organizational Careers*. Chicago: Aldine.

Glaser, Barney G., and Anselm L. Strauss

1967  *The Discovery of Grounded Theory: Strategies for Qualitative Research*. Chicago: Aldine.

Glaser, Daniel

1967  "National goals and indicators for the reduction of crime and delinquency." *Annals of the American Academy of Political and Social Science* 37:104–26.

Goffman, Erving

1959  "The moral career of the mental patient." *Psychiatry* 22:123–42.

1961  *Asylums*. Garden City, NY: Doubleday.

1967 "Embarrassment and social organization." Pp. 97–112 in Erving Goffman (ed.), *Interaction Ritual: Essays on Face to Face Behavior.* Chicago: Aldine.

Goldman, Fred

1981 "Drug abuse, crime and economics: the dismal limits of social choice." Pp. 155–82 in James A. Inciardi (ed.), *The Drugs-Crime Connection.* Beverly Hills, CA: Sage Publications.

Goldstein, Paul J.

1979 *Prostitution and Drugs.* Lexington, MA: Lexington Books.

1981 "Getting over: economic alternatives to predatory crime among street drug users." Pp. 67–84 in James A. Inciardi (ed.), *The Drugs-Crime Connection.* Beverly Hills, CA: Sage Publications.

1985 "The drugs/violence nexus: a tripartite conceptual framework." *Journal of Drug Issues* 15 (Fall): 493–506.

Gould, Leroy, Andrew L. Walker, Lansing E. Crane, and Charles W. Lidz

1974 *Connections: Notes from the Heroin World.* New Haven, CT: Yale University Press.

Gray, Susan, and Dean Morse

1980 "Retirement and re-engagement: changing work options for older workers." *Aging and Work* 3, 2 (Spring): 103–11.

Greenberg, Stephanie W., and Freda Adler

1974 "Crime and addiction: an empirical analysis of the literature, 1920–1973." *Contemporary Drug Problems* 3: 221–70.

Hall, Oswald

1948 "The stages of a medical career." *American Journal of Sociology* 53, 5 (March): 327–36.

Hanson, Bill, George Beschner, James W. Walters, and Elliot Bovelle

1985 *Life with Heroin: Voices from the Inner City.* Lexington, MA: Lexington Books.

Harper, Dean, and Frederick Emmert

1963 "Work behavior in a service industry." *Social Forces* 42, 2 (December): 216–25.

Harris, Mervyn

1973 *The Dilly Boys.* Rockville, MD: New Perspectives.

Hartjen, Clayton A.

1978 *Crime and Criminalization* (2d ed.). New York: Holt, Rinehart and Winston.

Hawkins, J. David

1979 "Reintegrating street drug abusers: community roles in continuing care." In Barry S. Brown (ed.), *Addicts and Aftercare: Community Integration of the Former Drug User.* Beverly Hills, CA: Sage Publications.

Hayano, David M.

1982  *Poker Faces: The Life and Work of Professional Card Players.* Berkeley, CA: University of California Press.

Hayim, G. J.

1973  "Changes in the criminal behavior of heroin addicts under treatment in the Addiction Research and Treatment Corporation: interim report of the first year of treatment." Pp. 1–62 in G. J. Hayim et al. (eds.), *Heroin Use in a Methadone Maintenance Program.* Washington, D.C.: U.S. Department of Justice, National Institute of Law Enforcement and Criminal Justice.

Henry, J.

1959  "Spontaneity, initiative and creativity in suburban classrooms." *American Journal of Orthopsychiatry* 29:266–79.

Heyl, Barbara Sherman

1977  "The madam as teacher: the training of house prostitutes." *Social Problems* 24, 5 (June):545–55.

Hong, Lawrence K., and Robert W. Duff

1977  "Becoming a taxi-dancer: the significance of neutralization in a semi-deviant occupation." *Sociology of Work and Occupations* 4, 3 (August): 327–42.

Hughes, Everett C.

1937  "Institutional office and the person." *American Journal of Sociology* 43 (November):404–13.

1958  *Men and Their Work.* Glencoe, IL: Free Press.

Hughes, Helen McGill

1961  *The Fantastic Lodge: The Autobiography of a Drug Addict.* New York: Fawcett World Library.

Hughes, Patrick H.

1977  *Behind the Wall of Respect: Community Experiments in Heroin Addiction Control.* Chicago: University of Chicago Press.

Inciardi, James A.

1974  "The vilification of euphoria: some perspectives on an elusive issue." *Addictive Diseases* 1:241–67.

1975  *Careers in Crime.* Chicago: Rand McNally Publishing Co.

1977a  "In search of the class canon: a field study of professional pickpockets." In Robert S. Weppner (ed.), *Street Ethnography.* Beverly Hills, CA: Sage Publications.

1977b  *Methadone Diversion: Experiences and Issues.* National Institute on Drug Abuse, Services Research Monograph Series. DHEW Publication No. ADM 77-488. Washington, D.C.: U.S. Government Printing Office.

1978  "The Uniform Crime Reports: some considerations on their shortcomings and utility." *Public Data Use* 6:3–16.

1979 "Heroin use and street crime." *Crime and Delinquency* 25 (July): 335–46.

1981 "Marijuana decriminalization research: a perspective and commentary." *Criminology* 19, 1 (May): 145–59.

1983 "On grift at the Superbowl: professional pickpockets and the NFL." Pp. 31–41 in Gordon P. Waldo (ed.), *Career Criminals*. Beverly Hills, CA: Sage Publications.

1986 *The War on Drugs: Heroin, Cocaine, Crime and Public Policy*. Palo Alto, CA: Mayfield Publishing Co.

1987 "Sociology and American Drug Policy." *American Sociologist* 18 (Summer): 179–88.

Irwin, John

1970 *The Felon*. Englewood Cliffs, NJ: Prentice-Hall.

James, Jennifer, Cathleen T. Gosho, and Robin Watson

1976 "The relationship between female criminality and drug use." Pp. 441–55 in Research Triangle Institute (ed.), *Drug Use and Crime: Report of the Panel on Drug Use and Criminal Behavior*. National Technical Information Service Publication No. PB-259-167. Springfield, VA: U.S. Department of Commerce.

Johnson, Bruce D., Paul J. Goldstein, Edward Preble, James Schmeidler, Douglas S. Lipton, Barry Spunt, and Thomas Miller

1985 *Taking Care of Business: The Economics of Crime by Heroin Abusers*. Lexington, MA: Lexington Books.

Kanter, Rosabeth Moss

1972 *Commitment and Community: Communes and Utopias in Sociological Perspective*. Cambridge, MA: Harvard University Press.

Kaplan, John

1983 *The Hardest Drug: Heroin and Public Policy*. Chicago: University of Chicago Press.

Kaplan, Max

1960 *Leisure in American: A Social Inquiry*. New York: John Wiley and Sons.

Katz, Fred E., and Harry W. Martin

1962 "Career choice processes." *Social Forces* 41: 149–54.

Kelley, Thomas M.

1983 "Status offenders can be different: a comparative study of delinquent careers." *Crime and Delinquency* 29, 3 (July): 365–80.

Kelly, Delos

1979 "The structuring and maintenance of a deviant identity: an analysis of lesbian activity." Pp. 592–603 in Delos Kelly (ed.), *Deviant Behavior: Readings in the Sociology of Deviance*. New York: St. Martin's Press.

Kelly, John R.

1983 *Leisure Identities and Interactions*. London: George Allen and Unwin.

King, Rufus

1972  *The Drug Hang-Up: America's Fifty Year Folly.* New York: W. W. Norton.

Kleinman, Mark A. R.

1988  "Crackdowns: the effects of intensive enforcement on retail heroin dealing." Pp. 3–34 in Marcia R. Chaiken (ed.), *Street Level Drug Enforcement: Examining the Issues.* Washington, D.C.: National Institute of Justice.

Klockars, Carl B.

1974  *The Professional Fence.* New York: Free Press.

Kolb, Lawrence

1925  "Drug addiction in its relation to crime." *Mental Hygiene* 9 : 74–89.

Krause, Elliot A.

1971  *The Sociology of Occupations.* Boston: Little, Brown and Company.

Kutner, Bernard, Carol Wilkins, and Penny Rechtman Yarrow

1952  "Verbal attitudes and overt behavior involving racial prejudice." *Journal of Abnormal and Social Psychology* 47 : 649–52.

LaPiere, Richard T.

1934  "Attitudes vs. actions." *Social Forces* 13, 2 : 230–37.

Lemert, Edwin M.

1951  *Social Pathology: A Systematic Approach to the Theory of Sociopathic Behavior.* New York: McGraw-Hill.

Lesieur, Henry R.

1977  *The Chase.* Garden City, NY: Anchor Books.

Letkeman, Peter

1973  *Crime as Work.* Englewood Cliffs, NJ: Prentice-Hall.

Leveson, Irving, and Jeffrey H. Weiss

1976  *Analysis of Urban Health Problems.* New York: Spectrum.

Lieberman, Leonard, and Leslie Lieberman

1983  "The second career concept." *Aging and Work* 6, 4 (Fall) : 277–89.

Lindesmith, Alfred

1940  "'Dope fiend' mythology." *Journal of Criminal Law and Criminology* 31 : 199–208.

1965  *The Addict and the Law.* Bloomington, IN: Indiana University Press.

1968  *Addiction and Opiates.* New York: Aldine. (Originally published in 1947.)

Linn, Lawrence S.

1965  "Verbal attitude and overt behavior: a study of racial discrimination." *Social Forces* 43, 3 : 353–64.

Luckenbill, David F.

1986  "Deviant career mobility: the case of male prostitutes." *Social Problems* 33, 4 (April) : 283–96.

Luckenbill, David F., and Joel Best
1981  "Careers in deviance and respectability: the analogy's limitations." *Social Problems* 29, 2 (December): 197–206.

Lukoff, Irving, and D. Quatrone
1973  "Heroin use and crime in a methadone maintenance program: a two year follow up of the Addiction Research and Treatment Corporation Program: a preliminary report." Pp. 63–112 in G. J. Hayim et al. (eds.), *Heroin Use in a Methadone Maintenance Program*. Washington, D.C.: U.S. Department of Justice, National Institute of Law Enforcement and Criminal Justice.

McAuliffe, William E., Mary Rohman, Paul Fishman, Rob Friedman, Henry Wechsler, Stephen H. Soboroff, and David Toth
1984  "Psychoactive drug use by young and future physicians." *Journal of Health and Social Behavior* 25 (March): 34–54.

McCaghy, Charles H., and James K. Skipper
1969  "Lesbian behavior as an adaptation to the occupation of stripping." *Social Problems* 17, 2 (Fall): 262–70.

McCall, George J., and J. L. Simmons
1966  *Identities and Interactions*. New York: Free Press.

Maddux, James F., Sue K. Hoppe, and Raymond M. Costello
1986  "Psychoactive substance use among medical students." *American Journal of Psychiatry* 143, 2: 187–91.

Manning, Peter K.
1977  "Rules in organizational context: narcotics law enforcement in two settings." Pp. 46–63 in J. Kenneth Benson (ed.), *Organizational Analysis: Critique and Innovation*. Beverly Hills, CA: Sage Publications.

Marshall, Eliot
1988  "Drug wars: legalization gets a hearing." *Science* 241 (September 2): 1157–59.

Martin, John M.
1978  "From morphine maintenance to methadone maintenance, 1919–75: the history, promise, and problems of narcotic clinics in the United States." Pp. 8–30 in Arnold S. Trebach (ed.), *Drugs, Crime and Politics*. New York: Praeger Publishers.

Matza, David
1964  *Delinquency and Drift*. New York: John Wiley and Sons.
1969  *Becoming Deviant*. Englewood Cliffs, NJ: Prentice-Hall.

Maurer, David W.
1955  *Whiz Mob: A Correlation of the Technical Argot of Pickpockets with Their Behavior Patterns*. Gainesville, FL: American Dialect Society.

Mead, George H.

1934 *Mind, Self and Society.* Edited by C. W. Morris. Chicago: University of Chicago Press.

Meier, Robert F.

1981 "Norms and the study of deviance: a proposed research strategy." *Deviant Behavior* 3 : 1–25.

Merton, Robert

1938 "Social structure and anomie." *American Sociological Review* 3 : 672–82.

Mieczkowski, Tom

1989 "Understanding life in the crack culture: the investigative utility of the Drug Use Forecasting System." NIJ Reports No. 217 (November–December).

Miller, Gale

1978 *Odd Jobs.* Englewood Cliffs, NJ: Prentice-Hall.

1981 *It's a Living: Work in Modern Society.* New York: St. Martin's Press.

Musto, David

1973 *The American Disease: Origins of Narcotic Control.* New Haven, CT: Yale University Press.

Nadelmann, Ethan A.

1989 "Drug prohibition in the United States: costs, consequences, and alternatives." *Science* 245 (September 1) : 939–47.

Nash, George

1973 "The impact of drug abuse treatment upon criminality: a look at 19 programs." Montclair State College, Upper Montclair, NJ.

National Institute of Justice

1988 "Attorney General announces NIJ Drug Use Forecasting System." NIJ Reports No. 208 (March–April).

National Institute of Law Enforcement and Criminal Justice

1978 *The Nation's Toughest Drug Law: Evaluating the New York Experience.* Washington, D.C.: U.S. Government Printing Office.

National Institute on Drug Abuse

1977 "Securing employment for ex–drug abusers: an overview of jobs." Services Research Report No. ADM 78-467. Washington, D.C.: U.S. Government Printing Office.

Niederhoffer, Arthur

1969 *Behind the Shield: The Police in Urban Society.* Garden City, NY: Anchor Books.

Oldham, Jack

1979 "Social control of voluntary work activity: the gift horse syndrome." *Sociology of Work and Occupations* 6, 4 (November) : 379–403.

Olson, Joan Toms

1979  "Role conflict between housework and child care." *Sociology of Work and Occupations* 6, 4 (November) : 430–56.

Packer, Herbert L.

1968  *The Limits of the Criminal Sanction.* Stanford, CA: Stanford University Press.

Parnes, Herbert S., and Gilbert Nestel

1981  "The retirement experience." Pp. 155–97 in Herbert S. Parnes (ed.), *Work and Retirement: A Longitudinal Study of Men.* Cambridge, MA: MIT Press.

Person, Philip H., Jr., Robert L. Retka, and J. Arthur Woodward

1977  *A Method for Estimating Heroin Use.* National Institute on Drug Abuse Technical Paper. Washington, D.C.: U.S. Government Printing Office.

Pittell, S. M.

1977  *Community Support Systems for Addict Aftercare.* Walnut Creek, CA: Pacific Institute for Research and Evaluation.

Platt, Jerome J.

1975  "'Addiction proneness' and personality in heroin addicts." *Journal of Abnormal Psychology* 84, 3 : 303–6.

Powell, Douglas H.

1973  "A pilot study of occasional heroin users." *Archives of General Psychiatry* 28 (April) : 586–94.

Preble, Edward

1982  Lecture and personal notes read in the memory of Edward Preble. Annual meeting of the American Anthropological Association, Washington, D.C., December.

Preble, Edward, and John H. Casey, Jr.

1969  "Taking care of business—the heroin user's life on the street." *International Journal of the Addictions* 4, 1 (March) : 1–24.

Rae, Andre

1981  *The Homemakers: The Forgotten Workers.* Chicago: University of Chicago Press.

Ray, Marsh B.

1961  "The cycle of abstinence and relapse among heroin addicts." *Social Problems* 9, 2 (Fall) : 132–40.

Ray, Oakley

1978  *Drugs, Society, and Human Behavior* (2d ed.). St. Louis: C. V. Mosby Company.

Roberts, Kenneth

1978  *Contemporary Society and the Growth of Leisure.* London: Longman.

Rosenbaum, Marsha
1981 *Women on Heroin.* New Brunswick, NJ: Rutgers University Press.
Rosenfeld, Rachel A.
1986 "U.S. farm women: their part in farm work and decision making." *Work and Occupations* 13, 2 (May): 179–202.
Rubington, Earl
1967 "Drug addiction as a deviant career." *International Journal of the Addictions* 2, 1 (Spring): 3–20.
Sackman, Bertram, M. Maxine Sackman, and G. G. DeAngelis
1978 "Heroin addiction as an occupation: traditional addicts and heroin addicted poly-drug users." *International Journal of the Addictions* 13: 427–41.
Savitz, Leonard D.
1978 "Official police statistics and their limitations." Pp. 69–81 in Leonard D. Savitz and Norman Johnston (eds.), *Crime in Society.* New York: John Wiley and Sons.
Scott, James Maurice
1969 *The White Poppy: A History of Opium.* New York: Funk and Wagnalls.
Shaw, Clifford R.
1930 *The Jack Roller: A Delinquent Boy's Own Story.* Chicago: University of Chicago Press.
Sherlock, Basil, and Alan Cohen
1966 "The strategy of occupational choice: recruitment to dentistry." *Social Forces* 44: 303–13.
Shulman, Harry Manuel
1966 "The measurement of crime in the United States." *Journal of Criminal Law, Criminology and Police Science* 57: 483–92.
Silver, Gary, and Michael Aldrich
1979 *The Dope Chronicles: 1850–1950.* New York: Harper and Row.
Singh, B. K.
1981 "The effects of community structure on drug treatment outcomes of methadone maintenance programs." *International Journal of the Addictions* 16, 7: 1183–96.
Skipper, James K., Jr., and Charles H. McCaghy
1970 "Stripteasers: the anatomy and career contingencies of a deviant occupation." *Social Problems* 17: 391–405.
Skoglund, John
1979 "Work after retirement." *Aging and Work* 2, 2 (Spring): 103–11.
Slocum, Walter L.
1966 *Occupational Careers: A Sociological Perspective.* Chicago: Aldine.

Smigel, Erwin O.

1964 *The Wall Street Lawyer.* New York: Free Press.

Smith, D. Randall, and William R. Smith

1984 "Patterns of delinquent careers: an assessment of three perspectives." *Social Science Research* 13 : 129–58.

Smith, D. Randall, William R. Smith, and Elliot Noma

1984 "Delinquent career lines: a conceptual link between theory and juvenile offenses." *Sociological Quarterly* 25 (Spring) : 155–72.

Smith, Jean Paul

1973 "Substances in illegal drugs." Pp. 13–30 in Richard H. Blum and Associates (ed.), *Drug Dealers—Taking Action.* San Francisco: Jossey Bass.

Speckart, George, and M. Douglas Anglin

1986 "Narcotics use and crime: a causal modeling approach." *Journal of Quantitative Criminology* 2 : 3–28.

Stagner, Ross

1979 "Propensity to work: an important variable in retiree behavior." *Aging and Work* 2, 3 (Summer) : 161–72.

Stebbins, Robert A.

1970 "Career: the subjective approach." *Sociological Quarterly* 11 (Winter) : 32–49.

1971 *Commitment to Deviance: The Nonprofessional Criminal in the Community.* Westport, CT: Greenwood Publishing Co.

1979 *Amateurs: On the Margin Between Work and Leisure.* Beverly Hills, CA: Sage Publications.

Steffensmeier, Darrell J.

1986 *The Fence: In the Shadow of Two Worlds.* Totowa, NJ: Rowman and Littlefield.

Sutherland, Edwin H.

1937 *The Professional Thief.* Chicago: University of Chicago Press.

Sutherland, Edwin H., and Donald R. Cressey

1974 *Criminology* (9th ed.). Philadelphia, PA: J. B. Lippincott.

Sutter, Alan G.

1966 "The world of the righteous dope fiend." *Issues in Criminology* 2 : 177–222.

1969 "Worlds of drug use on the street scene." Pp. 802–29 in Donald R. Cressey and David A. Ward (eds.), *Delinquency, Crime and Social Process.* New York: Harper and Row.

1972 "Playing a cold game: phases of a ghetto career." *Urban Life and Culture* 1 : 77–91.

Sykes, Gresham M., and David Matza
1957  "Techniques of neutralization: a theory of delinquency." *American Sociological Review* 22:664–70.

System Sciences, Inc.
1973  "A comparative analysis of 24 therapeutic communities in New York City funded by the Addiction Service Agency of the City of New York." Unpublished report, System Sciences, Inc., Bethesda, MD.

Tappan, Paul
1960  *Crime, Justice and Correction*. New York: McGraw-Hill.

Taylor, Mary D., and Shirley Foster Hartley
1975  "The two person career: a classic example." *Sociology of Work and Occupations* 2, 4 (November):354–72.

Terry, Charles E., and Mildred Pellens
1970  *The Opium Problem*. Montclair, NJ: Patterson-Smith. (Originally published in 1928 by the Bureau of Social Hygiene, Inc., New York.)

Thomas, W. I., and Florian Znaniecki
1927  *The Polish Peasant in Europe and America* (2d ed.). Chicago: University of Chicago Press.

Tieman, Cheryl R.
1981  "From victims to criminals to victims: a review of the issues." Pp. 239–67 in James A. Inciardi (ed.), *The Drugs-Crime Connection*. Beverly Hills, CA: Sage Publications.

Townsend, Aloen, and Patricia Gurin
1981  "Re-examining the frustrated homemaker hypothesis: role fit, personal dissatisfaction and collective discontent." *Sociology of Work and Occupations* 8, 4 (November):464–88.

Trebach, Arnold S.
1982  *The Heroin Solution*. New Haven, CT: Yale University Press.

United States Department of Justice
1988a  *Sourcebook of Criminal Justice Statistics*. Washington, D.C.: Bureau of Justice Statistics.
1988b  "Prisoners in 1987." Bureau of Justice Statistics Bulletin (April).

Van Maanen, John
1977  *Organizational Careers: Some New Perspectives*. New York: John Wiley and Sons.

Voss, Harwin L., and Richard R. Clayton
1984  "'Turning on' other persons to drugs." *International Journal of the Addictions* 19, 6:633–52.

Waldorf, Dan
1971  "Life without heroin: some social adjustments during long-term periods of voluntary abstention." *Social Problems* 18:228–43.

1973  *Careers in Dope*. Englewood Cliffs, NJ: Prentice-Hall.

1983  "Natural recovery from opiate addiction: some social-psychological processes of untreated recovery." *Journal of Drug Issues* 13, 2 (Spring): 237–80.

Wallace, Samuel E.

1965  *Skid Row as a Way of Life*. Totowa, NJ: Bedminster Press.

1968  "The road to skid row." *Social Problems* 16, 1 (Summer): 92–105.

Walters, James M.

1985  "'Taking care of business' updated: a fresh look at the daily routine of the heroin user." Pp. 31–48 in Bill Hanson, George Beschner, James M. Walters, and Elliot Bovelle (eds.), *Life with Heroin: Voices from the Inner City*. Lexington, MA: Lexington Books.

Warriner, Charles K.

1958  "The nature and functions of official morality." *American Journal of Sociology* 64: 165–68.

Weinberg, Martin S.

1966  "Becoming a nudist." *Psychiatry: Journal for the Study of Interpersonal Processes* 29, 1 (February): 15–24.

Wilensky, Harold L.

1961  "Orderly careers and social participation: the impact of work history on social integration in the middle class." *American Sociological Review* 26: 521–39.

Williams, Jay, and Martin Gold

1972  "From delinquent behavior to official delinquency." *Social Problems* 20: 209–29.

Winick, Charles

1961  "Physician narcotic addicts." *Social Problems* 9: 174–86.

1962  "Maturing out of narcotic addiction." *Bulletin on Narcotics* 14 (January–March): 1–7.

1974  "A sociological theory of the genesis of drug dependence." Pp. 3–13 in Charles Winick (ed.), *Sociological Aspects of Drug Dependence*. Cleveland, OH: CRC Press.

Wiseman, Jacqueline P.

1970  *Stations of the Lost: The Treatment of Skid Row Alcoholics*. Englewood Cliffs, NJ: Prentice-Hall.

Wish, Eric D., and Joyce Ann O'Neil

1989  "Drug Use Forecasting January to March, 1989." NIJ Research In Action (September). Washington, D.C.: U.S. Government Printing Office.

Wisotsky, Steven

1988  *Breaking the Impasse in the War on Drugs*. Westport, CT: Greenwood Press.

Wolfgang, Marvin E.
1972  *Delinquency in a Birth Cohort.* Chicago: University of Chicago Press.
Wolkstein, Eileen
1979  "The former addict in the workplace." Pp. 103–14 in Barry S. Brown
       (ed.), *Addicts and Aftercare.* Beverly Hills, CA: Sage Publications.
Yablonsky, Lewis
1965  *Synanon: The Tunnel Back.* New York: Penguin Books.
Zinberg, Norman E.
1984  *Drug Set and Setting: The Basis for Controlled Intoxicant Use.* New Haven,
       CT: Yale University Press.
Zinberg, Norman E., and Richard C. Jacobson
1976  "The natural history of 'chipping.'" *American Journal of Psychiatry* 133, 1
       (January): 37–40.

# Index

Addict ethics: contribution of career perspective, x; described, 52–53, 59–61;
effect of criminal specialization on, 93–
95; effect of drug availability on, 61,
93–94, 107–8, 125, 127; effect of life
structure on, 94, 124–27; as recurring
research issue, ix; stereotyped as moral
degeneracy, 11; variation of, over addict
careers, 135–36, 144; violation of, 59–
61, 124–27, 137. *See also* Subcultural
norms

Addiction: disease metaphor, 3; physiological basis of, 2; as social process, 2;
subcultural vs. middle class, 188n.4;
stereotypes of, 1, 111, 118, 127–28;
subjective understanding of, 5, 129–
30, 144. *See also* Drug consumption

Addictive personality, 3–4

American drug policy: history of, 149–
52; role of Chinese in, 150

Anomie: defined, 44; as lack of life structure, 108, 124–25, 141

Anslinger, Harry, 3

Appreciative understanding, 4, 144

Argot: importance of, for understanding
drug-using careers, 5

Arrest: effect of criminal skills on, 83–84,
163; effect of life structure on, 141,

164; reasons for, 117, 121–23, 140–42,
143, 163, 164–65

Big sting: defined, 101; and drugs-crime
connection, 103–5; effect of, on addict
life-styles, 101–3, 107–8; effect of, on
criminal specialization, 106–7; effect
of, on drug consumption, 101–5,
108–9; effect of, on life structure,
100–103; examples of, 101, 104, 105.
*See also* Crime

Brent, Bishop Charles, and Shanghai
Opium Commission, 150

Burglary, 30, 43, 79

Career: defined, 22–25; drug-using compared to conventional, 4, 37, 131;
phases of, 31–36, 130–31; types of,
25–28, 187–88n.3; typology of phases,
47–48

Career contingencies, 5, 37

Career history: as special application of
life history technique, 15. *See also* Life
history

Career perspective: contribution of, to
understanding addict life-styles, x, 5,
129–30; contribution of, to policy
issues, x–xi, 13, 162–66, 175–76